D1599314

CRIME AND PUBLIC ORDER IN ENGLAND IN THE LATER MIDDLE AGES

STUDIES IN SOCIAL HISTORY

edited by

HAROLD PERKIN

Professor of Social History, University of Lancaster

For a list of books in the series see back endpaper

CRIME AND PUBLIC ORDER IN ENGLAND IN THE LATER MIDDLE AGES

John Bellamy

Associate Professor of History, Carleton University, Ottawa

LONDON: Routledge & Kegan Paul
TORONTO: University of Toronto Press

First published 1973 in Great Britain by
Routledge & Kegan Paul Limited
and in Canada and the United States of America by
University of Toronto Press
Toronto and Buffalo
Printed in Great Britain by
Western Printing Services Limited, Bristol
RKP ISBN 0 7100 7421 2
UTP ISBN 0 8020 5257 6
UTP Microfiche ISBN 0 8020 0074 6
LC 73–163803

Contents

Preface and Acknowledgments

Although there are many histories of English law, legal administration, and government which deal with the later middle ages, the subject of crime and public order, a crucial issue in that period, has been sadly neglected. Only one full-scale work on the topic has ever been published and that nearly a century ago. Lawyers writing on the period have concerned themselves largely with the development of legal principles and institutions; historians have usually restricted themselves to administration and local government. Only recently has a revived interest in social history, emphasizing the need to view English society as a whole, drawn attention to the badly charted area of medieval crime and the urgent need for investigation.

This book is an attempt to summarize the present state of our knowledge in this field, to cover some aspects for which, surprising as it may be, there is nothing in print, and to suggest where further research might profitably be directed. Wherever it seemed suitable general trends have been illustrated by particular cases from the records to remind us that later medieval England was peopled with real men and women, delinquent or otherwise.

This book has been published with the help of grants from the Social Science Research Council of Canada, using funds provided by the Canada Council, and from the Publications Fund of the University of Toronto Press.

J.B.

I

Crime and Medieval Society

The effective preservation of public order, the protection of life, limb, and property from the malicious intent of the less tractable members of the community, has always been an integral element of good government. In most modern western countries the level of crime has been so reduced that the misdeeds of the few serve rather to provide the ordinary citizen with escapist entertainment than to instil a sense of fear. Very few of us believe that the main fabric of the state could ever be imperilled by those who practise crime, or that lawlessness could exist for more than a short period of time and within narrow territorial limits. In the England of the later middle ages the preservation of public order was very often the biggest problem the king had to face. It was not just a police matter. At heart were the crucial issues of royal authority and the structure of the state, whether they were to survive in their existing forms or wither away. Neither before that time nor since has the issue of public order bulked so large in English history.

Many of the reasons for this pre-eminence are to be found in the great social and economic changes which occurred in the fourteenth and fifteenth centuries. Famine and plague worked on feudal relationships, which were already decayed by time, so as to make many of the regulations for the upkeep of law and order quite unreal. The judicial system constructed laboriously by previous English kings, and perhaps their finest monument, was hardly equal to the task. The golden age of English common law, which extended from Glanvill to Bracton, was followed almost immediately, so many historians argue, by another in which the lack of public order made a mockery of the laws of property which they had so thoroughly expounded.

1

If such a contrast has been overdrawn there is certainly little evidence in the fourteenth and fifteenth centuries of a new ability to control crime. Long-serving police techniques were particularly undermined by the changes in society. The king and his ministers were unable to infuse any more life into the old system whereby the members of a group were collectively responsible for the misdeeds committed by any one of their number. Nor could the king find, or even imagine, a substitute for a system of law maintenance based very largely on the unpaid assistance of gentlemen and noble amateurs, yet there was a great need to do so since much of the crime originated in the misdeeds of those same classes. In brief, it was the large followings of the magnates which made the task of local law enforcement so difficult since the enforcers, the keepers or justices of the peace and the sheriff, were often attached in some way to one of the great lords, as were a considerable number of those they brought into court.

The factors which made the over-mighty subject so keen to increase the number of his dependants are not difficult to fathom but it is much less easy to assess their relative importance. Extravagance and the display of wealth and influence were undoubtedly fashionable. Once a magnate had acquired a following of some size a neighbouring magnate probably felt obliged to recruit a similar one in defence of his social position. It is possible that the magnates simply had their followers thrust upon them by social and economic pressures, quite often by the need for a strong protector in disturbed times. Perhaps the enlistment of supporters reflected the desire to dominate the king: there was a will to power, as the recurrent threat of baronial revolt clearly testified. Whatever was the cause, the tie which disturbed public order most was the one between magnate and gentleman, for it was the latter who was entrusted with so many of the tasks of local government. If, as often happened, the interests of his immediate master conflicted with those of the king, good government was the loser. Only in the later sixteenth century, when the gentry finally broke away from the leading strings of the great and rejected their livery, did widespread violence cease. One other reason may be adduced here for the poor quality of law and order in the later middle ages. Either because of short-sighted public complaint or from a lack of professional judges, the visitations of the general eyre which thoroughly investigated all the crimes committed over a period of years in a particular region were replaced by several types of commission which, because of their limited competence and *ad hoc* nature, were unlikely to have the same effect. Particularly was this so in the crucial field of unauthorized and corrupt behaviour on the part of office-holders. Except when the king had a personal reason for intervening or when the strength of parliamentary complaint necessitated royal action, the investigation of official corruption began to languish most noticeably. This was a serious failure.

Late medieval England was known throughout Europe for its high rate of crime, a reputation to which modern historians have frequently drawn attention. Unfortunately an accurate assessment of the incidence of criminal misdeeds during the fourteenth and fifteenth centuries may never be possible. Were there sufficient scholars and man-hours available to examine in exhaustive detail the massive legal records extant in the Public Record Office, it is still doubtful if any wholly acceptable statistics would be forthcoming. This is partly because the records are uneven in their coverage, being rich for some periods and localities and meagre for others, but primarily because the rolls of the keepers and the justices of the peace, who dealt with the majority of crimes in the first instance, have often not survived. It may be possible in one or two fortuitous cases to unravel the misdeeds committed in a single county over a period of say twenty or thirty years, but no historian has yet tried to do so. To estimate the general incidence of crime from the number of commissions issued for the appointing of justices to deliver gaols, hold assizes, or to hear and determine particular groups of crimes is hazardous. The issue of a commission is no proof that anything was done, nor were all commissions of equal importance. The justices might have to deal with no more than a few cases of theft or assault, or there might be presented before them an indictment of a well-organized criminal confederacy.

Thus the difficulties involved in compiling the general history of crime in this period are considerable, and only one general work on the subject has been produced.[1] Other historians, however, have been able to throw valuable light on particular and local aspects of the subject, usually by the editing of justices' rolls. The conclusions which they have been able to draw about the incidence of crime in the regions and periods covered by their records are of considerable interest. The first thing we notice is the close similarity. Everywhere there is a host of violent crimes, but appearances in court by the suspected malefactors are sadly few. Convictions are even fewer. Public order has

---

[1] L. O. Pike, *A History of Crime in England* (London, 1873–6).

badly decayed. L. O. Pike, a pioneer in English criminal history, who examined particularly lawlessness in 1348, the year preceding the Black Death, was so shocked by the misdeeds he uncovered that he classed that part of Edward III's reign as a time of widespread depravity.[2] E. G. Kimball, from her editing of Shropshire peace rolls of the reigns of Henry IV and Henry V, felt bound to comment that at that time serious crime was not being punished in Shropshire or for that matter anywhere in England.[3] Recently R. H. Hilton, examining rural society in the west midlands in the reign of Edward I, formed the opinion, largely from the assize rolls, that at the turn of the thirteenth century the sanctions of the common law were ineffective in curbing violence or corruption.[4] G. O. Sayles, from the records of the king's bench, was noticeably impressed by the criminal excesses of the reign of Edward II and the decline in the rule of law in the time of his father.[5] The names and the words of historians who have commented adversely on public order in the later Lancastrian and the Yorkist periods are too numerous and extensive to mention. Every verdict seems unfavourable and uniformly so. Not one investigator has been able to indicate even a few years of effective policing in the period 1290–1485.

We may fairly ask if the picture can have been uniformly black, if every decade can have been as bad as the next and the incidence of crime perpetually and universally high, for this is not the experience of modern times. Although the records of the law courts give little help in this direction there is still information to be gathered. It is to be found in contemporary comment and complaint, in incidental reference rather than in official memoranda, for example in the preambles to statutes and commissions to justices, in petitions to the king for the righting of some personal or local wrong, in the causes for the summoning of parliaments. There are also the occasional mentions by chroniclers and references in fifteenth-century family papers. The first open admission by a king that all was not well with public order was when Edward I, in the preamble to the statute of Winchester, complained forcefully about the wretched observance of the peace. Murders, robberies, and arsons, so it was said, were

[2] *Ibid.*, i, 297.

[3] *The Shropshire Peace Roll, 1400–1414*, ed. E. G. Kimball (Shrewsbury, 1959), p. 45.

[4] R. H. Hilton, *A Medieval Society* (London, 1966), p. 258.

[5] *Select Cases in the Court of the King's Bench, Edward II*, ed. G. O. Sayles (Selden Society, 74, 1955), p. liii.

more common than ever before, and jurors were refusing to indict or convict the offenders or those who received the proceeds from their misdeeds. Eight years later, in his instructions to the sheriffs, the king admitted to learning from the great number of complaints since the promulgation of the statute that more homicides, robberies, arsons, and other trespasses than ever before had been committed.[6] In 1294 Hugh Cressingham, a prominent royal justice, reported to his master that there were so many influential maintainers of false complaints, upholders of champerty, and conspirators in league together, all bent on the malversation of legal process by such tricks as altering writs, manipulating the election of jurors, and procuring appeals by approvers, that justice and truth were completely choked.[7] In 1300 the king acknowledged to the sheriffs that many more malefactors and disturbers of the peace were wandering about than in times past, and in 1304 the chronicler Langtoft, referring to the large number of men who specialized in violent assault, suggested that unless some drastic step was taken to stop the turbulence open warfare might well result.[8] Edward I has been regarded as one of the most able and legalistic of the English medieval monarchs but there must have been an element of truth in so many grave complaints. Unwisely he had become too absorbed by his wars and in his later years, by the bad example of his own high-handedness, had ruined respect for the law. At the end Edward realized his error and made a great effort to repair, if not completely restore, law and order in 1305–6.

In contrast to the forthright complaint of Edward I's reign there was little contemporary acknowledgment of the poor quality of public order in the time of his son. This might well have been because of the continuous bickering among the magnates and between the magnates and the king, which was serious enough to relegate local annoyances to temporary limbo. Modern historians incline to the belief that lawlessness in his reign was common, and that his successor Edward III had to face a problem which had become more serious as a result of the revolts of 1322 and 1326–7 and the poor quality of government by those who ruled in his name during his minority.[9] This may be true,

---

[6] *Statutes of the Realm* (Record Commission, 1810–28), i, 96; *Calendar of Close Rolls, 1288–1296* (Record Commission), p. 330.

[7] *Select Cases in the Court of the King's Bench, Edward II, ut supra.*

[8] *Cal. Close Rolls, 1293–1302*, p. 330; *Chronicle of Pierre de Langtoft*, ed. T. Wright (Rolls Series, 1866–8), ii, 361.

[9] Concerning perversions of the law in Edward II's reign G. O. Sayles says: 'it is hard to imagine that Henry II or the great justiciars would have tolerated

but widespread complaint was only renewed when the young king took over the reins of government himself. A petition in parliament in 1331 referred to those gentry who had banded together in great companies for the purpose of kidnapping for ransom or killing the king's lieges, churchmen, and royal judges. The reference was probably to the activities of gangs like the Folvilles and the Coterels.[10] Edward tackled the problem with vigour and, as was usual in the middle ages, expenditure of royal energy meant temporary success, but by the end of the decade, with the king often absent on expeditions against the French and their allies, complaint was heard again and it continued. In parliament in 1343 Edward admitted that the law of the land was not at all well kept. A petition by the commons in the parliament of 1347 claimed that the peace was very troubled and disturbed and that the law was almost ignored. This was said to be because some of the magnates were guilty of maintenance, which meant giving favour and support to felons and trespassers.[11] These were years when the king was very much engrossed in his war with France. The next period of complaint was after the treaty of Brétigny. In 1362 there was great clamour about the committing of felonies and trespasses and the excesses of officials. There were reports of large numbers of vagabonds congregating in warlike manner, as it was put, and living from ambush and pillage in Staffordshire, while felons were thought to be unusually thick on the ground in Devon. Soldiers who were accustomed to live by the sword in foreign parts were returning home and there was fear for the consequences.[12] The chronicler Henry Knighton, under the year 1364, described a wave of theft, pointing out how many churches were entered and robbed.[13] The rest of the reign is devoid of comparable evidence and suggests that relatively good order prevailed, although the first cause given for the summoning of the Good Parliament in 1376 was to legislate for the good keeping of the peace.

[10] *Rotuli Parliamentorum* (Record Commission, 1767–7), ii, 64; for the careers of the members of these prominent criminal bands see Chapter 3.
[11] *Rot. Parl.*, ii, 136b, 165.
[12] *William Salt Archaeological Society*, xiv (1893), 112; *Calendar of Patent Rolls, 1361–1364* (Record Commission), pp. 282, 396.
[13] *Chronicon Henrici Knighton*, ed. J. R. Lumby (Rolls Series; 1889–95), ii, 120.

for a moment the excesses of Edward II's reign' (*Select Cases in the Court of the King's Bench, Edward II, ut supra*).

A most notable feature of the reign of Richard II in regard to public order was the relatively slight damage done by the revolt of the peasants in 1381. There is no suggestion that any sizeable proportion of the followers of Tyler, Straw, and Ball, when they eventually dispersed, took to a life of crime or became outlaws in the woods, nor is there any reference to the subsequent depredations of those they freed from gaol. In fact there was no real outcry about the incidence of crime between 1378 and 1387. In the former year a statute referred to the raising of private armies which led to the setting aside of legal process, the illegal seizure of land, the abduction and ravishing of women, lying in ambush with murderous intent, and the imprisonment of men for purposes of ransom as though the land was at war. Justices were said to be fearful of doing impartial justice.[14] In 1387 there was popular clamour that evil-doers in great number were holding unlawful assemblies in several southern counties, and one cause that was given for the summoning of the first parliament of 1388, a session which turned out to be so hostile to King Richard, was the need for the better keeping of the peace.[15] Whether this wave of lawlessness was politically inspired and connected with baronial hostility to the king is an historical question which has not yet been answered. A problem which was broached in this parliament and the one of 1391 was the great danger from maintenance, and the legislation of 1390 on this matter, as well as against certain types of retaining, suggests that criminal deeds were being committed in increasing number under the protection of the magnates and the richer gentry. The later years of Richard's reign, which have been generally regarded as a time of increasing despotism, did not apparently produce a single major complaint about the lack of public order, nor did the usurper Henry IV ever suggest that his predecessor had been guilty of allowing it.

In the fifteenth century the first evidence that law and order were in serious jeopardy came not at the time of the rebellions of 1403 or 1405–8 but in Henry IV's last three or four years as king, when recurrent sickness had sapped his physical vitality. In Norfolk, secret societies were reported to be extorting money by threats, particularly from abbots and priors, and there were widespread riots and feuding in the north midlands and Yorkshire. In Staffordshire, at least, the years were noteworthy for the giving of livery to retainers illegally.

[14] 2 Richard II, st. 1. c. 6.
[15] *Cal. Pat. Rolls, 1385–1389*, p. 323; *Rot. Parl.*, iii, 228.

One of the reasons given for the summoning of the Leicester parliament of 1414 was the need to punish rioters and those guilty of homicide and other misdeeds, who were said to be more numerous in many parts of the realm than for a long time.[16] More likely it was the lack of firm governance in the previous half-decade than any Lollard machinations against the new king Henry V which caused the trouble: the rest of the reign seems to show a much greater respect for the law. Writing in about the year 1457 the chronicler John Harding, in wistful comment on Henry's reign, said that

> the pese at home and law so wele conserved
> Wer rote and hede of all his grete conqueste.[17]

When the child king Henry VI had ascended the throne complaint started again. In October 1426 the government admitted there were open and notorious robberies and misdeeds being committed in divers parts of the realm, and made special provision for the proclamation in public places of those statutes which concerned the safeguarding of the peace most vitally. Three years later the king, or rather his ministers, claimed to have reliable information from many sources that in every county a great number of robberies had lately been committed by thieves in criminal bands, 'more than used to be in times past'.[18] He was especially unhappy, he said, because ordinary citizens were doing little to capture the miscreants. This was very likely true for the frank-pledge system was virtually dead and it was a foolish man who quarrelled with the household followers and friends of the local potentate. A petition in parliament in 1429 referred to the daily occurrence of forcible entries into other men's property and claimed that the land so acquired was often being granted away to the locally powerful in order to have their maintenance. In 1433–4 the nobility and the gentry were asked to take an oath, as the king's councillors had done in 1429, promising not to maintain criminals of any sort either by influencing judges or jurors or by taking them into their service.[19] This was probably the result of the increasing number of petitions coming into parliament which complained of indictments against the illegal granting of livery being

---

[16] *Cal. Pat. Rolls, 1408–1413*, pp. 316, 374; *Rot. Parl.*, iv, 15; *William Salt Arch. Soc.*, xvi (1895), 83; *ibid.*, xvii (1896), 19, 29.
[17] C. L. Kingsford, 'Extracts from the First Version of Hardyng's Chronicle', *English Historical Review*, xxvii (1912), 745.
[18] *Cal. Close Rolls, 1422–1429*, pp. 316–17, 469.
[19] For the frank-pledge system see pp. 90–1. *Rot. Parl.*, iv, 422, 352–3.

prevented by 'great maintenance'. The later 1430s and the 1440s saw a growth in faction and acrimony within the king's council, and the rise of a court party around the persons of a number of royal favourites. There followed naturally from this a number of bitter baronial feuds which must have divided whole counties, but the period which from its general history we would surmise to have been the worst from the viewpoint of public order consists of the years from the fall of the duke of Suffolk to the time when Edward IV was reasonably well established as king, 1450–64. In 1450 the parliamentary commons declared the realm was troubled by a wave of lawlessness which was greater than ever before. Some seven years later John Harding spoke of public order as

> exilde bene away and foule ourterued
> In so ferr forthe that north and south and weste
> And este also is now full lytill reste.

The roll of the Coventry parliament of 1459 referred to the 'great and lamentable complaints of your true poor subjects universally throughout every part of your realm' about robberies, riots, and extortions, which forced them into payment of fines and ransoms.[20] In 1461 the oath not to maintain law-breakers was again taken by the upper classes, but within a year Margaret Paston was able to write that there had never been so much robbery and manslaughter in her part of East Anglia. The large number of bands of armed men and known evil-doers which secured mention at this period in the king's instructions to his law officers suggests she was telling the truth. By his personal intervention Edward IV was able to bring about an improvement, but there was another high period of criminal activity after the political upheavals of 1470–1, and possibly a lesser one after the French war of 1475.[21] By the end of the Yorkist period, however, there was less despair about public order, even if there were still outrageous crimes being committed and areas of continual high incidence.

The history of crime in late medieval England is therefore a tale of fluctuation. There were periods which struck contemporaries as being particularly bad and there were also times when the law was quite well obeyed and order was good, a fact which historians as a class

---

[20] *Rot. Parl.*, v, 200; *Eng. Hist. Rev.*, xxvii (1912), 745; *Rot. Parl.*, v, 367.
[21] *Paston Letters*, ed. J. Gairdner (Edinburgh, 1910), no. 435; J. G. Bellamy, 'Justice under the Yorkist Kings', *American Journal of Legal History*, ix (1965), 136–9.

have failed to comment on. Admittedly there were not many of the latter. In general terms the fifteenth century was worse than the fourteenth although, as will be seen later, less from the number of bad years than from the more pernicious organization of crime which developed. What caused the periods of great criminal activity and widespread disorder? Quite obviously war played a part, both foreign and domestic. Civil wars like those between the king and the barons in 1264–5 and 1321–2 may have resulted in elements of the defeated faction living a violent life outside the law for a time but the matter has not yet been properly examined. The same can be said about the effects of the factional battles between Lancaster and York in 1459–61 and 1469–71.

Campaigns overseas or in Scotland were more noticeably disruptive, and for one very good reason. It was not the depredations of the returning soldiery or the inflamed bellicosity of the participating nobility which had the deleterious effect on public order, but the prolonged absence of the king, usually at the head of his army. When the English monarch left his kingdom for any length of time in order to seek out his foreign adversaries, lawlessness and disorder were very likely to increase.[22] So great a king as Edward I by his prolonged sojourn in Gascony in 1286–9 seems to have been responsible for what has been called a change in social attitude whereby 'society at large ceased to place its trust in the workings of a royal centralized justice and sought instead the protection and support of the local magnates'. King Edward cannot have been blind to the possible consequences of his absence from England. In 1277 he commanded the sheriffs to swear to arms all the men of their bailiwicks for the better preservation of the peace and for the arrest of evil-doers, whose audacity, so he believed, was likely to increase during the absence of his nobles and himself on the forthcoming Welsh expedition. Similarly, in 1283 the sheriffs were told to summon to arms all men usually so instructed so as to intercept and arrest all malefactors wandering at large, who through the absence of the nobles and others

[22] The absence of Henry V in northern France for most of the period 1417–22 seems to have been the exception. Some credit should be given to John, duke of Bedford, who was lieutenant of the realm in his absence and to Thomas Langley, bishop of Durham, the chancellor, under whom the council was immensely efficient and noticeably active as a judicial body (E. F. Jacob, *The Fifteenth Century* [Oxford, 1961], p. 431). We may suspect, however, that it was the remarkable ability of Henry V to keep a firm control over the administration of England while abroad that preserved good order.

in the Welsh war were growing bold. While Edward was in Wales the Mayor of London, Henry le Waleys, found it necessary to introduce what were described as new punishments and new methods of trial for the castigation of the malefactors who were roaming round the city.[23] After Edward II had set out on his march to Scotland in 1314, information reached him about the loud complaints of his people against outrages committed by knights and others with which the sheriffs had not seen fit to deal, either from fear or from sympathy.[24] Edward III had as good a relationship with his nobility as any king of the later middle ages and his authority over his people was great, but his absences in Scotland, Flanders, and France between 1335 and 1347 gave rise to a stream of complaints about the level of public order as well as to a number of experimental devices meant to uphold the law, such as the extension of the power to arrest on suspicion and the construing of highway robbery as treason.[25]

As might be expected, the return of the king from a foreign campaign was often the signal for increased judicial and legislative activity. Edward I, by the so-called trailbaston ordinance of 1305, caused the sending out of high-powered commissions to investigate and determine serious crimes of violence. This followed his return from Scotland. In 1340–1 Edward III mounted a full-scale enquiry into the misdeeds committed by officials while he had been in Flanders, and in the period 1349–52 he caused the promulgation of what amounted to a new legal code. Many of the measures were in response to the complaints he received after his return from Calais. Another notable example was Edward IV's personal visitation, in a judicial capacity, of Hampshire and Wiltshire after the French war of 1475.

The beneficial effect of the royal presence at the scene of the crime, at the trials, or at any rate in the region where the disturbances had centred was an acknowledged fact. Edward III went with his most eminent judges to Stamford in 1332 when supporters of the notorious Folville gang were up for trial. Richard II went with Chief Justice Tresilian to the trouble centre of St Albans at the end of the peasants' revolt of 1381 and was probably present at the sessions in the moot hall where the rebel leaders William Grindcob and John Ball were

---

[23] *Select Cases in the Court of the King's Bench, Edward II, ut supra*; *Cal. Pat. Rolls, 1272–1281*, p. 218; *Cal. Pat. Rolls, 1281–1292*, pp. 66, 80.
[24] *Cal. Pat. Rolls, 1313–1317*, p. 122.
[25] See J. G. Bellamy, *The Law of Treason in England in the Later Middle Ages* (Cambridge, 1970), Chapter 4.

convicted.[26] Henry V visited the midlands in 1414 when the Lollards had recently been in revolt and when feuding among the gentry had been particularly virulent. He remained with his bench at Lichfield for more than two months, receiving presentments from every hundred in Staffordshire and hearing every kind of complaint, both private and concerning his own peace. Then he proceeded to Shrewsbury to deal with all the Shropshire presentments.[27] Edward IV, in his great endeavour to correct the lawlessness bequeathed by Henry VI, sat in his bench at Westminster for three days on one occasion. He travelled with a number of oyer and terminer commissions and made a point of being present in court in person when he was particularly keen to have a verdict of 'guilty' returned against the accused. The council of the Duchy of Lancaster in May 1482 must have expressed what was in the minds of most men when in reference to the local 'great strifes, variances, controversies and debates' it declared they were of such depth that they could be remedied 'by no person but only by the king himself if it would like his grace to come into those parts'.[28] This is why historians concerned with the medieval period are wont to lay such emphasis on the king's personality. Without his will and his ability to govern effectively there could be little public order since so much in the medieval state depended on the monarch alone.

Almost as productive of lawlessness as the king's absence on his military campaigns was the corruption of officials. In all but the most sophisticated societies the holding of office allows suitable opportunity for illegal gain since the relative paucity of officials per head of the population does not permit a comprehensive system of surveillance of one by another. The England of the later middle ages was short of trained officials as the employment of the gentry in many different administrative and judicial capacities demonstrates. Tenure of office was usually for no great length of time except for the judges of the two benches, who in theory held their posts at the king's pleasure but in practice were often secure for life. These factors, together with the insecurity which must have arisen from the lack of regular pay, created the wish to make profit while one could, especially as many had purchased their office. Office-holding had great attraction

[26] *Thomae Walsingham Historia Anglicana*, ed. H. T. Riley (Rolls Series, 1863–4), ii, 24–32.
[27] *William Salt Arch. Soc.*, xvi (1895), 4–5.
[28] Public Record Office, Duchy of Lancaster 5/1, f.62.

even if it was rarely the sole means of a man's income. The knights and esquires who held so many local administrative and judicial positions in the fourteenth and fifteenth centuries must also have been corrupted by the example of the great, being constant witnesses to the misapplication of the law and the misuse of office on the part of their social and feudal superiors.

The position concerned with public order which offered the greatest opportunity for dishonest behaviour and on which contemporaries cast the gravest aspersions was that of sheriff, an unpaid elective post which from the mid-fourteenth century was held in theory for one year at a time. On the sheriff devolved most of the work of bringing a suspect or indicted man before the courts, as well as empanelling the juries and carrying out the verdicts. The writs concerned with the various stages of judicial process were largely directed to him. Without his co-operation the central government was virtually powerless. If, for example, the sheriff untruthfully said, as sometimes happened and particularly in cases of appeal of felony by women whose husbands had recently been killed, that a man in his custody was too ill to be sent into the king's bench, little could be done about it. On many occasions when the sheriff made this response the prisoner was probably not ill at all, but the deception was rarely revealed. An exception was a case concerning Felicia Pycheford who, having appealed Henry de Bysshebury, was told he was taken but was too ill to be sent into the king's bench.[29] Luckily Felicia was able to show that Henry de Bysshebury and the Staffordshire sheriff who made the return were one and the same. No return at all was almost as bad and quite as common as a false return, but punishment by the king for these misbehaviours was rare. In England in the later middle ages trial by jury was firmly established and the principle behind it never questioned. The practice suffered, however, from many attempts to influence the verdicts of the jurors, and few men interfered more in this respect than the local sheriff. It was he who was in the most advantageous position to do so, having the power to empanel men of known and particular sympathies as jurors. Sheriffs were known who put their own servants on a panel, and who even deliberately seated a number of outlaws as jurors. Complaints against the sheriffs were common. In 1340 and again in 1368 the parliamentary commons questioned the practice of their holding office for more than a year. In 1404 they petitioned against the embezzlement of revenues by

[29] *William Salt Arch. Soc.*, xiv (1893), 3.

sheriffs and in 1439 against their taking of bribes to empanel juries for corrupt reasons. The malpractices of sheriffs were most clearly stated in the statute of 23 Henry VI, which laid particular emphasis on the taking of bribes to let men out on bail or to forestall arrest despite royal command.[30] The practice of refusing bail to men who were in gaol following personal actions or on indictment for trespass was also condemned, as was the custom of taking fees in those cases for the return of panels of jurors and charging more than fourpence for a copy of their names. It is no wonder that John Heydon, the notorious Norwich recorder and an enemy of the Paston family, was said to have been willing to spend a thousand pounds in order to have in office in Norfolk a sheriff who was favourably inclined towards him.[31]

In a position comparable with that of the sheriff and likewise able to affect public order and the fate of local criminals was the coroner. Unlike the sheriff he was elected for life, but in fact few remained in office until they died. As with a sheriff, an escheator, and other locally based royal ministers, only the very worst sort of misbehaviour could lead to a coroner's forcible dismissal. Every coroner, it has been said, practised some form of extortion, and bribes became an invariable prelude to the performance of his duties.[32] Corruption amongst officials such as these seems to have been as bad in the fifteenth century as it had been in the thirteenth.

In contrast, the standard of conduct among the professional judges may have improved. W. S. Holdsworth, looking across the years from Thomas Wayland to Sir John Fortescue and Thomas Littleton, felt sure this was the case, and the history of judicial corruption seems to bear him out.[33] When Edward I returned to England in 1289 after an absence of three and a half years in Gascony he invited complaints against corrupt officials of all sorts. Many judges were denounced, including Hengham and Wayland, the two chief justices. Wayland had to abjure the realm and Hengham, though pardoned in 1291, was not restored to public life until 1299.[34] The crimes alleged against

[30] *Statutes of the Realm*, ii, 334.   [31] *Paston Letters*, ed. Gairdner, no. 117.
[32] See R. F. Hunnisett, *The Medieval Coroner* (Cambridge, 1961), pp. 118–126.
[33] W. S. Holdsworth, *History of English Law* (London, 1923), ii, 566.
[34] *State Trials of the Reign of Edward I, 1289–1293*, ed. T. F. Tout and H. Johnstone (Camden Society, 3rd Series, ix, 1906), xl. F. W. Maitland called the episode 'our one great judicial scandal': *Mirror of Justices*, ed. W. J. Whittaker (Selden Society, 7, 1895), xxiv–xxv.

them included allowing the taking of inquests in wrong counties and by unsuitable persons, failure to make arrests or execute writs, delaying judgment in return for bribes, making jurors condemn innocent persons or change their verdict, and acting in dictatorial manner in their courts. The last of these offences could hardly have been avoided since the rules of pleading and of the actual trial procedure were rudimentary, and cases would have lasted for a very long time had the judges not intervened decisively on occasion so as to stop the pursuit of bewildering side-issues. An investigation with comparable results occurred when Edward III, who was desperately short of funds, returned from Flanders to England on the last day of November 1340 and purged the administration which had failed to send him the money he required. Judges were among those who were tried for misconduct and found guilty. The complaints of the men of Nottinghamshire and Lancashire against Chief Justice Wylughby stated he had sold the laws as if they were oxen or cows.[35] He had procured indictors, and taken bribes to lessen fines and gifts to deliver those who had been indicted. In 1350 Chief Justice William Thorpe was accused of having accepted money payments in five different cases, and he did not venture a denial. He was sentenced to be hanged, but suffered only a year's imprisonment and the loss of a great part of his possessions. In 1365 Edward III arrested the judges Henry Green and William Skipwith for what were called heinous breaches of faith, presumably corrupt behaviour.[36] They had to redeem their errors by payment of large fines. This is the last evidence of proven corruption amongst the judges of the two benches. There was obsequious compliance with the wishes of Richard II on occasion, but no obvious impugning of judicial integrity.

During the century which followed there were, in contrast, at least two occasions when eminent judges were so loyal to the cause of justice that they braved the enmity of the king. In 1405 Chief Justice William Gascoigne left the court rather than sit in judgment on Archbishop Scrope, who had been taken in open insurrection. In 1468 Chief Justice Markham seems to have been responsible for a verdict of guilty of misprision rather than treason in the trial of the London mercer Sir Thomas Cook.[37] These examples of incorruptibility, which

---

[35] *Year Books, 14–15 Edward III*, ed. L. O. Pike (Rolls Series, 1889), pp. 258–262.

[36] *Chronicon Henrici Knighton*, ii, 121.

[37] *Historians of the Church of York and Its Archbishops*, ed. J. Raine (Rolls

were really refusals to bend the law to suit the king, must be set against the peculation of men like William Paston, a judge of common pleas, who in 1434 was accused, but not convicted, of taking a number of rewards and fees from parties. There were also the graphically described practices of judges like Chief Justice Prisot, who would not give so much as 'a bek nor a twynclyng of the eye' to the special pleas put in by the counsel of Sir John Fastolf, the Pastons, and the city of Norwich, but 'toke it to deriscion'. Later on Prisot, to the Pastons' annoyance, moved the sessions from Norwich to Walsingham, where the other party was stronger.[38] This was naturally held as open partiality, an opinion which the Pastons must have felt was substantiated when Prisot refused to allow counsel to plead for the plaintiff uninterrupted but 'took them by the nose at every thred woord'. Such criticism we should accept only with reservation, for the unfavourable comment came from the unsuccessful party and the point at issue was the bench's handling of the pleading, a delicate matter which often gave rise to debate. The charge that Prisot moved the case to Walsingham unfairly was not well founded either, since had it been concluded at Norwich the Pastons' enemies might well have suffered from the hostile climate there. Medieval men were not slow in seeking to influence the judges by non-monetary means. Usually friendship, blood-relationship, and sheer rhetoric were the vehicles used. In 1457 Sir John Fastolf wrote to Justice Yelverton asking for his favour on behalf of his chaplain Thomas Howes in a suit against John Andrews. He also sent a letter to the son-in-law of Sir Richard Bingham, the justice of the king's bench, asking him to speak to the judge about the same matter. Margaret Paston in 1465 advised her husband to talk to the justices of assize appointed for Norfolk before they came down from London.[39] She thought this would be the best way of protecting three of the Pastons' servants against charges made by their enemies. It is of course impossible to say how much effect such supplication had, but if it did the petitioner and his friends no positive good it certainly did not do their cause any great harm.

Court officials and lawyers might also be corrupt. In 1348 the chief clerk of the king's bench was accused by a gentleman of Lancashire of accepting a bribe of four marks to delay proceedings on behalf of

[38] *Paston Letters*, ed. Gairdner, nos. 19, 158.
[39] *Ibid.*, nos. 308, 309, 513.

Series, 1879–94), iii, 290–1 ; J. Stow, *Annales or A Generall Chronicle of England* (London, 1631), p. 419.

a particular monastery. A Buckinghamshire jurors' clerk in 1350 wrote down in the presentments some felonies which the jury responsible had not mentioned. In the same year there was some very questionable behaviour in a suit between the abbots of Pershore and Westminster. Geoffrey Aston, so it was later reported, declared himself as counsel for the abbot of Pershore and received a fee to obtain a commission of enquiry. The case was moved into the king's bench and the sheriff of Worcestershire returned a panel of jurors. Somehow the return came into the hands of Aston and Adam le Clerk, agents of the abbot of Pershore, who decided to destroy it. In its place they substituted one of their own making which gave the names of jurors who had been suborned. Then Aston pretended to betray his client, the abbot of Pershore, and approached the abbot of Westminster, intimating a wish to become his counsel instead. The offer was accepted and an increased fee was promised. But when the day of the trial arrived Aston reverted to his original side, no doubt taking with him a knowledge of the abbot of Westminster's planned court strategy.[40]

The king was well aware that many of those concerned with the administration of justice were corrupt. In the thirteenth century culprits were often brought to book by the general eyre, which was a prolonged visit to one particular county or region by the judges of the central courts and a few administrators. The articles of the eyre usually required investigation into the excesses, misdeeds, taking of bribes, and other dishonest practices of sheriffs and bailiffs. It overhauled the work of officials and local courts since the previous eyre. The sessions of the eyre were extraordinarily thorough by medieval standards, the judges being entitled to hear all pleas, not just a special group, but from about the year 1300 the system began to collapse. This may have been because there was more work than the small number of professional justices could manage, for they had an increasing amount of other work awaiting them at Westminster. Visitations in eyre became increasingly rare, often being bought off by the local inhabitants, and substitutes were developed. Commissions of gaol delivery and of oyer and terminer, the former being meant to try the prisoners in a particular gaol, while the latter dealt with a wave of crime in a particular area, must have taken on more work. In 1305, when particularly perturbed by the lawlessness and judicial corruption which had arisen during the protracted Scottish war, Edward I

[40] Pike, *A History of Crime in England*, i, 280–1.

ordered a campaign against crime by a nation-wide commission of oyer and terminer directed against wandering felons. Until the later fourteenth century there were spasmodic complaints in parliament about oyer and terminer commissions but the king never wavered in his belief in their efficacy, and in many ways his faith was justified. They were less successful, it would seem, in dealing with the malpractices of the justiciary. This may have been because it became less easy to make effective complaint when answers to the articles in eyre were no longer supplicated. Normally, unless accusation was by the old process of appeal, a jury had to be persuaded by the person aggrieved to indict the corrupt official. This most juries were loth to do as the official might possibly be the receiver of the indictment. Legal action had to originate with a jury or an individual because in medieval England the king could not prosecute on his own account. To encourage men to reveal the misbehaviour of officials Edward I in 1290 allowed complaints to take the form of the mere lodging of information in writing, and Edward III in 1340 was ready to investigate mere public clamour, which offered no surety for prosecution at all. There was also preventative legislation. In 1346 Edward III decided he must forbid by statute the taking by judges of fees, robes, or rewards from any man except for meat or drink of small value; their fees from the king were increased in compensation. In the same year the king gave power to justices to enquire into the misdemeanours of sheriffs and presumably report them for trial in the king's bench.[41] It was over a century before the justices of both benches—of assize and of the peace—were empowered to hear and terminate sheriffs' offences as a matter of course and without the necessity of a special commission. By that time the shrieval office was often in the pocket of the great lords.

If those who wished to pervert justice were for some reason unable to secure the favour of justices by gifts, rewards, or the abuse of friendship, they might still gain their ends by other means. One method much favoured was the use of force or the threat of force against either the justices themselves or against jurors, witnesses, or rival parties. Examples of these offences are both plenteous and colourful. Usually they occurred at the time of the local sessions. It was there that the frustrated anger of the accused against his known or suspected accusers boiled over, and to prevent his own humiliation

[41] *Statutes of the Realm*, i, 303; *Chronica Adae Murimuth et Roberti de Avesbury*, ed. E. M. Thompson (Rolls Series, 1889), pp. 196–8.

through indictment or outlawry he might try to stop the court from sitting. One summer early in Edward II's reign Sir Roger Swynnerton of Swynnerton, Staffordshire, and his kin-folk and supporters went armed to a county court being held at Stafford and forcibly closed the doors of the hall. They placed guards so that no one could get out and threatened to kill both the sheriff, Hugh de Croft, and Sir William Stafford, with whose family they were at odds, unless the court was stopped. At Tredington, Worcestershire, in 1347 the justices of oyer and terminer were kept from holding sessions in the house of Thomas Baddely, the king's clerk, by a large band of men who were already in occupation. In 1464 John Troys and Thomas Persons of Ely assembled men from the surrounding villages and went to Cambridge where they threatened with death the jurors who had indicted them. This was to prevent the peace sessions from being held thereby delaying their own trials.[42]

Sometimes interference took a still more violent form and the judges' lives were in jeopardy. At Eynsham in 1350 two justices of the peace were attacked by a gang of miscreants who were described as behaving like madmen or men possessed by an evil spirit. One fled into the abbey chamber to escape further assault and the sessions were called off.[43] When the bishop of Lincoln's steward, two other justices, and the under-sheriff were preparing for sessions at Huntingdon in 1440, an attempt was made by a band of armed men to reach the room where they were at work by means of ladders and also to fire the house. A jury at Colchester in May 1350 accused a number of men by name (and said there were others whom they dare not mention) of chasing Peter of Buxted, the sheriff, into a chamber adjacent to the hall where sessions were held and forcing him to make a fine with them.[44] Attacks such as these, although revealing the inability of the local authorities to keep an orderly court, resulted in relatively few violent deaths. Far more likely to result in serious injury or cause major concern were attacks on justices away from the court room. Violence of this type was more likely to be premeditated and not committed in a fleeting moment of passion. In 1332 the Leicestershire Folville gang captured Sir Richard Wylughby, a justice of the king's

[42] *William Salt Arch. Soc.*, x (1889), 54; *Cal. Pat. Rolls, 1345–1348*, p. 386; I. D. Thornley, *England under the Yorkists* (London, 1920), p. 160.
[43] *Cal. Pat. Rolls, 1348–1350*, p. 594.
[44] B. H. Putnam, *Proceedings before the Justices of the Peace, Edward III to Richard III* (London, 1938), cxi; *Select Cases in the Court of the King's Bench, Edward III*, ed. G. O. Sayles (Selden Society, 82, 1965), p. 76.

bench, and held him for a ransom of 1,300 marks (£866 13*s*. 4*d*.). A Rutland gang first warned and then murdered Sir John Wittlebury, a local keeper of the peace, in 1336. In 1350 John Legat, a Hertfordshire justice of the peace, was ambushed and murdered on his way to Hertford assizes. There is evidence to suggest that the Coterel gang deliberately set out to destroy the property and injure the persons of those who had crossed their path in a judicial capacity.[45] The most notorious attack on a judge occurred not in the remote countryside but in London, in Fleet Street, in 1358. Thomas Nesebit, a chaplain, was hired to kill Thomas Seton, a justice of common pleas. He succeeded in stabbing him in the belly and death soon followed. This attack was considered outrageous even by the standards of the fourteenth century and official records referred to Nesebit's hirers as 'satellites of the devil'.[46] The mid-fourteenth century was the high period for attacks on justices, although they were by no means unknown in the Lancastrian and Yorkist periods. No doubt as society became more sophisticated men found subtler ways to gain their ends and take revenge.

The use of threat of violence against the rival party in a lawsuit either at the sessions or elsewhere was equally common. In August 1323 Sir William Bradshaw appeared at the Lancashire county court with sixty armed men and prevented Cecilia le Boteler from proceeding with her appeal against him for the death of her husband. He persuaded the jury, doubtless by threats, to give judgment against her 'as one who had not prosecuted her appeal at all'.[47] While the justices of assize were sitting at Somerton, Somerset, in 1348 Robert Mansel assaulted Robert Brente in the hall of justice. Friends of Mansel who were present drew their weapons and chased Brente to the bar of the court. What injuries were suffered we are not told.

More likely than anyone else to suffer from threats or overt violence were the jurors, both those responsible for the indictment and those

---

[45] For the history of the Folvilles and the Coterel gang see E. L. G. Stones, 'The Folvilles of Ashby-Folville, Leicestershire, and Their Associates in Crime, 1326–1341', *Transactions of the Royal Historical Society*, 5th Series, vii (1957), 117–36, and J. G. Bellamy, 'The Coterel Gang: An Anatomy of a Band of Fourteenth Century Criminals', *Eng. Hist. Rev.*, lxxix (1964), 698–717. The murder of John Legat is in P.R.O., K.B. 27/361 Rex m. 43.

[46] *Cal. Pat. Rolls, 1358–1361*, p. 280.

[47] *South Lancashire in the Reign of Edward II*, ed. G. H. Tupling (Chetham Society, 3rd Series, i, 1949), li.

who gave the verdict. Sir Roger Swynnerton was indicted before the sheriff and coroners of Staffordshire for the death of Henry Salt at Stafford in 1326. Thereupon he went to Swynnerton, where the deed had been committed, and forced all the witnesses to come before him and pay a fine of fifty marks each for indicting him. All those involved he then made swear they would take no further proceedings against him. Part of the charges against Robert Bulwick in the sessions of the king's bench at Lincoln in July 1331 was that he had said that if anyone indicted him of felony, conspiracy, or confederacy, he would be acquitted by his neighbours, or if he was found guilty by others who were not his neighbours those jurors would be punished by having their property burned or in some other way.[48] At the outset of a notorious Staffordshire feud Hugh Erdswick and his confederates, John, Thomas, and William Myners, went to Stone on 12 October 1408 with a great company of followers in order to kill John Boughay, a duchy of Lancaster tenant, because he had indicted them at the Newcastle leet. They would certainly have killed him had he not fled to the parish church. There was another good example in the same county fifteen years later. In August 1423 Sampson Meverel, his wife, and his supporters collected a band of malefactors and outlaws and laid in wait to kill the jurors empanelled for a particularly important inquest. One juror was compelled to swear he would find a verdict in Meverel's favour and two others were threatened with death and the burning of their houses if the verdict went against him.[49] When the trial had finished the juror was still exposed to danger, as a case from about the year 1336 illustrates. A number of petty jurors who had just adjudged to death Roger Alford were seen by Gilbert Twyt, then lying in the king's marshal's prison at Lincoln. He cursed them in the foulest of language, saying they had perjured themselves. He cried that all the young men of Lincolnshire would be accursed if they did not avenge Roger's death on the jurors.[50] To tamper with the jury was to upset the most sensitive part of the English legal system. The offence was as prevalent at the end of the fifteenth century as it had been at the beginning of the fourteenth.

The roots of crime lie more in social institutions and attitudes than in the personalities of the individuals who compose society. The bane

---

[48] *William Salt Arch. Soc.*, x (1889), 54; *Select Cases in the Court of the King's Bench, Edward III*, ed. G. O. Sayles (Selden Society, 76, 1957), p. 63.
[49] *William Salt Arch. Soc.*, xvi (1895), 86–7; *ibid.*, xvii (1896), 98.
[50] *Select Cases in the Court of the King's Bench, Edward III* (1957), p. 87.

of late medieval England above all else was the widespread maintenance that was practised, that is to say the illegal support which magnates offered to a lesser man's suit by word, writing, or physical deed.
It could take a form which we have just noted, attempting to influence a jury. For this the technical name was embracery. Maintenance
was rampant before the fourteenth century began. A judge who was
sent to Yorkshire in 1294 reported to the king that there were great
complaints about maintainers of false causes and about champertors
(those who supported a suit or plea in return for a share of any profit)
by whose deeds truth and justice were completely choked.[51] The
crimes unearthed by this judge and his fellows justified his alarm, but
the problem was beyond the power of Edward I to solve, and his
successors had a similar lack of success. Statutes against maintenance
were passed from 1275 but they were all largely ineffective. Commissions to judges to enquire the names of those who maintained parties
in court occurred so regularly that they cannot have cured the evil
even if they caused a temporary abatement. One obvious reason,
possibly the principal one, for the rise of maintenance was the increasing local influence of those who were already powerful and the way
the law was corrupted by this influence. What historians have not yet
established is whether influence increased because of the lowering of
the quality of public order or public order deteriorated because of the
magnates' desire and ability to attract supporters. The more common
view is that the known partiality of justice compelled men with
complaints, and defendants too for that matter, if they wished to win
their suit, to resort to dishonest means. This meant ultimately seeking
the good offices of a lord who was so powerful in the region that none
would readily wish to offend him—neither sheriffs, nor jurors, nor
court officials, nor even justices. It was said of John Somery early in
the reign of Edward II that he had such a mastery in the county of
Staffordshire that no one could obtain law or justice. His power was
like that of a king and no one could dwell there unless he bought his
protection, either by money or by assisting him to build his castles:
so said the record. He was wont to attack people in their own houses,
intending to kill them unless they paid a fine to secure his protection.[52]
The charges made by the commons against the duke of Suffolk in the
parliament of 1450 show a similar dominance but over a greater part
of the country. Any cause he favoured was likely to prosper, any

[51] *Select Cases in the Court of the King's Bench, Edward II*, p. liii.
[52] *Cal. Pat. Rolls, 1307–1313*, p. 369.

lacking his favour was badly hindered. Suffolk's influence was very great partly because he was the royal favourite, but there were many other members of the nobility at this period whose authority over two or three counties was quite stifling.

Closely connected with maintenance was the giving of livery, usually clothing in the colours and bearing the badges of the donor. In an indented deed the man who received promised the performance of a number of services to the lord who gave. In return he was offered certain monetary rewards as well as what was called 'good lordship'. This took the shape of advice, protection, and maintenance in law-suits. There is little doubt that powerful men were very keen to develop this relationship and that social prestige was founded to some degree on the display of liveried retainers and rumour of numerous 'well-wishers'. Few of either group were their master's tenants. His wish for authority was now satisfied by a much less permanent following than had been the case in the twelfth and early thirteenth centuries, but one which was greater in number. This meant, of course, that a magnate was more likely to be asked to interfere on behalf of one of his followers. The acquisition of 'feed' (paid) men and more particularly of 'well-wishers' (who had no formal agreement with the lord) snowballed until the limits of a lord's influence actually overlapped those of the neighbouring magnates. Few men who owned a little land were able to withstand being drawn into one camp or another, though there was always the chance of changing loyalties later on.[53]

Maintenance and livery, as numerous petitions in medieval parliaments pointed out, afforded comfort and employment to criminals and thereby crimes of all kinds were caused to multiply. There is little to support the argument sometimes propounded that by increasing the power of the baronial class local authority and therefore local order were improved. As dangerous to good government as maintenance and the giving of livery was the inability of many who had suffered injury to limb or to property to secure redress or to communicate details of their injuries to the king. The 'over-mighty' subject, as he has been called, was often able to control the sheriff and through him the juries, and thus satisfaction was only to be had under the

---

[53] There is little indication that the late medieval English kings made serious efforts to suppress the giving of livery let alone destroy it root and branch. Edward IV seems to have been the first to take a proper stand: see my 'Justice under the Yorkist Kings', 150–5.

common law if the injured party was on friendly terms with the magnate. In theory, redress could also be sought outside the common law, through petitions in parliament or to the council or to chancery. In practice, a successful parliamentary petition usually needed the support of the commons as a whole, and since most members of parliament were 'feed' men they were not likely to oppose baronial interests. Petitions to council would get no sympathetic consideration if the magnate or the lord of the men who were complained against were members of the council or influential at court. Petitions to the chancellor were also likely to be defeated by influence in high places, although sometimes the same end was achieved by the simple ambushing of the would-be petitioner on his way to Westminster.[54]

There must have been much abuse of power and interference with legal process by the baronial class which never came before a court and was known to the king, if at all, only by rumour. This is suggested by one of the few ways such misdeeds did become generally known in the fifteenth century, through the disgrace and fall from power of a great figure at court. Then the king or political opponents might seek to besmirch the reputation of the fallen magnate by digging up every possible charge which could be made against him. This was what happened on the fall of William de la Pole, duke of Suffolk, in 1450 and of George, duke of Clarence, in 1477. One of Clarence's misdeeds which came to light the following year concerned his compelling a jury to indict and find guilty of murder an innocent woman. He had been persuaded to believe that his wife had been poisoned by a serving woman call Ankarette Twynho. He sent his men across several counties to seize her and then forced justices of the peace then sitting at Warwick to put her on trial for petty treason. The jurors were so frightened that despite their consciences they found the woman guilty and execution followed.[55] The case was closely connected with Clarence's quarrel with his brother Edward IV. When the duke had been attainted of treason by act of parliament another act in the same parliament declared the judgment at Warwick void. The efforts of the political opponents of the duke of Suffolk brought against him through the parliamentary commons a number of articles relating to the administration of justice. Interestingly enough, al-

[54] R. L. Storey, 'Disorders in Lancastrian Westmorland: Some Early Chancery Proceedings', *Transactions of the Cumberland and Westmorland Antiquarian and Archaeological Society*, liii (1953), 73.
[55] *Rot. Parl.*, vi, 173; *Cat. Pat. Rolls, 1476–1485*, p. 72.

though they give us a rare insight into gross abuse of power in this particular field, they were not the very best of ammunition. The Paston letters by chance reveal examples of interference with justice and of extortion by Suffolk's henchmen and his officers in East Anglia which would have served even better but which obviously were not available. We must suspect that the number of crimes promoted or supported by the magnates which became known to the king and resulted in cases in the courts was only a small percentage of the total committed. It is small wonder that the kings of the later fifteenth century instituted the practice of informing for profit.

The request of clients for illegal assistance, the frustration arising from an inability to secure justice in what were considered to be righteous causes, and the number of fighting men at beck and call made members of the upper classes turn against each other in open violence. Vicious feuds were the result. Also to blame, though to a lesser degree, were the conventions and manners of late medieval society. Because men of lower rank as a matter of course carried knives and the gentry swords, any quarrel was likely to end in the shedding of blood, especially since society viewed martial deeds and a willingness to engage in them as a valuable quality in any man. Men were very quick to take affront, particularly over matters to do with precedence and rank, title to land, advowsons, and claims to office. Injuries suffered by their followers could also drive magnates to seek revenge and lead to the spilling of blood. One such case occurred in 1385. When Richard II and his army were marching to Scotland, an archer of Ralph Stafford, the eldest son of the earl of Stafford, killed one of Sir John Holland's squires in a quarrel. Froissart, the chronicler, says that the same evening Ralph Stafford rode to visit Holland in order to appease his anger. At the same time Holland was riding to demand an explanation from Stafford. They met up with each other in the darkness. Holland asked who was passing by.[56] When the name of Stafford was given in answer he acknowledged his own identity and struck Ralph Stafford down. The feud between Adam Banaster and Sir Robert Holland in Lancashire in the earlier part of Edward II's reign flared up from the time when Holland occupied certain manors, castles, and wapentakes of Thomas, earl of Lancaster, in the south of the county without, as it was later reported,

[56] J. Froissart, *The Chronicle of Froissart*, translated by Lord Berners, 1523–5 (New York, 1967), iv, 52–5.

showing any charter or authorization from the earl.[57] Banaster may have been affronted as one of the tenants of the earl in those parts but the roots of the feud probably went back to the mid-thirteenth century. Hatred, we may note, had not been assuaged by the marriage of Banaster to Holland's sister.

The prolonged nature of late medieval feuds is well illustrated by an example from Staffordshire. In June 1324 Thomas Brumpton and William Ipstones quarrelled over the rectorship of Church Eyton church. Brumpton enlisted the support of Sir William Stafford and of James Stafford, his brother, a leader of a notorious criminal gang, while Ipstones got the support of Sir John Ipstones and Sir William Chetulton, another leader of outlaws who was known as a common malefactor and maintainer of false quarrels. This feud may well have been a continuation of an earlier one between Sir William Stafford and Sir Roger Swynnerton which had flared up in the thirteenth and fourteenth years of the reign but which dated from at least 1312–13, even perhaps from an obscure murder attributed by jurors to Swynnerton which had occurred in 1307–8. The Staffords were still feuding with the Ipstones in 1331 when a John Ipstones defeated an appeal for the killing of Thomas Stafford on a technicality. This extended and extensive quarrel must have seriously upset public order in Staffordshire and there is evidence that, although basically it was between gentry, at least one member of the nobility sent armed men to assist one of the parties.[58]

A Yorkshire feud which erupted in 1387 caused even more disturbance since it developed into quite a serious insurrection. The cause in this case seems to have been the failure of the rebel leader to secure an office he considered hereditary. William Beckwith, the disappointed candidate, on failing to obtain for himself a forestership in the forest and chase of Knaresborough, pursued for more than four years a private war against the local duchy of Lancaster officials, especially Sir Robert Rokeley, the steward and constable of Knaresborough castle.[59] Beckwith was able to raise a large number of active supporters and could rely also on the assistance of many sympathizers among the poorer classes. His gang, which according to one chronicler numbered five hundred men, wandered over the countryside seeking

[57] *South Lancashire in the Reign of Edward II*, xlii.

[58] *William Salt Arch. Soc.*, x (1889), 66, 50, 54; *ibid.*, xiv (1893), 23.

[59] See J. G. Bellamy, 'The Northern Rebellions in the Later Years of Richard II', *Bulletin of the John Rylands Library*, xlvii (1965), 254–74.

out Rokeley's friends, attacking their homes, bent on the murder of those who had indicted its members. About the beginning of the year 1392 Beckwith was betrayed and murdered by Thomas Blande, who was said to have been paid five hundred marks by the dead man's enemies. In July 1393 Beckwith's kinsmen met Blande and asked for part of the blood money to pay for prayers for the soul of their relative. Blande agreed but was then treacherously murdered. The king viewed the feud as open insurrection, though this was probably unfair. However, it does seem to have encouraged a rebellion in south Yorkshire in 1392 and may have helped to cause the revolts in Lancashire and Cheshire a year later.

The fifteenth century was the high period for feuds among the magnates, and especially the last two decades of the reign of Henry VI. As far as we can ascertain, many quarrels sprang from causes which we have already met. The feud between William, Lord Bonville and Thomas Courtenay, the thirteenth earl of Devon, seems to have erupted in 1440 when the king, by an administrative error, granted the earl the office of steward of the duchy of Cornwall when Bonville already held an office which was essentially the same. The quarrel between the Staffords of Grafton and the Harcourts of Stanton Harcourt probably stemmed from the levying of a distress.[60] Bad feeling was later turned into open warfare by a murder done at a chance meeting. One cause of rivalry and strife which was associated particularly with the fifteenth century was an attempt by one magnate to encroach on the zone of influence of a neighbour. To attempt to win supporters by the giving of livery and the like in an area where the loyalty of most men was already pledged would cause great hostility. Thus it has been suggested that Thomas Percy, Lord Egremont, quarrelled bitterly from 1450 with his uncle, the earl of Salisbury, and his sons John and Thomas Neville, over his desire to build up his influence and authority in their part of the Scottish march.[61]

Feuds such as these disrupted public order because of the large numbers of armed men who were periodically employed in riding round the county and harrying their masters' enemies by open violence. The numbers were great enough to act as a smoke-screen for

---

[60] R. L. Storey, *The End of the House of Lancaster* (London, 1966), pp. 86-7. Ill feeling, though not open feuding, may have been engendered by the social advance of Lord Bonville. He married an aunt of the twelfth earl of Devon. *Paston Letters*, ed. Gairdner, no. 60.

[61] Storey, *The End of the House of Lancaster*, pp. 125-6.

men who wished to commit individual crimes. Also, if the sheriff was of sufficient independence to try to stop the quarrel, the numbers of the contestants were great enough to drive off any posse he might recruit for the purpose. Sometimes there were as many as a thousand men on one side, as when Lord Berkeley faced his enemy Thomas Talbot, Viscount Lisle, at the 'battle' of Nibley Green on 20 March 1470. In 1453 Lord Egremont had a reported 5,000 men in the force which he assembled to attack the Nevilles in Yorkshire. When in mid-October of that year both families had eventually mustered all their strength there may well have been 10,000 men poised for action. Juries, it is true, were wont to use round figures like '500' and '1,000' too readily to convince us of their strict accuracy, but even when allowance is made for inflation the reputed numbers of the earl of Devon's private army in late 1455, 800 horse and 4,000 foot, are still impressive.[62]

Feuds also gave employment to outlaws and to the 'common malefactor', those who made their living from crime. A Staffordshire indictment spoke of Hugh Erdswick of Sandon and his brothers assembling at Amerton, Staffordshire, 1,000 disturbers of the peace who had been purposely collected from all over England, Ireland, and Wales. The intention was to kill Edmund Ferrers, lord of Chartley. In 1423 Sampson Meverel, bent on the ambush of a number of jurors and two coroners, got together a band of alleged malefactors and outlaws from various parts of the country. Whether it was common for men such as these to form a sizeable part of a great lord's retinue we cannot tell. Certainly a plundering mentality existed. John Bromyard, the Dominican, referred scathingly to the magnates' retainers and their great greed for spoil.[63] He pointed out how they used their livery as a shield. 'No hounds', he said, 'were ever readier for the chase, no hungry falcon for the bird it has spied than are these to do whatsoever their great lords bid them, if he should want to beat or spoil or kill anyone.' Although the numbers of those who supported the magnates in their open feuding might be large, we must not imagine they were all in the field continuously. The private armies rarely held together for as long as a week at any one time, even if the hard core, the members of the magnates' households, were willing to

[62] *English Society and Government in the Fifteenth Century*, ed. C. M. D. Crowder (Edinburgh, 1967), p. 107; Storey, *The End of the House of Lancaster*, pp. 132, 172.

[63] *William Salt Arch. Soc.*, xvii (1896), 7, 98; G. R. Owst, *Literature and Pulpit in Medieval England* (Oxford, 1961), p. 325.

campaign a great deal longer. Hostility was long lasting but military operations were not.

When the violence slackened, sometimes even while it was rife, the parties at feud continued their quarrel in the law courts. No doubt each felt compelled to do so to prevent his rival obtaining a legal title to any disputed territory. It has been argued that as more land came to be held by lease rather than by feudal service men discovered that title could be challenged more successfully.[64] Not that any title to land was obtained except after the expenditure of a great deal of time and money. A long purse or influence at court could enable a poor claim to stave off defeat for many years, and the law itself gave endless opportunities for delay. Suits were started before other suits were finished, with the result that John Paston, for example, had twelve actions pending in one term on his sister's behalf alone. Litigation provided an umbrella of protection from flank attack and an action which was eventually successful raised the victor's prestige in the county. Often litigation was also the continuation of a struggle at stalemate by other means. We may suspect that it provided the parties with the thrill of combat vicariously. On certain occasions a lawsuit might actually be benefited by the use of violence, as when a man collected rents by forcible entry or gained possession of a manor court and held sessions so that his claim to that manor would be improved. At other times during litigation violence occurred without any clear purpose, and it sprang directly from the frustration experienced by the laborious progress of the action in the courts.

The squabbles of the gentry and nobility greatly disrupted the king's peace but other classes and social groups also made a contribution. Who these other criminals were is a question which has rarely been asked by historians. In fact crimes were committed by all social groups in numbers roughly proportionate to the size of their membership. The types of crime were distributed in a similarly even manner, and relatively few offences were confined to a single class. The nobility and the gentry, as is perhaps already apparent, were quite as likely to use violence and to commit felony as their inferiors. Unlike today,

[64] H. S. Bennett, *The Pastons and Their England* (Cambridge, 1932), p. 172. P. S. Lewis in 'Sir John Fastolf's Lawsuit over Titchwell, 1448–1455', *The Historical Journal*, i (1958), 1–20, suggests that litigation could arise on account of the uncertainty of the land law and especially because titles had become continuously more complicated since the thirteenth century by increasing employment of entail.

a man might break the law quite seriously when an opportunity for profit or revenge offered itself but then revert back to obedience to the law, even to upholding it, for the rest of the year, the decade, or even a lifetime.[65] There was thus less of a gulf between honest men and criminals than in modern society. As in the twentieth century, a great deal of medieval larceny, in contrast with crimes such as homicide, abduction, extortion, rape, and economic offences such as the use of non-standard weights or forestalling, was probably the work of men who lived by crime. In contemporary records of the courts these men were referred to as common or notorious malefactors: what we would call persistent offenders or men with a criminal record. They often had a string of aliases both of surname and of locality where they were supposed to have been originally domiciled. Many must have been persistent wanderers. W. A. Morris pointed out how the Bedfordshire eyre of 1287 found that in almost every case involving a serious offence the criminal was a vagabond or came from another locality.[66] The assize rolls of the period show the same thing. The manner in which the processes of justice were weighted against those with a reputation or record of misbehaviour suggests that medieval man was sure he knew where the blame for much of the crime lay even if on occasion he took advantage of these men by loading them with the responsibility for crimes he had not the desire or ability to investigate properly. The vagueness and unsubstantiated nature of some charges against hapless wanderers, sometimes without the introduction of one definite felony or trespass, caused condemnation of the practice by judges of the bench several times in the fourteenth century. 'Notorious' misdoers were the only offenders who were persistently sentenced to death in the king's bench, although this may have been because the king, until 1380, was reluctant to allow justices of the peace, before whom most of the convictions for trespass and felony occurred, to determine cases of this type.

Those who wrote histories in the fourteenth and fifteenth centuries and those who administered justice made little effort to classify criminals according to type except perhaps for highway robbers, 'roberdesmen and drawlatches', and thieves. Medieval records tell us very little about the social origins of criminals or why men ventured into crime in the first place. Not until the Tudor chronicler Holinshed considered the matter was there any real interest or eager speculation.

[65] See Chapter III.
[66] W. A. Morris, *The Frank Pledge System* (Harvard, 1910), p. 152.

Holinshed believed that most persistent offenders were 'rogues', that is to say able-bodied men without employment. He argued that crimes were also commonly committed by two other groups.[67] There were the 'young shifting gentlemen which oftentimes doo beare more port than they are able to maintaine' (i.e. live above their station) and the 'servingmen whose wages cannot suffice so much as to find them breeches'. Both types turned periodically to larceny to support themselves. Whether this was sound criminology or not, contemporary comment is always valuable and medieval history suffers from the lack of it. Impoverished men of this sort, says Holinshed, turned to horse stealing, highway robbery, and breaking into and entering richer men's houses. Very probably these were the criminal activities which the persistent misdoer of medieval times also preferred.

Most crimes, in Holinshed's opinion, took a form of theft, and the reason for it was poverty. Medieval man had little curiosity about causation of crime, although he was aware of the importance of opportunity. Revenge was understood, but not much else. Chief Justice Fortescue only got as far as speculating that England's many robberies indicated a rather praiseworthy determination not to be overawed by the law, an independence of spirit which gave and took hard knocks in good part.[68] The law itself reflected society's lack of concern with motivation. Not until the end of the fourteenth century did the idea of secret or stealthy killing arouse sufficient concern as to be given special treatment by the law. A statute of 1390 distinguished pardonable homicide from non-pardonable. In the first category were those killings committed in self-defence or by misadventure, and in the second those done by ambush, deliberate attack, or with felonious intent. The law of treason showed a similar interest in the intention of the perpetrator. In 1415 to conceal a knowledge that treason was intended was held to be always malicious despite the argument of an accused, Henry, Lord Scrope of Masham, that in his case the concealment was to elicit further information about the crime.[69] One clue about the motivation of medieval criminals is provided by contemporary ballads. A common theme and obviously

---

[67] R. Holinshed, *Chronicles of England, Scotland and Ireland* (London, 1807), i, 313.

[68] J. Fortescue, *The Governance of England*, ed. C. Plummer (Oxford, 1926), pp. 141–2.

[69] See J. M. Kaye, 'The Early History of Murder and Manslaughter, Part I', *Law Quarterly Review*, lxxxiii (1968), 365–95; *Rot. Parl.*, iv, 65–6.

one much in demand among the hearers was the downfall of unjust lordship. The unjust lord manipulated the law to his own advantage and lesser men could get no satisfaction for the insults, injuries, and loss of property suffered, in the courts which he dominated. They must therefore go outside the uncertain law and by using force to settle their quarrels make an appeal to the judgment of God.[70] There is very little in medieval writings to suggest that Englishmen thought that economic and social grievances caused criminal acts. This was probably because when they considered the ills of society and anti-social behaviour, they thought in terms of obligations shirked, wrongs done, and rules broken or badly administered. Even Wat Tyler's complaints at Smithfield in 1381 were largely about the workings of the law.

Almost alone among medieval men in giving evidence of a desire to probe beneath actual misdeed in order to reach motives in the mind were the preachers. Conditioned by the religion on whose behalf they spoke they found all misbehaviour to spring from man's spiritual frailty. Native sin rather than the pressure of external events was the prime motivator. Pride and vanity were always prompting the deeds of the nobility, greed and lust for pleasure those of the gentry, deceit those of the merchants, and idleness and trickery those of the labouring classes.[71] To the clergy crime was a natural consequence of man's original fall from grace. At times laymen also must have felt that many criminal acts, particularly those involving violence, had an inevitable quality about them since few tempers were under good control and a dagger or sword might flash and a life be ended in a moment.

The incidence of the different types of crime in the later middle ages, as in any other period, was determined by the prevailing social conditions. Abduction of heiresses, to take one example, seems to have become commoner towards the end of the middle ages when competition for ladies, their hands in marriage, and thus their lands and other wealth, increased. This may have been because of the decline of the incomes of those of the nobility and gentry who still exploited their estates directly. Another example is suicide. No doubt it was on account of the teachings of the Catholic Church that far fewer people seem to have killed themselves each year in the four-

[70] *Anglo-Norman Political Songs*, ed. I. S. T. Aspin (Oxford, 1953), pp. 69–73; *The Political Songs of England*, ed. T. Wright (Camden Society, vi, 1839), 201–2.
[71] Owst, *Literature and Pulpit in Medieval England*, pp. 319–74.

teenth and fifteenth centuries than in Tudor times.[72] These crimes, like all the others, came within the two great categories of felony and trespass. Most crimes had to be one or the other, but a few could be either, depending on how the charge was brought forward initially. Felony was the more wicked offence with the more serious consequences and included homicide, rape, larceny, burglary, arson, petty treason, and breaking out of prison. Trespass included such crimes as assault, breaking into houses, taking goods, issuing threats, abduction, conspiracy, extortion, obstruction of sewers and dykes, resisting officials, forestalling, and using non-standard weights and measures. In the mid-fourteenth century there suddenly appeared a new group of trespasses which had its origins in the extensive labour legislation which followed the Black Death. Listed as offences were the taking of excessive prices, the giving or receiving of excessive wages, quitting one's master or normal locality of residence, refusing to work at the proper wage rates or even to work at all. For a short period crimes of this sort were as common in some of the courts as ordinary trespasses.

The total of presentments for felony comprised approximately twenty-five per cent for homicide and fifty per cent for larceny. In the rolls of eight counties covering the century 1314–1414 used by B. H. Putnam, E. G. Kimball, R. Sillem, and M. Gollancz, there were some 1,695 presentments for felony, of which 411 were for homicide. Larceny was the largest category of all crimes, whether felony or trespass. It carried the death penalty if the goods stolen were valued at more than a shilling. The rolls of five counties for the period 1357–1414 contain 703 presentments for felonious larceny out of 1,422 for felony in general. In the fourteenth century the cases tried in any one peace session might contain considerably more felonies than trespasses or the reverse; there was no hard and fast rule.[73] In the fifteenth century, or rather in its early years, for it is

[72] This information about suicide was given in a lecture in 1965 to the University of Nottingham History Society by Dr R. F. Hunnisett.
[73] The figures are calculated from the plea rolls printed in: B. H. Putnam, *Proceedings before the Justices of the Peace; Rolls of Northamptonshire Sessions of the Peace*, ed. M. Gollancz (Northamptonshire Record Society, xi, 1940); *The Shropshire Peace Roll, 1400–1414*, ed. E. G. Kimball; *Records of Some Sessions of the Peace in Lincolnshire, 1360–1375*, ed. R. Sillem (Lincoln Record Society, xxx, 1936); *Records of Some Sessions of the Peace in Lincolnshire, 1381–1396*, ed. E. G. Kimball (Lincoln Record Society, xix, 1955); *Rolls of the Warwickshire and Coventry Sessions of the Peace*, ed. E. G. Kimball (Dugdale Society, xvi, 1939); *Yorkshire Sessions of the Peace, 1361–1364*, ed. B. H. Putnam (Yorkshire Archaeological Society, Record Series, c, 1939). The five

for this period that records survive, felonies tended to outnumber trespasses. The fifteenth-century rolls of the justices of the peace of five counties show 387 presentments for felony, or about seventy-five per cent of the total, as against 131 for trespass. In comparison, in the fourteenth-century rolls of fifteen counties, presentments for felony amounted to about thirty-six per cent of the total. Robbery, that is to say larceny with violence, was isolated as a separate crime in 1348 and was a capital offence. It amounted to less than 5 per cent of all felonies. Burglary meant breaking into some enclosed place with intent to commit a felony. Unlike today, it was not particularly common. Perhaps the reason was the difficulty of defining 'breaking in' at a time when many buildings were incapable of being closed off from the outside world. As we might expect, the greater part of any list of offences investigated by any judicial commission was composed of appropriations of property. In the field of trespass the commonest offence was assault, which sometimes totalled as much as two-thirds of the crimes tried. It had to be described by the indicting jurors as being committed 'by force and arms' and they usually added descriptions of beating and wounding. Less important statistically, but very common, were cases of resistance to officials, extortion, which was the unlawful taking of money by officials for the performance of some official act, and conspiracy. Rape, which could be either a trespass or a felony, was not rare but it was less common. It was more than a sexual attack and was often accompanied by charges of abduction or theft of goods.

According to the rolls of the justices of the peace, economic offences had their zenith in Edward III's reign and were commonest in eastern England, the cloth-producing region with access to the continent. The surviving records of the Yorkshire sessions of the peace in 1361–4 show 78 felonies, 165 trespasses of a non-economic sort, 107 commercial trespasses, and 222 offences against the labour laws. Indictments surviving from Norfolk for the years 1372 and 1375–9 give 71 charges of felony, 40 of ordinary trespass, and 256 for offences in some way economic, but the various peace rolls which survive for Yorkshire from the reign of Richard II show only four economic offences out of a total of 179 presentments. Usually the

counties from whose rolls the presentments for grand larceny are drawn are: Lincolnshire, 1360–75 and 1381–96; Salop, 1400–14; Somerset, 1357–8; Staffordshire, 1409–14; Yorkshire, 1361–4, 1380–5, 1389–92, 1391–6 and 1390–2.

giving or receiving of excess wages bulked largest in offences against the labour laws and the use of illegal weights and measures in what may be called the field of economic trespass. In the fifteenth century charges of either type became much less common, for example there were only eight economic offences in 185 presentments in the Staffordshire peace rolls of 1409–14, but the records of peace sessions are not extant in sufficient quantity to allow any proper investigation of why this was.[74] It may have been because the labour laws were no longer enforced. Certainly the period was a golden one for the agricultural labourer, and after a brief flurry at the end of Henry IV's reign organized agrarian discontent was virtually unknown. What economic offences were presented tended to be connected with the sale of commodities in the towns, such as falsifying measures and attempting to corner the market in a particular commodity. This may account for the generally higher level of trespasses as against felonies in urban plea rolls.

Whereas the modern historian is often appalled by the violence which prevailed in this period, contemporary man commented and criticized only at what seem to have been times of excessive incidence. Monkish chroniclers, who cannot have been ignorant of the illegal acts committed in the countryside around them, did not feel they called for mention unless the offences concerned their own house directly, such as when it suffered from a daring theft or from arson. Like the lay community, men of religion had come to accept a relatively high level of lawlessness and planned their lives so that it interfered only a little. Men travelled long distances regularly even in periods of civil war without coming to grief, and only rarely did merchants lose their goods on the journey. There were, of course, some areas where men were wise not to go unless they went in a group. The regions bordering Scotland and Wales had a higher rate of crime than, for example, the south-east of England. The northern frontier in particular bred a warlike spirit and the outlaws of Tynedale and Redesdale were renowned for their violence and effrontery. Yet, in general, danger lay less in the spite of magnates whose territories one must cross or in the depredations of highway robbers than in the plots and machinations of one's own neighbours. In the fifteenth century disaster struck not so much the traveller as the goods, lands,

[74] *Yorkshire Sessions of the Peace, 1361–1364*, ed. B. H. Putnam, pp. xxix–xxxiii; B. H. Putnam, *Proceedings before the Justices of the Peace Edward III to Richard III*, pp. 108–29, 295–341, 434–67.

and the family he left behind. Most crimes were committed by mis-doers in their own neighbourhood. John Paston was in much greater danger in Norfolk than in London or *en route* between the two. By the later middle ages violence was for the most part rational in its aims and came as a climax to a quarrel which had previously been fought by other means. If retaliation and an escalation of aggression were to be prevented, then reliable local peace officers were essential. Unfortunately they were lacking. Few locally based royal officers escaped being drawn into the following of a great lord because the king chose his provincial servants from the gentry of the region and their possessions and lands exposed them to the pressure of any local tyrant. If they were not in league with a nobleman and maintained in their quarrels when they were appointed, they were soon after. Hardly ever was a royal representative, who had no local ties there, sent to a region equipped with strong judicial powers to take up residence for an extended period, even though this was the ideal solution, particularly if the official was supplied with a military force to enforce his decisions. Generally, public order had to be maintained by traditional machinery and it was an uphill struggle.

II

Misdeeds and Misdoers

Most of the crimes committed in late medieval England were either assaults or petty larcenies. There must have been tens of thousands of these offences every year. Most of the assaults were made in hot blood. The sight of an old enemy renewed the memory of scores to be settled, and the desire for revenge overcame all scruples. Larceny also was often practised without a proper plan, even if there was intent in the mind. A robber frequented places where there were the best chances of ambush or of easy access into buildings and awaited the right opportunity. Such modest crimes, lacking careful preparation, tell us very little about what was in the medieval criminal's mind, or his criminal capabilities. Another handicap in this respect is the lack of good descriptions of most sorts of crimes. Court records, the only records of so many medieval crimes, were extremely terse. Indictments were framed according to the laws thought to have been broken, which caused the exclusion of much interesting detail. Any courtroom argument between the accused and the justices was nearly always omitted. Only if the crime was novel enough to capture the interest of the clerk who compiled the court record, or if a notorious criminal made a full confession, or an injured party petitioned the king, is there recorded more than the minimum of information. Monkish chroniclers, it is true, were not averse to mentioning the more celebrated crimes in lay society, but very often they did so inaccurately. If we would discover anything worth while about the motives, the audacity, the weaknesses, the competence, perhaps even a little about the personalities of medieval criminals, it is best to inspect not the vast number of assaults and larcenies but the limited

37

number of more renowned misdeeds about which more than the usual amount of detail happily remains.

Not all medieval crimes involved the use or the threat of force. In a fair number of examples quite sophisticated forms of trickery were used. The medieval confidence trickster was not common but his existence cannot be doubted. An interesting example of criminal deceit occurred on 7 April 1354 at Barnstaple, Devon. Three men, Gervase Worthy, Geoffrey Ipswich, and William Kele, visited the house of Roland Smalecombe, who himself was absent at the time, and informed his wife that once they had been pagans but were now Christians. This was done apparently to convince the woman of their ability to foretell the future and perform feats of magic.[1] They talked so convincingly about their magical powers that Mrs Smalecombe brought before them various precious articles then in her keeping. These included cups, belts, rings, and brooches, all of gold or silver. The articles were put first into a linen bag and were then, as far as the woman could tell, placed in a box which the men locked with a key. Gervase Worthy, the trio's spokesman, pocketed the key and told the woman that if she went to church and had three masses a day celebrated for nine days, she would, when the men returned on the tenth day, find the belongings in the box to have doubled. The three men then left but of course they never returned. Eventually the woman broke open the box and found only a linen bag filled with pieces of lead and stones. It was as a consequence of this, or so the indictment of the tricksters claimed, that she took sick and died.

This was only one of a number of swindles which Worthy and his associates committed in Devon. The jurors who presented the information about the case reckoned they persuaded the people of that county to part with more than 200 marks. The ruse was obviously well tried and the victim and the opportunity sought out with care. The tricksters made their visit seemingly when the woman's husband was absent. Their number no doubt enabled one of them to remove the valuables while the others engaged the victim in conversation. Perhaps they made use of a simple conjuring trick. They played on the woman's greed, her desire to know the future, and her belief in fortune-telling and magic. Although indicted soon after committing their Barnstaple offence, at least two of the misdoers were not put on trial until years later. Worthy was outlawed and then pardoned.

[1] *Select Cases in the Court of the King's Bench, Edward III*, ed. G. O. Sayles (Selden Society, 82, 1965), p. 104.

He accepted jury trial but on account of the failure of the jury to appear was not actually tried until Easter term 1362 when he was found not guilty. Proceedings against Kele lasted even longer, until 1374, when he was acquitted because of an error in procedure. Despite the obvious value of the goods stolen the justices did not reckon the crime constituted a felony, which suggests that the common lawyers were unsure how to classify thefts of this sort. The three tricksters, like many of their kind since that time, were probably one jump ahead of the law.

In the competitive world of medieval begging, enterprise was essential for success. Two supposed beggars, brought before the mayor, aldermen, and sheriffs of London in October 1380, John Warde of Yorkshire and Richard Lynham of Somerset, were really fully fledged confidence tricksters. To obtain alms they had concocted a thoroughly deceitful routine. They pretended to be mutes, to have been deprived of their tongues. They went about the city carrying in their hands two ell measures, an iron hook, pincers, and a piece of leather shaped like a human tongue which was edged with silver and bore the words 'This is the tongue of John Warde'.[2] With these props, and by the use of signs, they gave people to understand they were traders, and that their tongues had been drawn out with the hook and cut off with the pincers. They gave authenticity to their mime by making roaring noises in accompaniment, and even opened their mouths as if to show their tongues were lacking. The ell measures and the pose as traders were probably intended to win the sympathy of the mercantile and commercial sections of the London citizenry. The men were no doubt trying to capitalize on the fears of traders of suffering similar penalties. The two tricksters must have met with some success for they were accused not only of defrauding poor and infirm persons but also of acting in manifest deceit of the whole people. The court found Warde and Lynham, who had made a confession, guilty, and sentenced them to an hour a day in the pillory for three days and then a term in Newgate prison until order was given for their release.

Another type of medieval confidence trick involved the offer by a man of rank or an office-holder to perform a service in return for cash. When the money was paid he went away with no intention either of returning or of completing his part of the bargain. The need

<hr />

[2] *Memorials of London and London Life in the Thirteenth, Fourteenth and Fifteenth Centuries*, ed. H. T. Riley (London, 1868), p. 445.

of men and women who could not travel themselves to be represented legally at the papal curia or have an agent watching over their affairs there gave great scope for clerical swindlers. Nowhere are such deceits better exemplified than in the career of the rascally Master Robert Colynson, a fifteenth-century priest who had a remarkable taste for crime.[3] In 1453 Colynson was accused before the king's council of informing a number of priors in Cheshire that they had been cited to the papal curia and must appear there on a certain day. Each said he could not. Colynson then offered that if they paid him he would 'ease them' of their difficulty, presumably by getting the summons annulled. The priors gave him money but seem to have received no satisfaction, even if Colynson did in fact visit Rome. We know he was there on at least one occasion because another charge stated that while he was at the curia he made the acquaintance of a fairly wealthy canon of Guisborough, who was probably pursuing a suit there but who had been laid low by illness. Colynson persuaded the canon to entrust him with a sum of money in order to expedite the case in the courts. He used it not for the intended purpose but to spend. When the canon recovered from his sickness and asked Colynson for any money remaining, he was met with the cool answer that none had ever been given. The outraged canon then enlisted the support of Lord Camois, which so frightened Colynson that he fled the curia for good. Another charge made before the council was that Colynson, by deceit, had obtained from a woman of Hedon (near Hull) a large sum of money with which she intended to purchase residence in an abbey. The roguish priest had persuaded her to part with the savings by promising that her soul would never suffer pain if he said a mass for her at Scala Coeli. On another occasion, in 1450, Colynson paid a visit to Swine abbey in Yorkshire and told the prioress he had been sent by Cardinal Kemp to preach to them and to teach them. Then by a glib speech, in which he promised to get them absolution at Rome, he was able to extract a shilling from each nun to a total of 20s. 8d. The ruse was so successful that he tried it again elsewhere.

These offences were only a section of Colynson's misdeeds and perhaps not the most reprehensible. He was a thoroughgoing villain who exploited his ecclesiastical rank and other men's credulity to the uttermost. He must have been notorious in many parts of the country. He was banished from Cambridge University for his sermons,

[3] *Calendar of Patent Rolls, 1452–1461* (Record Commission), pp. 93–101.

which were described as erroneous and seditious, and at Leicester he had preached 'perilous matter' and spoken against the king's estate. In 1453, when accused before the council, he was known to the authorities as a 'misgoverned person'. This was true enough for his private life was most unpriestly and contained several very unsavoury episodes. At St Albans he lived with another man's wife, calling her his sister. On one occasion he tried to kill the woman's husband by taking him a letter and then stabbing him with a knife while he was reading it. When he was a chantry priest at a parish church in Canterbury he was said to have behaved 'horribly' with a young woman but no other details are known. On another occasion, at Southwark, early one morning he entered a tavern much frequented by prostitutes, seized a boy aged eleven in his arms, and 'kiste him many tymes as it hadde been a woman'. Only when the lad cried out loudly did Colynson release his hold and ask if there was any woman available, 'for he wolde fayne have a woman'. Being rebuked by Leventhorp, the marshal of the king's bench, not because of his behaviour towards the boy but because of his drinking so early in the day, Colynson, no whit abashed, retorted sharply that he had already said mass at St Magnus' and had worked up a rare thirst.

For his many frauds and his overtly loose way of life Colynson should have been put on trial in an ecclesiastical court, but there was little determination to do so among the church authorities. Despite the serious accusations made against him before the council, and despite his indictment for treason on another occasion, he remained until his death the rector of Chelsfield in Kent.[4] He obtained papal dispensation to hold an additional incompatible benefice in April 1459 and was provided by the Pope with the bishopric of Ross in Ireland in March 1460. The trickery of Colynson was recorded in detail only because he had fallen foul of |Ralph, Lord Cromwell, by accusing him of involvement in the treasons of John Wilkyns, a leader of popular revolt. Colynson claimed to have acquired his information from Wilkyns just before he was dragged on a hurdle to execution. Lord Cromwell was able to show that Colynson had not been near Wilkyns on that occasion, and while proving his own good character made detailed counter-charges against the priest which give us our information. There seems no weighty reason for doubting the substantial veracity of these accusations.

[4] P.R.O. K.B. 9/273/134; A. B. Emden, *A Biographical Register of the University of Cambridge to 1500* (Cambridge, 1963), pp. 152–3.

Highway robbery, perhaps the most colourful form of a crime which existed in a great number of varieties, was very common in the England of the later middle ages. Robin Hood and his men were reputed in popular lore to make their living from it, and many of the ballads feature a highway ambush. Perhaps, of all the types of robbers, highway robbers were the most professional with reputations which were more than local. It was the man who robbed on the highway who was referred to most frequently in indictments as a common or notorious criminal, and this served to make the charges laid against him the more weighty. Unlike most other offenders, only a minority of 'notorious' criminals were acquitted by trial juries, and thus the occupation of highwayman, if it promised lucrative rewards, was a relatively dangerous one. There was another hazard also. Because highwaymen interfered with merchants whose goodwill was needed for the purpose of loans and taxation, the late medieval king was wont to view highway robbery with the greatest detestation. In the years 1346–50 Edward III or his judges made several attempts to classify robbery on the highway as treason and inflict the penalties associated with that crime.[5] Henry IV did likewise in 1401–2, when a number of highwaymen were actually convicted as traitors, but then apparently he had to desist.[6] Highway robbers usually operated in one particular locality. Even those who were the most mobile favoured particular stretches of road. This was usually because of the opportunities offered for ambush and the proximity of a safe retreat. The wooded defile at Trimpley on the edge of Wye forest, three miles north-west of Kidderminster, Worcestershire, was the stamping ground of a gang which specialized in robbing travelling merchants.[7] Where the three counties of Lincolnshire, Leicestershire, and Rutland joined was a place particularly beloved by robbers.[8] Several roads ran nearby, and because the shire boundaries were so ill-defined sheriffs and justices of the peace were reluctant to assume responsibility for the suppression of crime there. Since it was the wealth of the passer-by which was of prime importance to the highway robber, merchants were a major quarry and roads which led to towns with important fairs and markets were the most profitable.

One robbery on the highway which attracted more attention than

[5] *Chronicon Galfridi le Baker*, ed. F. M. Thompson (Oxford, 1889), p. 92; P.R.O. K.B. 27/349 Rex m. 23.

[6] P.R.O. K.B. 9/189/10.

[7] R. H. Hilton, *A Medieval Society* (London, 1966), p. 254.

[8] *Cal. Pat. Rolls, 1272–1281*, p. 178.

nearly all others was an ambush in 1248 at the pass of Alton, in Hampshire, on the London to Southampton road. The spot was notorious for its robberies and murders.[9] On this particular occasion it was a number of important merchants from France and Flanders who suffered the loss of their goods and their money. One of them, called Reyner de Lewe, was eventually recompensed by the king from the issues of Hampshire eyre in the sum of £106.[10] The chronicler Matthew Paris tells us that just before the beginning of Lent in 1248 two merchants of Brabant, one probably Reyner and the other called Fulmar, went to the king on arrival at Winchester and told how they had been attacked and robbed of 200 marks.[11] They said that if those whom they accused dared to deny the accusation they would settle the matter judicially by duel. Most surprisingly they claimed that members of the royal household were involved. This was quite true, but they were by no means the only offenders. As the king's council pointed out to its master, a great number of local inhabitants were incriminated also, particularly the men of Alton and of the liberty of the bishop of Taunton.

At first there was considerable difficulty in getting a jury to make the necessary indictments and a second one had to be elected. Those who were eventually named as the culprits were no ne'er-do-wells but men of substance, each possessing, according to Matthew Paris at least, between fifty and eighty librates of land. Also named were a number of men who were members of the king's household, as had been suggested originally. Some of those indicted were arrested immediately, but many sought sanctuary in churches and others were able to flee the region for good. If the chronicler is to be believed, 300 misdoers were convicted and hanged, and as many more were placed in prison to await a similar judgment. There was also a substantial number of men who were merely fined. If the men of Alton and the men of the king's household were involved together, the robbery must have been a carefully laid plot. Although the Alton defile would give any ambusher a great advantage, the robbers had to make provision for the permanent watch mounted there by a number of king's sergeants, unless of course the sergeants were in the plot as well. Very few of the robbers' names are to be discovered. There is

---

[9] *Calendar of Miscellaneous Inquisitions, Henry III and Edward I* (Record Commission), no. 269.

[10] *Calendar of Liberate Rolls, 1245–1251* (Record Commission), p. 222.

[11] *Matthaei Parisiensis Chronica Majora*, ed. H. R. Luard (Rolls Series, 1872–1884), v, 56–60; P.R.O. J.I. 1/776 m. 27

reference to William le Escot, possibly a former approver, to Nicholas de Winceleis, who must have won royal favour since he was a sergeant in the king's service in May 1255, to John de Bercham and John Beddings, but that is all. All other names, which were the subject of indictments or appeals, were of men or women who had received or comforted the actual robbers. They were numerous.[12] Despite Matthew Paris's emphasis on indictments by jury a number of men were accused by approvers. The chronicler mentions only one approver, a notorious man called William Pope, whom he says appealed fifteen confederates and killed six of them in judicial combat. The legal records which mention others seem to suggest that the one named William le Escot had been an approver before and was placed in gaol by the king so that, from the conversations he overheard among those arrested for the Alton robbery, he could make accurate accusations.[13] There was nothing subtle about many of the robbers' motives. They stole to get rich quickly. Those of the Alton locality who participated probably banked on the refusal of presenting jurors drawn from that neighbourhood to name names, a possibility which caused the king's council much concern. At the gallows the condemned members of the king's household admitted their greed and guilt, but made a most interesting and revealing request. They asked the hangman to tell the king that he was responsible for their deaths because he so delayed their pay that they had been forced to steal. William Pope, the approver, was an Alton merchant who was in debt to a Jew.[14]

When he heard of the robbery, King Henry made a point of visiting Winchester so that his presence might help in the discovery of the criminals and make their conviction the more certain. He showed that he was particularly incensed by the attack being made on the merchants of a friendly power, the duchy of Brabant. He told the bailiffs and freemen of Hampshire, whom he had summoned to Winchester castle, that he was ashamed of the county and reminded them that he himself had been born there.[15] He talked of calling men

[12] *Calendar of Close Rolls, 1247–1251* (Record Commission), pp. 403, 411; *ibid., 1251–1253*, p. 315; *Cal. Pat. Rolls, 1247–1258*, p. 121; P.R.O. J.I. 1/776 mm. 27, 27d, 30, 37.

[13] *Matthaei Parisiensis Chronica Majora*, v, 60; *Cal. Close Rolls, 1247–1251*, pp. 66, 69.

[14] *Matthaei Parisiensis Chronica Majora*, v, 60; *Cal. Close Rolls, 1254–1256*, p. 197.

[15] *Matthaei Parisiensis Chronica Majora*, v, 57–8.

from all the other shires of England to ferret out the Hampshire misdeeds. At one stage he even intended to imprison his audience, but was dissuaded by the bishop of Winchester. Despite the punishments inflicted on the criminals, the pass of Alton continued to be infested by robbers, fugitives, and rebels. There is reference to an attack on the king's baggage there just before March 1260, and it was in the woods near Alton that in 1266 the Lord Edward hunted down Adam Gurdon, a persistent Montfortian and a forester of Woolmer, who with a band of die-hard adherents was in retreat there.

The great Alton robbery shows that the most unlikely of medieval men, even members of the king's own household, might on occasion turn their hands to crime. What tempted them in the Alton case was probably the combination of wealthy merchants with inadequate protection, knowledge of a perfect place for ambush, and a belief that, having the sympathy and assistance of the men of the neighbourhood, they were unlikely to be indicted. Normally those with gentle blood in their veins showed little inclination to be highway robbers. They might commit forcible entry, abduction or assaults regularly but interference with travellers who were unknown to them was quite rare, at least in the central shires of England. One of the few examples of highway robbery which involved local gentry and which is reasonably documented occurred on 2 February 1341. According to a petition they addressed to the earl of Arundel, two merchants, William Drakelowe and Richard Horninglowe, sent their servants with two horses laden with fardels of spices and textiles worth £40 to a market to be held at Stafford.[16] When they reached Cannock wood they met Sir Robert Rideware, accompanied by two followers, and were taken captive. They were led to Lapley priory, but one man escaped on the way. In the priory were gathered a number of Rideware's friends and accomplices, some of them knights. According to the petitioners, it was here that the plunder, their merchandise, was divided up, each man taking a share according to his social rank. The following day the company of robbers and captives rode from Lapley to the priory of Blythebury, where Rideware sought rest and food, claiming they were all retainers of the king. The prioress, perhaps suspicious, refused the request but the robbers nonetheless stayed the night and broke open the barns to take hay and oats for their horses. The servant, who escaped, had resolutely trailed the misdoers at a distance, and having established they were at Blythebury went to the

---

[16] *Archaeological Journal*, iv (1847), 69–71.

king's bailiff errant at Lichfield and told him the facts. Taking with him some Lichfield townsmen the bailiff went to Blythebury and summoned the robbers to surrender, but they refused and a fight took place. The bailiff and his men had the better of it and the robbers fled. Four were caught in the pursuit and apparently decapitated straightaway. Possibly because he lost the trail, or because of nightfall, the bailiff turned back towards Lichfield. Between Blythebury and Ridware Parva he was overtaken by Sir Robert Rideware, who had rallied the robber band and had been reinforced by Sir Walter Rideware, the lord of Hamstall Ridware. A sudden attack recovered the plunder for the malefactors. The following Thursday the two petitioners went to Stafford to make their complaints but were unable to enter the town since confederates of the robbers were posted at the gates. Thus the merchants had recourse to petitioning the earl of Arundel at his sessions at Lichfield. What happened subsequently we do not know.

Unlike in the Alton robbery, the merchants were local men, not foreigners. The journey the goods were travelling was only short and their value was probably not particularly great. The number of servants who accompanied the goods was not mentioned but they were forced to deliver them up to a mere trio of bandits. No doubt a single mounted and well-equipped household servant of a knight, perhaps with experience in the wars, was the equivalent in a fight of two or three servants of a merchant, but the small number of original ambushers suggests either a chance and unpremeditated meeting or, more likely, a number of small parties simultaneously watching the many roads across Cannock Chase. Some confirmation of the second alternative is provided by the sinister gathering at Lapley priory.

The knights who were involved in the episode are worthy of individual attention. Sir Robert Rideware appeared on few local commissions, but if not a notable figure in shire government, he was no persistent criminal and was not, as far as we know, addicted to feuding. Nor does Sir John Oddingseles, one of those waiting at Lapley, seem at this time to have been suspected as a lawbreaker. Another of the gang, however, Edmund Oddingseles, was quite possibly the leader of a criminal band of his own. In February 1342 the king commissioned Richard de Monte Caniso to find and arrest Oddingseles and a score or so of his followers, and deliver them into the custody of the constable of the Tower of London. A second order to the same effect, signifying failure hitherto and showing concern at the situation, was issued to John Legat of Langley, Hertfordshire, about five weeks later.[17] The outcome is unknown. The chances are that those accused by the two merchants escaped conviction. Sir John Oddingseles, who held land in Staffordshire and Hertfordshire, was favoured with local duties by the king in 1344 and 1347, but since both tasks concerned the arrest of malefactors, and it was at that time a fairly common practice to set a thief to catch a thief, his character is by no means vindicated. In 1350 he was responsible for the slaying of a justice of the peace, in fact the John Legat mentioned above.[18] The king tried to call the crime treason and Oddingseles was imprisoned in the Tower for a time.

The use made of Lapley priory as a hide-out should not surprise us. There is evidence of a number of religious houses in the fourteenth century having close connections with bands of criminals, frequently from choice. They were used for such purposes as collecting rents and intimidating ecclesiastical and secular foes. If Rideware and his associates had no such 'business' relationship with Lapley priory they could easily have obtained hospitality by a mere show of strength. The formal division of the spoil which took place is an important detail. It suggests both a fair number of robbers in the band and a careful plan of campaign. While the determination of the king's bailiff shows royal officials in a good light, the resilience of the robbers and their counter-pursuit are very significant, as is their ability to stop the petitioners from entering Stafford. Very probably the band was no ordinary collection of outlaws turned robbers but a well-led and carefully organized gang with a number of knights and esquires and their household servants as its core.

During the last two and a half centuries of the middle ages the English counties which suffered most from a lack of good governance were those furthest from London, and particularly the shires which bordered on Scotland. The keeping of public order there proved too much for the king, and he left the problem in the hands of the great nobles of the region. They recognized it as a task which could be brought to no satisfactory conclusion, particularly as the near continuous fighting with the Scots gave men an excuse to be always well armed as well as the opportunity to commit crimes which they could blame on the national enemy. There was little respect among the inhabitants of the English northern border counties for their distant

[17] *Cal. Pat. Rolls, 1340–1343*, pp. 442, 449.
[18] P.R.O. K.B. 27/361 Rex m. 43.

king and his policies at any time, but they were particularly incensed when he refused to make peace or even a truce with the Scottish enemy and yet was unable to offer them any protection from Scottish raids. This was the situation in Northumberland in 1315–17. Feelings were exacerbated by the oppressions of a number of royal officials such as John le Irys, who was keeper of Barnard castle in 1315–16 and then under-keeper of Bamborough castle, and also by the king's choice of a new bishop of Durham. Instead of the nominee of the monks there had been elected Lewis Beaumont, a relative of the queen and a man thought by many to be avaricious, insufficiently learned, and quite unsuitable.

On 1 September 1317 the bishop-elect and his brother, Sir Henry Beaumont, the constable of Norham, were travelling towards Durham for the consecration. With them were two cardinals, Gaucelin of Eauze and Luca Fieschi, who had been sent by Pope John XXII to arrange a peace between the English and the Scots and were travelling north for that purpose. They had also been instructed to reconcile the rival baronial factions in England, and this may have been an additional cause of the events which followed. At a place called Aycliffe, near Durham, a large band of northern gentry and their followers led by Sir Gilbert Middleton, a Northumberland landholder and apparently a member, past or present, of the king's household, stopped the travellers, kidnapped the two Beaumonts, and robbed the cardinals.[19] In captivity the Beaumonts may have been separated, the bishop being held at Sir Gilbert's castle at Mitford and Sir Henry at his fortress at Morpeth, or they may both have been kept at Mitford: either is equally probable. One argument is that the intent behind the kidnapping was to stop the consecration at Durham, but this does not explain the ransom which Sir Gilbert exacted from the two Beaumonts. The amount paid to secure their release is unknown, but we have the information that Middleton gave a receipt for the payment. If the bishop and his brother were held to ransom why not the cardinals? This would have made the ambush at least twice as profitable. If Sir Gilbert's quarrel was solely with the Beaumonts why should he rob the cardinals? Perhaps he felt that the kidnapping of cardinals was so heinous an offence as to result in his own destruction; perhaps

[19] A. E. Middleton, *Sir Gilbert de Middleton and the Part He Took in the Rebellion in the North of England in 1317* (Newcastle-on-Tyne, 1918), pp. 28–59. The amount paid to ransom the Beaumonts is unknown but Sir Gilbert's chattels were later found to be worth £2.615 12s. 4d., a very large sum: *Abbreviatio Placitorum, Richard I to Edward II* (Record Commission, 1811), p. 330.

the cardinals were robbed by mistake, their possessions not being distinguishable from others; perhaps Middleton's followers stole against their master's instructions. No answer is totally satisfactory. Since there is reference to Sir Gilbert holding other prisoners to ransom in Mitford castle we may take it that this was not his first criminal venture.

When he heard of the crime Edward II was furious. His inability to protect ecclesiastical visitors of the highest importance was revealed, and by a member of his own household at that. Quite unreasonably he called the crimes of Middleton treason, pretending the knight had levied open war against his king. He must have hastily sought to arrange for nobles of those parts on whom he could rely to seize Middleton, but nothing was accomplished until December. By then both Lewis Beaumont (17 October) and his brother Henry (December) had been ransomed and released. Very likely only a matter of days after the latter event Sir Gilbert's castle of Mitford was captured by a group of local gentry, supposedly with the aid of some hostages within. Middleton was himself taken and then sent by sea and land to London. There he was convicted as a traitor on the king's record, the most summary way of condemning a man in the later middle ages, and execution followed.[20] Those of his adherents who escaped capture at Mitford fled to the peel of his ally, Walter Selby, at Horton, which fell after a siege of about ten weeks. In retrospect it is obvious that the ambush at Aycliffe was not a typical case of fourteenth-century highway robbery. What it exemplified were the special conditions prevailing in the Scottish marches and the temerity of the inhabitants. What should perhaps be surprising is the relatively quick capture of Sir Gilbert Middleton. This was caused no doubt by his determination to stand his ground and remain in one of his castles. Even when public order was so weak, unless the misdoer was a great noble, he was best advised to go into hiding on committing a notorious crime, or to leave the locality.

If larceny on a small scale was very common in the later middle ages the theft, as distinct from the malversation by officials, of a really large sum of money, or of a great number of valuable objects, was rare. Only very infrequently were such things deposited together or transported in a single load. When it was a matter of storage over an extended period men often preferred to leave their prized possessions

[20] *Select Cases in the Court of the King's Bench, Edward II*, ed. G. O. Sayles (Selden Society, 74, 1955), p. 78.

in a monastery, trusting in the honesty of the monks and the fear any would-be thief should have for ecclesiastical sanctions. The English kings themselves favoured this device and made particular use of Westminster Abbey as a treasure-house. Usually the king, despite all his wanderings, was on hand every two or three months to keep a watchful eye on the royal hoard, but when, during the Scottish war, Edward I moved the exchequer, chancery, and the law courts to York (1298–1303), royal visits became increasingly rare and few royal servants were left in London. Thus was afforded a golden opportunity for a daring robber to raid the wardrobe treasury then located in the crypt under the Westminster Abbey chapter house. The bold man who attempted this most sensational of medieval robberies was not a notorious criminal but a merchant named Richard Pudlicott.[21] Pudlicott had been trading in wool, cheese, and butter in Flanders when he was arrested as a surety for the debts which Edward I had left behind him there. He managed to escape to England, but lost vouchers for £14 17s. for wools taken for the king's use. Intending to sue for his losses in court, Pudlicott took lodgings in London, and soon became acquainted with John Senche, keeper of both the king's palace at Westminster and the Fleet prison, and with his deputy William of the Palace. These two, who obviously had time on their hands and no one to answer to, were members of a disreputable band of men and women who congregated at the palace keeper's lodge, and whose drunken revelry was notorious in the neighbourhood of Westminster.

The abbot of Westminster was an old man at this time and his authority must have been waning. Soon a number of his monks had joined in the local festivities. Pudlicott became an acquaintance and perhaps even a friend. When he failed to gain satisfaction from the king in the courts the idea was germinated that he should recompense himself from the treasure in the abbey. His monkish companions had most likely already shown or described to him their house's silver plate, and his own visits to dine in the abbey refectory had revealed to him how the ground lay. Pudlicott seems to have made preparations for robbery while the king was still in London and to have decided to

---

[21] T. F. Tout, *Collected Papers III* (Manchester, 1934), pp. 93–115; *Willelmi Rishanger Chronica et Annales*, ed. H. T. Riley (Rolls Series, 1865), pp. 420–21; *Flores Historiarum*, ed. H. R. Luard (Rolls Series, 1890), iii, 115, 117, 121, 131; *Chronicles, Edward I and Edward II*, ed. W. Stubbs (Rolls Series, 1882–3), i, 130–4; H. Hall, *The Antiquities and Curiosities of the Exchequer* (London, 1891), pp. 25–8.

steal first the abbey's own valuables rather than those in the wardrobe treasury. Thus on the day the king left Westminster, after a fleeting visit, in March 1302, Pudlicott broke in through the chapter house window and stole plate from the refectory. The proceeds were spent on riotous living and Pudlicott must have become a very popular member of the Westminster revellers.

By December 1302 all was gone and he turned to a new scheme, nothing less than the removal of the king's treasure from the crypt. Access to this part of the abbey was properly from the sacristy, not from the chapter house but, according to the juries which indicted Pudlicott later, he chose to make a frontal assault on the latter. Instead of procuring the assistance of the sacrist or of some of the monks and breaking into the crypt from inside the church, he elected to try to break through the wall of the chapter house from the outside, that is from the churchyard on the east side of the abbey. In parts this wall was thirteen feet thick and although medieval stonework could be in parlous state of disrepair the fact that Pudlicott himself claimed it took him many winter nights' work to effect an entry suggests a truly gargantuan task. According to the indictments he sought and obtained the assistance of a number of masons and carpenters. To lessen the risk of discovery Pudlicott sowed hempseed near the hole so that, when grown, it might serve to camouflage his excavations. He was also assisted, deliberately or not we do not know, by the sending of passers-by round by another path. By 24 April 1303 he had gained entry. His elation was so great that for more than a day he merely gloated over his prize. Then on the 26th he left with as much treasure as he could carry. Finding perhaps his load too heavy, he concealed a part in the churchyard of St Margaret's and went on, bearing the remainder. He next seems to have joined his old drinking companions for two nights of revelry in a house inside the Fleet prison, after which they went armed to Westminster and returned before dawn loaded with valuables. In all it was reckoned that treasure to the value of £100,000 had been stolen. It has been argued that this account of events, which is the one to be found in Pudlicott's confession, was only distantly related to the truth, which was that the sacrist of the abbey, Adam of Warfield, and perhaps a number of other monks, had assisted him in entering the crypt from the abbey church. The hole in the wall was fictitious or perhaps diversionary. Certainly its failure to excite alarm is very suspicious despite Pudlicott's story about the hempseed.

Suspicions that the abbey had been robbed were first aroused when valuable objects appeared in unlikely places. Silver goblets were fished out of the Thames, and dishes and cups were discovered in St Margaret's churchyard and other plate in the surrounding fields. Those who dealt in coins and precious articles, the city goldsmiths and the money changers, were either reported as having, or were found to have, plate and foreign coin in their possession which came from the Westminster treasure. No doubt Pudlicott's drinking cronies found it hard to refrain from displaying or spending their newly acquired wealth. One local whore, noticed wearing a precious ring, explained that it had been given to her by Adam of Warfield, the sacrist, 'so that she should become his friend'. When King Edward, who was encamped at Linlithgow, heard reports of the robbery, he appointed a special commission for an enquiry. On 20 June the keeper of the wardrobe, John Droxford, came to Westminster to make an official examination of his treasury. By that time a considerable amount of the treasure had been recovered: some from Pudlicott's lodgings, some from under the bed of William of the Palace, and some in the possession of a number of Westminster monks, including Adam of Warfield. Pudlicott was himself arrested on 25 June when in sanctuary in the church of St Michael in Candlewick Street, and William of the Palace captured soon after. Grave suspicion fell on the whole of the Westminster convent, causing the arrest on indictment of 49 monks, including the abbot, and 32 laymen. Later the vast majority were released on bail. Judging by the bitter complaints to the king demanded further enquiry, some injustices had been done and the commissioners were not making proper progress. As a result a second commission, which included Roger Brabazon, chief justice of the king's bench, and William Berford, later chief justice of common pleas, was appointed in November and held sessions from January to March 1304. Those found guilty included Pudlicott, who made a confession, Adam of Warfield, who was suspected of being the principal deviser of the robbery, William of the Palace, and a number of monks and laity. Pudlicott, Warfield, and the monks claimed their clergy, and only William and five other lay culprits eventually went to the gallows that year. Pudlicott at least had only delayed the end. He was kept in gaol until October 1305, and then, for some reason unknown to us, he was hanged.

The story of this great robbery is a remarkable one. Pudlicott achieved success because of the slackness, even the wickedness, of the monks of Westminster. The monkish chroniclers of later years put the blame on Pudlicott squarely enough, but it is obvious that without some sort of assistance from within the abbey neither of his two robberies could have been carried out. The help he received may have been nothing more than useful information, but we may fairly suspect it was substantial and practical. From gallantry, or because he was prompted by justices who did not wish the monks to receive too much of the blame, Pudlicott confessed to committing the crime on his own, but the statement must be regarded with suspicion. By the fourteenth century, perhaps before, a fair number of religious houses had been involved in criminal misdeeds, through both the wilful employment of malefactors to assist in their quarrels and the errant behaviour of their own members. Edward I must himself take some of the blame for the robberies. The absence of the king from Westminster was of course common, but not for periods as prolonged as in Edward's case. Because of the removal of the exchequer, the law courts, and chancery to York, there must have been fewer royal servants at Westminster at the time of the robbery than at any other period in the later middle ages. The untrustworthiness of John Senche, and particularly of William of the Palace, should remind us of the unreliability of many medieval office-holders. It serves particularly to illustrate the fact that those who in medieval times were entrusted with the custody of malefactors were quite likely to be drawn by their charges into the world of crime. Pudlicott's statement in his confession, that he intended in August 1302 to sue in the king's courts for compensation for his losses, reveals him as either ingenuous or a liar. If there was a court at Westminster at that time in which to sue he was still likely to be disappointed, for no man could sue the king: he could only petition him for justice. The delay in bringing Pudlicott and his allies to trial suggests that the king was himself slow to move against the robbers, perhaps because of his fear of ecclesiastical scandal. The appointment of a second, more powerful, commission points to the discovery of the definite involvement of the Westminster monks and of royal officers at that stage in the enquiry rather than the failure of the first commission to do anything. Whatever the degree of Pudlicott's guilt there can be little doubt that the robbery of the wardrobe treasury in 1303 was one of the most enterprising of all medieval crimes.

Murder, perhaps surprisingly, is not a well-documented later medieval crime. Murder meant not so much premeditated killing as

homicide by stealth. It was heinous, not because of any evil preparations, but because it caught a man off his guard. One of the few cases
known to us which contained elements of the modern murder drama
occurred in Lincolnshire in 1375.[22] Sir William Cantilupe, a Lincolnshire knight of some stature in his home county, was, according to
a jury of presentment, murdered in his room in his home at Scotton.
Those named as guilty of the deed were not unknown felons, or
notorious robbers, as in so many indictments, but twelve members of
Sir William's own household, including his esquire, his steward,
Maud his own wife, and Agatha her maid. This made the crime
technically one of petty treason. The indictments, of which there
were several, said that Sir William had been violently done to death
while lying on his bed in his room at night. His murderers had then
bathed the mortal wounds in water, presumably to staunch the flow
of blood, put the body naked into a sack, carried it for four miles,
and then, having first reclothed it in fine garments and with spurs and
belt, had thrown it into a field. They intended quite obviously to give
the impression that the knight had been killed by common robbers
while travelling on the highway. No two juries offered the same date
for the committing of the crime. It varied from 13 February to 11
April, and in view of this surprising divergence of opinion we may
wonder if the other details reported by the jurors were at all accurate.

Eventually, at the Lincolnshire quarter sessions in June 1375,
sixteen men and women, including a landowning neighbour of Sir
William, Sir Ralph Paynel, were indicted of the murder. One of the
accused, Maud, the widow of the dead man, then appealed the
others of the crime, but the case was not proceeded with at that
sessions. Only when the king's bench visited Lincoln in the autumn
of 1375 did trial take place. Maud then withdrew her appeal and she
and Sir William's steward, the only two of the original accused who
seem to have appeared in court, were tried on the indictments. They
were both acquitted while all the other suspects save one were outlawed. The exception was Sir Ralph Paynel, who was then indicted
anew of harbouring Maud, Richard Gyse, Sir William's esquire, and
Agatha the maid, in his house at Caythorpe knowing them guilty of or
complicitous in the murder. At Easter term 1377 Paynel was eventually acquitted and in time, so it would seem, all the outlawed
members of Sir William's household were able to secure pardons.

[22] *Records of Some Sessions of the Peace in Lincolnshire, 1360–1375*, ed.
R. Sillem (Lincoln Record Society, xxx, 1936), pp. lxx–lxxiv.

As in most other medieval criminal cases it is difficult to define with anything approaching exactitude the motivation of the evil-doers, or even to hazard a guess at the name of the killer. Sir Thomas Kydale, to whom Maud was married not long after, has come under suspicion as perhaps prompting the murder. He had on occasion associated with Sir Ralph Paynel, who is known to have been an enemy of Sir William's brother Nicholas Cantilupe. But quarrels were commonplace among the late medieval gentry and widows with property were soon persuaded to embark on matrimony again. No doubt Maud made her appeal in the county court because she knew it was expected of a wife whose husband had been killed while she was in the house. Withdrawing the appeal later on does not necessarily throw any more suspicion on her conduct, for this was common too. We must leave the identity of the killer an open question.

The most interesting feature of the murder was undoubtedly the attempt to shift the blame from the real culprits on to footpads or highwaymen. Moving the corpse any distance and changing the victim's attire are rarely found in medieval records. The killing of a master by his servants or a husband by his wife, statutorily classified as petty treason in 1352, though it had long been acknowledged as such, was an uncommon offence. It was regarded as particularly heinous by all ranks of society, and we know that in such cases juries were more likely than usual to find the accused guilty. This might account for the flight of nearly all the members of the Cantilupe household. Another notable aspect of the case was the inability of the presenting juries to place the date of the murder with any degree of unanimity. Very likely the corpse was not found for some time after it had been placed in the fields or, more likely still, the first finders failed to report their discovery to the proper authority. In all, ten juries framed indictments, which gives the impression that more than the usual efforts were made to gather information. However, the inability of the king and his officers to unravel a fairly subtle crime like this was only to be expected.

Killing in cold blood in time of peace, quite openly, and with a complete disregard for the consequences, was not likely to be under-taken by anyone but a magnate in a region where his own authority was paramount, and then only in one of the few periods when the king's prestige was at its lowest ebb. Thus only the fact that the killing was in Devon in October 1455 explains the remarkable circumstances of the murder of Nicholas Radford, a misdeed which has been called 'the most notorious private crime of the century'. Radford, an eminent apprentice of law (barrister), who had served in his time as a Devon justice of the peace, woke up at his home at Upcott on the night of Thursday, 23 October, to discover his outhouses on fire and a hundred armed men in his yard. When he found they were led by Sir Thomas Courtenay, he opened the door to allow the marauders entry, having been solemnly promised that no harm would befall him or his property. However, while Courtenay ate and drank sustenance provided by Radford, his men stripped the house of all valuables. Then Courtenay told his unwilling host he must go with him to speak to his father, the earl of Devon. When Radford pointed out that all his horses had been taken, Courtenay told him he would soon ride well enough: with that he bade farewell and rode off. Thereupon six of his men leaped at Radford with drawn swords and daggers, stabbing him to the heart, cleaving his skull, and spattering his brains on the ground. Courtenay and his father showed no remorse at the killing. The following Monday on the earl's instructions a number of his men went to Upcott to hold a mock coroner's inquest. They indicted Radford of his own death and brought in a verdict of suicide. Radford's household servants were forced to carry the body to the grave, singing a lewd song as they went. There it was tipped from the coffin and crushed by stones dropped from the grave-side.[23]

The motive behind this brutal homicide was not a desire to rob, despite the stripping of all valuables from the victim's house, but a deadly feud. Radford was a friend and very probably legal counsellor of Lord Bonville, the sworn foe of the Devons. The war between these two factions, sometimes clandestine but often overt, was racking the whole county. Public order was perhaps at the lowest level it was to reach that century. Much of the information about the crime is to be discovered in a parliamentary petition of January 1456. In response to this the king agreed that the crime should not go unpunished, but nothing was done until the duke of York, a friend of Bonville, became protector later that year. Then at last an Exeter jury indicted Courtenay, although, as we might have suspected, to little purpose. The mock inquest was probably something more than a macabre joke. A magnate was demonstrating to the county that he

---

[23] The detail is to be found in P.R.O. S.C. 8 138/68/64 (printed by Mrs G. H. Radford in *Transactions of the Devonshire Association*, xxxv [1903], 264–8) The background to the crime is explained in R. L. Storey, *The End of the House of Lancaster* (London, 1966), pp. 167–70.

could assume at will the functions of the king's legal officers and pervert the law as he wished.

Sir Thomas Courtenay made no effort to conceal the cold-hearted killing of Radford because he was confident he would never be brought to book. Malicious magnates, who sought to settle scores in most other decades of the century, usually acted more covertly. Sometimes they even used the existing machinery of justice and the king's law officers to revenge themselves on their foes. George, duke of Clarence, brother of Edward IV, at a time when he had lost royal favour and was eager to retaliate against his personal enemies, was greatly grieved by the death of his wife, Isabel, whom he believed they had poisoned.[24] His grief soon turned to fury, but, hot-headed as he was, he dealt with the supposed poisoner in a manner which, though quite illegal, might have caused no outcry at all had not his star been on the wane so markedly. In April 1477 he sent a number of his men, perhaps as many as eighty, to Cayford in Somerset to seize Ankarette Twynho, a middle-aged widow. Until a short while before she had been a household servant of Clarence and his wife. The duke believed she had administered the poison to the duchess six months previously in a drink of ale. His men arrived at Cayford at 2 p.m. on Saturday afternoon, 12 April, and carried Ankarette off to Bath during the afternoon. They travelled to Cirencester on Sunday, and from there to Warwick on Monday, arriving at 8 p.m. Ankarette was separated from her daughter and son-in-law, who had accompanied her, and lodged in the duke's prison there for the night. At 9 a.m. the following morning Clarence had her brought to the Warwick guildhall, where the justices of the peace were holding their sessions, and caused her to be indicted of poisoning his wife. Ankarette was arraigned, tried, and a jury found her guilty of murdering her mistress. Almost immediately she was drawn at the horse's tail through the town to the gallows at Myton where she was hanged. All this took place before noon.

The verdict of the jury had not been arrived at fairly. It had been influenced by the duke, whose tampering made him guilty of the crime of embracery. The jurors had given a decision, which was contrary to their real beliefs, out of fear of the duke. Before Ankarette was executed several of them sought her out and remorsefully asked for forgiveness. Very likely Clarence had also acted illegally in

---

[24] *Cal. Pat. Rolls, 1476–1485*, p. 72; *Rotuli Parliamentorum* (Record Commission, 1767–77), vi, 173.

seizing and detaining the woman: 'the unlawful taking of Ankarette through three shires' was the description used. The inordinately hasty process about which the petitioner also complained might have been unfair, but it was not illegal; neither was the priming of the indicting jurors, for Clarence was a member of the Warwickshire bench. There were, of course, many other occasions on which magnates forced juries to go against the dictates of their consciences, but they are not so clearly documented. The crime of Clarence was revealed so clearly because the moment was politically opportune for a petition like that of Ankarette's grandson, since the duke was attainted of treason in the same parliament and the king was very ready to receive any information which added to his brother's discredit. Whether Clarence's suspicions against Ankarette had any sound basis is unknown. By 1477 the duke's behaviour had become quite irresponsible, even unbalanced, and he was very willing to believe that his waning fortunes and undoubted ill-luck were the result of the machinations of his enemies.

Charges of abduction and rape were very common in the fourteenth and fifteenth centuries. The hands of unmarried women who were heiresses were sought in marriage assiduously and often ruthlessly. No woman of any wealth was allowed by society to stay unwed for very long. Since marriages among the wealthier classes were arranged by parents, relatives, or guardians, affection played little part in the selection of conjugal partners. A woman of station who could marry the man she preferred must therefore act without the permission of those in authority over her. Often she would allow herself to be abducted by her admirer, but at the same time seek to show that the abduction was carried out against her will. Usually such an elopement and the subsequent marriage meant a financial loss for the superior lord, who was often the king. The indictment of the new husband would follow and he would have to purchase a pardon. It was common for the lord or king to accept this train of events, but he did not always do so. One most daring abduction upset Edward III very much. Just before dawn on Good Friday 1347 Margery de la Beche, the wealthy widow of Sir Nicholas de la Beche, once keeper of the Tower of London, who held land in ten counties, was taken by intruders from her manor of Beams in Wiltshire.[25] In the course of the abduction two of Margery's household servants were murdered,

[25] *Cal. Pat. Rolls, 1345–1348*, p. 310; P.R.O. K.B. 27/350 Rex m. 55; *Cal. Close Rolls, 1346–1349*, pp. 271, 305.

several were wounded and her chaplain, who lay in sick-bed, died of fright. Some other servants were forced to accompany their mistress, and the intruders took with them goods and chattels to the value of over £500.

At the time of the abduction Margery was the lawfully, perhaps the recently, wedded wife of Gerard del Isle. The leader of the intruders, Sir John Dalton, who had land in Northamptonshire and Lancashire, had probably been an unsuccessful candidate for Margery's hand: when they were well away from Beams they were married. As well as members of his own family, Dalton's allies in the enterprise seem to have included six or seven knights and the constable of Banbury castle. According to the indictments of various juries he also received shelter and sympathy from the priors of Bristol and Holland (Lancashire) and, rather remarkably, from justices commissioned to effect his capture. What made the deed outrageous was that it had been done on Good Friday, and, most heinous of all, when the king's son Lionel, who was keeper of England while his father was besieging Calais, was staying at Beams. The crime was therefore committed within the verge of the marshalsea of the keeper's household and to the terror, so said the king, of Lionel and the rest of the royal children, who as it happened were with him at the time. The king's officers, who claimed that Margery had been abducted against her will, used every means at their disposal to secure the abductors' arrests. On one occasion they believed they had them in their grasp and ordered the keeper of the Tower of London to be ready to receive prisoners, but the quarry escaped. Then they commissioned Gerard del Isle to search for his lost spouse, giving him a licence to travel with a band of armed followers. Again there was no success. The fugitives, who were soon outlawed, found hiding places in Lancashire, even perhaps on the Scottish border for a time. Eventually, two or three years later, when the king's wrath had subsided, the main culprits were allowed to purchase pardons and resume their old positions in society. The king was popular and had great prestige, but he had lost. He possessed no machinery capable of capturing abductors who had the sympathy of the gentle classes. His attempts to add to the gravity of the crime by references to Good Friday and the danger to the royal children fell on deaf ears. Gerard del Isle had lost his wife for ever.

According to a royal command of 1429 most contemporary crimes were committed not in villages or the open fields but in woods and towns. Certainly it was in the towns where cut-purses, petty thieves, and tricksters tended to congregate, and many town taverns had the reputation of being meeting places for the criminal fraternity. It was in towns also, particularly the larger ones, that prostitution flourished. No doubt common harlots usually worked for themselves and in competition with others of their kind, but there is some evidence that in London at least, as in the royal household where there was a marshal of prostitutes, prostitution was well organized by the fourteenth century, and pimps and procuresses were plentiful. A confession made in July 1385 by one Johanna, the serving woman of Elizabeth, wife of Henry Moring, an eminent London citizen, claimed that Elizabeth, under the colour of the craft of embroidery which she pretended to follow, took a number of women including herself as apprentices in that art.[26] In fact they did not work at perfecting their embroidery techniques but were inveigled into living a most immoral life. Johanna was asked to consort, as she put it, with friars, chaplains, and all other such men as desired to have her company both in her own house and elsewhere. The embroideresses in reality were being hired out by Elizabeth to the friars and chaplains at an agreed rate. Discipline was rigorous. On 4 May Elizabeth sent Johanna to accompany a chaplain and carry a lantern before him to his chamber: there she was to stay the night with him. Johanna did as instructed, returning to her mistress next morning. When asked to hand over her fee she said she had not been paid. Elizabeth therefore sent her back the following night with orders to take from the chaplain's lodgings anything she could lay hands on. The instructions to Johanna were common to all the embroideresses and a London court decided from this evidence that Elizabeth Moring was a common harlot and procuress and must quit the city for three years.

That there existed a connection between vice and crime was readily acknowledged. On 20 April 1417 the common council of London was summoned to consider the problem of the 'many grievances, abominations, damages, disturbances, murders, homicides', and larcenies there 'by reason . . . of the common resort, harbouring and sojourning which lewd men and women of bad and evil life have in the stews belonging to men and women in the city and suburbs'. Men and women, so it was said, were slain, spoiled, and robbed there, and wives, sons, daughters, apprentices, and servants of the reputable

---

[26] *Memorials of London and London Life in the Thirteenth, Fourteenth and Fifteenth Centuries*, pp. 484, 647–8.

men of the city were corrupted by the inhabitants through the 'illicit works of their lewd flesh'. The outcome of the council meeting was the fixing of new penalties for such offenders, a common medieval answer to a persistent problem of crime. On occasion a town might try to expel once and for all the prostitutes in its midst, but even if it succeeded they were soon back.

Sorcery figured in a fair number of late medieval crimes and its appearance became more frequent as the fifteenth century wore on. Its practice was a reflection of the value placed on magic by society as a whole. Both Henry VI and Edward IV, for example, had schemes for the solving of their financial difficulties by the transmuting of base metal into gold and there is evidence that from the thirteenth century, or even before, quite a number of prominent men and women dabbled in the occult with malicious intent. Adam de Stratton, the infamous chamberlain of Edward I, was thought to have preserved nail parings of his personal enemies in a cabinet for magical purposes. Edward I's treasurer, Walter Langton, bishop of Lichfield, was accused before the Pope by his stepson of many crimes, including sorcery and homage to Satan. In 1310 the Templars were charged with the same thing. In 1441 Eleanor Cobham, duchess of Gloucester, did penance for procuring Roger Bolingbroke to prognosticate by magical means the death of Henry VI. Jacquetta of Luxemburg, the ex-duchess of Bedford, was thought to have caused by magic the infatuation of Edward IV for Elizabeth Wydvile, and in Richard III's reign Jane Shaa, lately the mistress of Edward IV, was summoned before the council to answer an accusation based on the same premise. Most fifteenth-century men had a great dread of sorcery. It was seen as the cause of many mysterious afflictions. In 1453 an approver from Southwark said that Henry VI's mental breakdown was due to the dabblings in sorcery of a number of Bristol merchants, and another approver confessed that he himself had cast a spell over one of the king's cloaks on the prompting of Lord Cobham.

An excellent example of the sorcerer at work is provided by a case which came before the king's bench in Hilary term 1325.[27] Apparently at the end of November 1323 twenty-seven men of Coventry went to the home of Master John of Nottingham, a necromancer in that town, and told him that if he could counsel them in secret it would be

[27] *Select Cases in the Court of the King's Bench, Edward II*, p. 154; *Parliamentary Writs and Writs of Military Summons*, ed. F. Palgrave (Record Commission, 1827–34), II, ii, 269.

to his great profit. Master John agreed to help and once mutual security had been provided the supplicants told their tale of woe. They said they were so badly treated by the prior of Coventry that they could no longer endure it. They claimed that he was seeking to destroy the town and that in this he was supported by the king, Hugh Despenser the elder, earl of Winchester, and Hugh Despenser the younger. Thus they asked if, in return for a gift, Master John would undertake by his necromancy and his arts to kill these great men and the prior. John agreed to do so if they paid him £20 sterling and gave him his keep in the religious house of his choice. The townsmen gave him a part of the sum as a down-payment and all was settled. With seven pounds of wax Master John and his assistant made seven images: one each of the king, the Despensers, the prior, a fifth in the likeness of the priory's cellarer, a sixth like the prior's steward, and a seventh like Richard of Sowe, one of the Coventry men. The last image was to be used, with the man's consent, as a test piece to see if all the other images were reliable.

Master John began to ply his arts on 7 December 1323 at an old house half a league from Coventry and near Shortley park, and worked at his magic continuously until the end of May the following year. On 27 April Master John handed his assistant a lead pin and told him to drive the sharpened end two inches deep into the forehead of the image of Richard of Sowe. This he did, and the next morning John sent him to Sowe's house to see what condition he was in. He found Richard screaming and 'crying harrou': he was unable to recognize anyone because he had gone out of his mind. He lay sick until Sunday morning, 19 May 1324, when John drew the lead pin out of the image's head and thrust it in again under the heart. It remained there until the following Wednesday, when Richard died. All this information derived from John's assistant, Robert le Mareschal, who was persuaded to appeal his master. The jury acquitted Master John, but he was kept in custody and died a few months later, still in the sheriff's custody. Robert, his assistant, was sent to the Marshalsea prison while further investigations were made: what happened to him eventually is unknown.

The king's bench jury had to consider an offence which was held to amount to killing by magical means. Robert's appeal made no reference to the misdeed as a felony, or a treason, or a trespass for that matter. It was left carefully unclassified. The reason was, no doubt, the anomalous position of sorcerers under the law. Was sorcery merely a secular offence or did it come within the category of heresy and thus pertain to the ecclesiastical courts? No one knew. The writer *Britton* in the late thirteenth century had suggested that the church courts should try such offenders in the first instance and deliver them, if found guilty, to the king's court to put to death: there are cases to suggest his statement was accurate. However, he hastened to add that the king, as a good marshal of Christianity, might proceed against them himself if he so pleased. From the fair number of cases which appeared in secular courts we may conclude that this was also the view of the king. With the passing of the statute against heresy in 1401 came commissions for the arrest of sorcerers in general (1406), or in particular areas of the country. In the 1420s and the 1430s several men and women of importance, some of them clerics, were haled before the king's council accused of magical practices. For example, in May 1432 the order was given to arrest for that purpose Thomas Northfelde, professor of divinity of the order of friars preachers: in addition all his books on 'sorcery and wickedness' were seized. In 1441, the year that Eleanor Cobham and her associates were brought to justice, rewards were offered to all those who could discover witches. The agenda of the king's council in the fifteenth century periodically included these cases up to the end of the Yorkist era.

Usually sorcerers like Master John of Nottingham sought to conjure up spirits for malicious purposes. Less frequently they worked to relieve pain by such methods as extracting wooden nails fixed in an image. They also performed services of divination, discovering by magical means who had committed a certain misdeed. Thus in a case reported in October 1382 Robert Berewold of London promised Alan, a water carrier, that he would find out who had stolen a mazer from the house of Matilda of Eye.[28] Thereupon he took a loaf, fixed a wooden peg in the top, placed four knives on each side in the form of a cross, and then 'did soothsaying and art magic' over them. Having completed the ritual he then named the culprit as one Johanna Wolsy. Johanna for this took him to court, which decided that by such soothsaying and magic arts people might have their good name tarnished, and that furthermore such sorcery was manifestly opposed to Christian doctrine. Alan was sentenced to the pillory and to make public

---

[28] *Memorials of London and London Life in the Thirteenth, Fourteenth and Fifteenth Centuries*, p. 472.

confession of his offence. According to this court's decision those who practised sorcery, whatever their intent, were committing a crime.

One of the most skilful and daring of medieval criminals was the seal counterfeiter. He was bold because, for the greatest chance of profit, he often turned to forging the king's seal, an offence which was often rated as treason and thereby carried the most fearsome penalties. All written royal commands had to be authenticated by a royal seal of some kind. Without sealed instructions the machinery of justice ground to a halt, royal financial operations ceased, and no king's minister need take action. Opportunities for counterfeiting the king's seal were many, for writs were not the sole preserve of the sheriff and his officers. There were messengers whose business it was to obtain writs in chancery on behalf of any private citizen who was seeking legal action. In the fourteenth century the writs required were drafted initially by a number of chancery clerks in Westminster and then carried by the messengers to the chancery itself for sealing. The messengers therefore had the opportunity of tampering with the writs, even of affixing a seal themselves. We know of a number of men in the fourteenth century who were able to acquire a lead matrix counterfeiting the king's seal. Another device was the one adopted by a chaplain named Philip Burdon in 1324. He purchased in chancery a writ close of novel disseisin, together with a writ patent in agreement with it, both under his own name.[29] He then had two forged writs made under his name against a number of his enemies. Finally he removed the wax seals from the proper writs and put them on the forgeries. This was no isolated offence, for Philip was a member of a gang which specialized in such misdeeds. In fact the crime may have been more heinous than Philip cared in court to admit, for evidence was given that the gang had possession of a metal impression of the king's seal and that it had been used in this particular instance. Perhaps Philip, like other criminals later on, was hoping by his story to avoid a charge of treason, believing erroneously that the substitution of one seal for another was not counterfeiting.

Often the counterfeiting of seals together with the forging of documents was for the purpose of obtaining money. In 1348 a chaplain, who was a member of a notorious band of Suffolk robbers, disguised himself as a merchant of Ghent in the employment of Queen Philippa. He went to her bailiff, showed him a forged seal, and asked for a large

---

[29] *Select Cases in the Court of the King's Bench, Edward II*, p. 158.

sum of money.[30] The bailiff refused to disburse, considering the seal insufficient proof of authority. The chaplain returned a little later bearing this time a forged letter which asked for a larger sum. This trick also failed. Next another member of the gang visited the bailiff, pretending to be a sheriff's officer, and showed him a writ to the sheriff of Suffolk under the king's secret seal ordering the distraint of the bailiff's goods and chattels for the sum required by the merchant from Ghent. He even produced a receipt for the money supposedly signed by the queen. This, like all the other documents, was a forgery but the bailiff, although he may have had strong suspicions, thought the time had come to cease his opposition and so he paid up. In another case, which came into the courts in the same year, Nicholas Boylet said that Walter Yarmouth, one of the king's ministers, brought him a bill supposedly sealed with the seal of the king's wardrober and showing that the king owed £312 to Lord John Beaumond. On this security Yarmouth borrowed £10, leaving the document as pledge. He returned later with three more bills sealed in the same way, which showed a foreign merchant was the king's creditor for more than £1,000, and was able to get an advance of £31. To obtain still more money Yarmouth presented other bills whose face value totalled several thousand pounds before his swindle was exposed. In court he confessed to forging bills and seals and was sentenced to imprisonment for life. The counterfeiting of seals was a very specialized form of criminal activity involving a most skilful type of criminal. He was probably literate and quite likely possessed good connections with royal officials and clerks. Perhaps he had been one himself at some stage, or at least had been in holy orders. The game he was playing was a dangerous one for, since counterfeiting the royal seal was usually held by judges to be treason, there could be no benefit of clergy and delivery to the mild regime of the church.

Violence was part of the pattern of life in the later middle ages and men did not shed tears over it easily. Crimes which stirred contemporaries to passionate protest on the issue of physical hurt inflicted had to be quite outrageous. There was, for example, the disembowelling by John Carpenter of his newly-wed wife while on a pilgrimage (1433), and the death by torture of the Carmelite friar who had accused John of Gaunt of treason (1383), but such instances were not

---

[30] The case is followed through carefully by L. O. Pike, *A History of Crime in England* (London, 1873–6), i, 271–2.

common.[31] An over-abundance of violent deeds, perhaps also the very harshness of life, seems to have bred a certain callousness which regarded blood-letting as commonplace and even as a form of grim jest. To say that late medieval man exulted in bloodshed is going too far. In the fourteenth and fifteenth centuries there was still considerable adherence to the idea that to settle quarrels by the use of arms was to appeal to the judgment of God. The *duellum* or trial by battle existed as a popular spectacle until past the middle of the fifteenth century. This notion, combined with a belief that proficiency in arms was proof of virility, was a sizeable obstacle to the progress of good government. When medieval men were cruel there was usually good reason for it. Rarely were they brutal out of sheer sadism. The heroes in contemporary ballads, such as Robin Hood, Gamelyn, and the like, when they acted brutally did so to achieve a particular end. When Little John and Much the miller's son captured and murdered the monk who had betrayed Robin Hood to the sheriff, they also killed the boy who rode with him 'Ffor ferd lest he should telle'. When Robin killed Guy of Gisborne he cut off his head and fixed it on the end of his bow. He then drew his knife and nicked the face so that no one would know whose head it was. Presumably there would have been difficulty in identifying the decapitated body as well.

A small number of cases appeared before the courts which involved the torture of men and women by thieves who had broken into their homes. Usually the intention was to elicit information about the location of concealed valuables. Thus a Lancashire jury reported that in January 1397 a gang of men led by Roger, son of John of the Blith of Lathum at Crossens in the vill of Northmeles, broke into the Northmeles rectory, seized the parson, John Lyurpull, who was then abed, and forced water into his mouth through a water pipe, tormenting him until he told them where his treasure lay.[32] Sometimes the intention was to force a man to give his land away. A commission of oyer and terminer appointed in February 1319 had as its task the investigation of the complaint by Adam, son of John Bertram, that Peter Nerford of Saxlingham and his confederates cut off his genitals and imprisoned him until he enfeoffed Peter of all his tenements in

---

[31] *Rot. Parl.*, iv, 447b; *Thomae Walsingham Historia Anglicana*, ed. H. T. Riley (Rolls Series, 1863–4), ii, 112–14.

[32] *Plea Rolls of the County Palatine of Lancaster*, ed. J. Parker (Chetham Society, New Series, lxxxvii, 1928), p. 62.

Saxlingham and placed him in seisin thereof.[33] Occasionally, when a house had been broken into and looted while the owner was present, the misdoers decided to cover their tracks by making sure they should not be identified by the victims at a later date and that no detailed information about the offence should be given to the sheriff. To this end they might gouge out the eyes and cut out the tongues of the men and women they had robbed. Deosculation, the cutting off of lips, may have been intended for the same purpose. Unfortunately for the protection of society, these crimes were considered as no more than trespass in themselves until 1404. Then by the statute 5 Henry IV c. 5, because, as it was said, offenders were daily beating, wounding, imprisoning, and maiming the king's lieges and purposely pulling out their tongues and putting out their eyes, it was ordained that those found guilty of such deeds done of malice prepense should incur the pains for felony. For all this, during the later middle ages as a whole, crimes involving deliberate cruelty against the victims were relatively few. One of the reasons is perhaps to be discovered in English legal custom. Misdoers are often influenced in their criminal behaviour by the methods used to maintain public order in their country. Those who used torture had little in English common law to copy from. Only when the accused stood mute in court refusing to plead was a form of torture used, and mutilation was generally a punishment associated only with borough custom.

The criminal of the later middle ages was not just a boorish oaf with a propensity to violence who committed misdeeds as the fancy took him, but quite often a man with a well-laid plan and the competence to carry it out. Pudlicott's great venture, and the devices of confidence tricksters like Gervase Worthy and Robert Colynson, show a degree of sophistication we might not expect of medieval society. Some of the criminal schemes showed a good knowledge of the English machinery of government and its weaknesses, as well as the inefficiency or corruptibility of officials. This is demonstrated by the successful attempts to forge bills, writs, and seals, the capitalizing on the king's failure to guard the wardrobe treasury at Westminster, the disregard of the duke of Clarence for the proper processes of law, and the help afforded by justices to the kidnappers of Margery de la Beche. The involvement of members of the king's household in the ambush at Alton demonstrates not the mere turning of a blind eye but officials actually assisting in the perpetration of a robbery; so does the

[33] *Cal. Pat. Rolls, 1317–1321*, p. 359.

behaviour of Adam the sacrist and some of the monks of Westminster in 1303, and that of chancery clerks and messengers when cases involving the forging of seals erupted. Only very rarely did those who held office aid criminals out of fear, and assistance offered on account of admiration felt for the bold villain must have been even rarer. When help was given it was nearly always because they too wished for quick profit, having perhaps discovered, like those of the king's household involved in the Alton robbery, that an official position did not guarantee either good pay or regular pay, whereas the information which it provided could be turned to definite profit.

III

<hr>

The Criminal Bands

<hr>

Medieval English crime is celebrated in ballad not simply through the individual career of Robin Hood, but also through the exploits of the other members of his outlaw band. There seems little doubt that this was a truthful reflection of the times. There were accomplished rogues like Robert Colynson and Robert Pudlicott who committed gross offences virtually on their own, but perhaps the biggest danger to public order was the organized gangs of misdoers which we hear of so frequently in late medieval records. The indictments of jurors, when the offence was no mere petty larceny or assault in anger, often referred to a number of misdoers, principals and accessories, varying from two or three to two or three hundred. Criminals banded together not out of a desire for jolly company but for purposes which were strictly utilitarian. A great many of the commoner types of crime such as the seizure of land, the committing of mayhem, abduction, highway robbery, the carrying on of feuds, were offences which by their nature demanded a considerable number of misdoers to ensure success. As most men carried weapons of some sort, the armed attacker had less of an advantage over a potential victim than his modern counterpart, and therefore a band of confederates was necessary to ensure quick surrender and certain profit. The customs of society also assisted the formation of criminal bands. Kinship counted for so much in the middle ages that a miscreant could usually rely on assistance from his family. Many gangs seem to have had as their core a band of brothers or men closely related. The system of outlawry was responsible for the creation of numerous bands. In law a man was only a criminal when convicted by trial in court, or, as happened more frequently, when he failed to appear in court and was outlawed. The new outlaw very often thought it best to take evasive action, to change his habitat, to cross county boundaries, or to take to the forest. In flight he would meet men of similar condition and they would band together for mutual protection and profit. Thus a petition in the parliament of 1439 referring to the activities of Piers Venables of Derbyshire, a fugitive from justice who had helped to rescue a prisoner being taken to Tutbury castle, said he had gathered around him a great number of misdoers 'beyng of his clothinge, and in manere of insurrection wente into the wodes in that county like it hadde be Robyn Hode and his meynee'.[1] Many criminal bands must have been founded in the halls of the nobility and the squirarchy, for of many outlaws it was stated that they were members of a lord's household. The lord might lead or he might merely plan their activities. He was certainly not ignorant of their past history or their criminal potential. In the fourteenth century there were many complaints in parliament about the extent of this evil. In the fifteenth century it lost some of its notoriety with the prevalence of 'bastard feudalism' and the increase in the size of retinues. Yet the outlaws and other criminals were still there, and they must have contributed greatly by expert example to the disorder of the times.

The first question which needs to be asked about medieval criminal gangs concerns the size of their membership. Here we must be careful to separate the criminal himself from his hirers or maintainers, and especially those he relied on for shelter and food, his receivers. James Coterel, a gang leader who flourished around 1330 in northern Derbyshire, regularly had with him as the hard core of his band his two brothers and three or four other men of local origin.[2] When outlawed after two or three years of misdeeds, in March 1331, the gang roved through the Peak district and northern Nottinghamshire from hide-out to hide-out. Coterel was joined as he wandered by a number of recruits, some already outlawed but most not.[3] They must have numbered at least twenty, and with their assistance the gang leader was able to extend his criminal activities noticeably, particularly in the direction of extortion.

Eustace Folville, leader of a Leicestershire gang in the same period and an occasional ally of Coterel, was obviously very reliant on four of his brothers and more loth than the Coterels to operate with

---

[1] *Rotuli Parliamentorum* (Record Commission, 1767–77), v, 16.
[2] *English Historical Review*, lxxix (1964), 689–717.
[3] Middleton MSS. (in Nottingham University Library), 6/179/1 mm. 3, 4.

criminals not of his own blood.⁴ Nonetheless when the occasion demanded, if a big crime was to be committed, like the kidnapping of Sir Richard Wylughby on 14 January 1332 near Melton Mowbray, extra help was sought. For this misdeed Coterel and his brother joined the Folville fraternity and so did a number of other small groups. In all they totalled between twenty and thirty bandits. This was an important feature of medieval criminal organization, the assistance supplied by one group to another. Equally impressive was the interlocking nature of the gangs: a criminal appeared with one gang one moment and with another soon after. Sir William Chetulton of Staffordshire, an infamous gang leader both there and in Lancashire, served for a time in the band of James Stafford and then made common cause with the Coterels in Nottinghamshire and Derbyshire in 1331.

There are one or two references to very large bands of criminals but they are not common. William Beckwith of Beckwith, Yorkshire, who waged a private war from 1387 to 1392 against the officials of the duchy of Lancaster in Knaresborough and Ockeden chases, had as the basis of his band a score of kinsfolk and friends from the Knaresborough region.⁵ In 1390, when the forces of law were closing in, he was reported to have fled to the deepest part of the forest with no fewer than 500 confederates, all of whom had been indicted in court. This was exceptional, and for the fourteenth century it is perhaps best to postulate 'core' units in gangs as being of no more than six members, and often all from the same family. They would periodically combine with similar groups to their mutual benefit, and occasionally seek additional and perhaps specialized help in time of need. In the fifteenth century, with the growth of maintenance and the giving of livery, bands which engaged frequently in criminal activities may have been larger. The gang of Charles Nowell, Robert Ledham, and Roger Church in Norfolk in the 1450s seems to have numbered between forty and sixty men.⁶ Persistent evil-doers must have found a place easily amongst household retainers (Nowell and his followers, for example, were retainers of the duke of Norfolk), and this, together with the continuous failure of juries to indict known miscreants, the lack of subsequent outlawry, and the low level of public order in

---

⁴ *Transactions of the Royal Historical Society*, 5th Series, vii (1957), 117–36.
⁵ *Bulletin of John Rylands Library*, xlvii (1965), 254–74.
⁶ *Paston Letters*, ed. J. Gairdner (Edinburgh, 1910), no. 179. Nowell and his friends, although retainers of the duke of Norfolk, were not averse to attacking other members of the retinue.

general, very often makes it impossible to determine whether a group of misdoers was a criminal band of long standing and record, as can be done with the fourteenth century.

Quite often indicting juries were able to provide lists of men and women who had assisted criminal gangs not actively, but in a passive capacity as what were called receivers. Usually this meant supplying food and shelter, carrying messages, and showing them little-known paths and by-ways. Receivers, as might be expected, were far more numerous than the active gangsters. The Coterel band, during its wanderings in 1331–2, received help from over 150 such folk.[7] Whether they assisted out of sympathy or from fear is unknown. Juries frequently named maintainers. They were not really members of the gang: rather they were those who instigated and commissioned the crimes and who took a large share of any proceeds. Maintaining was a more active form of support than receiving, and for that reason maintainers must have been fewer than receivers. In general they were of a higher station in society as well.

The social status of the members of criminal gangs is an important issue. For the most part the leaders were drawn from the gentry, the knights, and esquires, the very members of society on whom para-doxically the task of preserving local law and order increasingly devolved. The Folville brothers were the sons of John de Folville, lord of Ashby-Folville (Leicestershire) and Teigh (Rutland). Eustace Folville, the unchallenged leader, died a knight in possession of three parts of a knight's-fee in Teigh. Sir William Chetulton, periodically an ally of the Coterels, held two knight-fees and other lands and manors in Cheshire. Roger le Sauvage, another of their allies, was the son and heir of John le Sauvage (or Savage), lord of Stainsby manor (Nottinghamshire) and of a moiety of Gunshelf (Surrey). Lord John Fitzwalter, an Essex gang leader of the 1340s, was left by his father Castle Baynard, the advowson of St Andrews, London, and extensive holdings in Norfolk, Suffolk, and Essex. James Coterel and his brother John started off with fewer advantages in life. They were, most likely, younger sons of a Ralph Coterel, who owned small parcels of land in central Derbyshire and who, had he lived in the fifteenth century when ranks had to be given in all legal records, would perhaps have been called a gentleman. The other members of criminal bands were usually of lower station in society and were drawn from a wide variety of occupations: it is impossible to general-

[7] P.R.O. K.B. 27/291 Rex m. 27.

ize. The Coterel and Folville gangs may have had more than an average percentage of men of gentle blood, whereas William Beckwith's band was drawn almost entirely from menials, tradesmen, and poorer landholders.[8] The nobility, who were outlawed only on very rare occasions, were found in such bands infrequently, although in the fifteenth century in particular they were to be discovered leading household followers and 'well-wishers' on many a foray in the course of a feud. Bailiffs and other local officials often gave assistance to the gangs: the Coterels, for example, could count on the support of half-a-dozen or more bailiffs in the High Peak. Yet they were often no more than maintainers and receivers for rarely were they active participants in the carrying out of criminal enterprises. Men in holy orders figured quite frequently in indictments concerned with gang activities and some were capable of operating without lay assistance. In December 1317 six monks of Rufford abbey (Nottinghamshire) were reported as having gathered around them a large band and to have seized a passer-by, robbed him of his goods, and held him for a ransom of £200.[9] As with the bailiffs, however, most clerics who helped the gang leaders did so in a passive capacity as receivers and maintainers.

A criminal band might be in business for itself, so to speak, or, as often happened, be in the employ of a magnate or a religious house. The Coterels were hired by the canons of Lichfield cathedral to remove the vicar of Bakewell from his church, and to collect tithes and defend jurisdictions which the chapter possessed in the parishes of the Peak district. There was a danger that these might be appropriated by Vale Royal abbey or Lenton priory. The Folvilles were hired on one occasion by a group, which included a canon of Sempringham and the cellarer of the Cistercian house of Haverholm, to destroy a rival's water mill. The abbot of St Mary's, York, seems to have employed one who called himself 'Lionel, king of the rout of raveners' to stop by threats of violence Richard de Snaweshill, parson of Huntington, from supporting a particular priest for the position of vicar in Burton Agnes.[10] In 1327 at the time of the disturbances at Bury St Edmunds we hear of six friars minors of Babwell giving encouragement to the rioters, who included malefactors from

[8] P.R.O. K.B. 27/533 Rex m. 7.
[9] *Calendar of Patent Rolls, 1317–1321* (Record Commission), p. 93.
[10] *Select Cases in the Court of the King's Bench, Edward III,* ed. G. O. Sayles (Selden Society, 76, 1957), p. 93.

London. Among the lay maintainers of criminal bands was to be found Sir Robert Tuchet, lord of Markeaton (Derbyshire) and of Ashwell (Rutland), who was perhaps the chief patron of the Folvilles and the Coterels. Eustace, Laurence, and Walter Folville were actually members of his and his brother's household 'wearing their robes and living with them'.[11] It was in Markeaton park that the ransom money of Sir Richard Wylughby was divided up among the kidnappers. In Northamptonshire, during the same period, the constable of Rockingham castle, Sir Robert de Vere, was notorious for maintaining groups of armed men. He was reported as harbouring malefactors both at Rockingham and at his home at Sudborough. One indictment said, most sinisterly, that 'sometimes twenty armed men, sometimes thirty come to Vere at the castle and leave at dawn or during the night'.[12] Robert Doufbygging, a forester and acting master forester in the chase of Knaresborough, who was the sworn enemy of William Beckwith, was said to have made use of the services of felons from 1377 for almost twenty years.[13] There can be little doubt that the services of outlaws and criminals who had banded together were in considerable demand among religious houses, and that many of the gentry recognized that such gangs could be used for profitable ends.

Most important for the success of any criminal band was an able leader. Why James Coterel or Eustace Folville should turn to crime is a question well worth asking, even if the answer must be incomplete. Feud was a common cause, undoubtedly. The criminal careers of the Folvilles began when, in January 1326, they murdered an unpopular neighbour, Roger Bellers, a baron of the exchequer. According to the chronicler Henry Knighton, Bellers had threatened them and done them actual injury.[14] William Beckwith became leader of a criminal band when his hopes of succeeding to a forestership in the forest and chase of Knaresborough, which had once been held by an ancestor, were dashed. Sir William Aune, an ex-constable of Tickhill, and Roger le Sauvage, close associates of James Coterel, probably went into crime because of straitened circumstances. In 1330 Aune petitioned in parliament for compensation for the loss of the manor of Lee (near Gainsborough), which had been recently taken

[11] Middleton MS. 6/179/1 m. 5.
[12] *Trans. Roy. Hist. Soc.*, 5th Series, vii (1957), 124.
[13] P.R.O. K.B. 27/534 Rex m. 6.
[14] *Chronicon Henrici Knighton*, ed. J. R. Lumby (Rolls Series, 1889–95) 432.

from him. He had been promised, but not actually given, a constable-ship or some other *grande baillie*.[15] William de Uston, lord of Rad-manthwaite (Nottinghamshire), who was a confederate of Aune, a counterfeiter, and the Coterel spy in Nottingham, probably joined the gang for the same reason. There is, however, no positive indication why James Coterel and his brothers turned to crime. They started their misdeeds in a small way, evicting the vicar of Bakewell from Bakewell church in August 1328.[16] Perhaps their proficiency in such violence and the ability to make a profit made them attractive leaders and caused a band to grow around them. Political affiliations and disappointments have been suggested as reasons for gang forma-tion, but the Coterel band at least contained men who had shown very different political inclinations in the preceding years.

Criminal gangs often possessed a considerable degree of internal organization. They were more than a mere collection of men with one or two leaders. The instigator and planner of a band's activities was sometimes dignified by the title of captain. Indictments awarded this rank to both Eustace Folville and James Coterel. Sir William Chetulton was also said to have had a gang, or 'society' as they were called in legal records, of his own.[17] In medieval ballads, outlaws were often portrayed as having their own peculiar hierarchy with their leaders as 'yong men of prys'. Gentle blood was apparently esteemed among criminals as it was by most other members of medieval society. One very interesting feature of gang organization was the division of labour, the specialization in particular forms of criminal activity, practised by the members. The gang captain might be a pivot round which revolved a number of smaller units, each practising its own brand of crime. James Coterel, for example, seems to have presided over a federation of criminal units rather than commanded a single monolithic structure. Roger le Sauvage and another member of Coterel's gang called William Pymme, of Sutton Bonnington, specialized in extortion by means of threatening letters carried by their own bearers.[18] William de Uston was the Coterels' spy in Nottingham and their means of communication with Sir Robert Ingram, a clandestine ally, who was mayor of Nottingham and sheriff of that county on a number of occasions.[19] Perhaps only when a major crime was to be undertaken were several of these

---

[15] *Rot. Parl.*, ii, 366.   [16] *Eng. Hist. Rev.*, lxxix (1964), 699, 701.
[17] P.R.O. K.B. 27/254 m. 23.   [18] Middleton MS. 6/179/1 mm. 7, 8d.
[19] P.R.O. J.I. 1/166 m. 51d; J.I. 1/1411b mm. 6, 6d.

units brought together. Thus for the kidnapping of Sir Richard Wylughby, Eustace Folville recruited the specialist assistance of the Coterel brothers, Robert Lovet, parson of Ashwell, Roger le Sauvage, Anketil Hoby, a renowned highway robber, and probably Robert Helewell and Alan de Baston. Helewell was a clerk who had previously assisted Folville in the Bellers murder, and Baston was a canon of Sempringham who the year before had himself hired Eustace's services.[20] After Wylughby had been ransomed the kidnappers carefully divided up the proceeds at Markeaton park, just as Sir Robert Rideware's gang was to do with its profits at Lapley priory a few years later. Of the 1,300 marks paid, Eustace, Lawrence, Walter, Robert, and Richard Folville received 300 and the Coterels a much more modest 40; who received the large remainder is unknown.[21] At this robbers' meeting the division of spoil may well have been carried out according to an accepted procedure, but even so it was hardly as formal a gathering as the one held by William Beckwith and his followers in 1388 when carrying on their private war against the officials of the duchy of Lancaster near Knaresborough. Their assembly, which they called 'Dodelowe', was held on a number of occasions for what was referred to as 'the subversion of the law, oppression of the people, disinherison of the duke (of Lancaster) and the loss of his ministers lives'.[22] There are many other references in legal records to conventicles and assemblies of criminals of one sort or another. The king sometimes affected to believe that such gatherings heralded an onslaught on the fabric of government but more likely it was the criminals aping the institutions of the society from which they were excluded.

Some criminal bands were bold enough to claim that they operated a law of their own. They were not referring to the gang rules of membership or articles of discipline, if such existed, but to their hegemony over a particular region. Lionel, the 'king of the rout of raveners', pretended to believe that Richard de Snaweshill was his vassal, and that a fine or forfeiture could be exacted from him if he failed to carry out the instructions contained in a letter which was itself composed along the lines of a royal writ. Other letters also in the royal style were dispatched for purposes of extortion to a number of wealthy men by Roger le Sauvage and William Pymme. The

[20] *Trans. Roy. Hist. Soc.*, 5th Series, vii (1957), 123, 124.
[21] Middleton MS. 6/179/1 m. 4.
[22] *Cal. Pat. Rolls, 1391–1396*, p. 551.

Coterel gang on one occasion kidnapped John Staniclyf, a tenant of the local knight Roger Wennesley, who for a time had been entrusted with the task of hunting them down, and imprisoned him until he took an oath that he would never be against them. On release they took from him a bond of £20, to be paid if he ever opposed them.[23] William Beckwith and his followers in their parliament called 'Dodelowe' ordained among themselves to make a number of unlawful appointments, presumably to install their nominees in local offices. At Ipswich in 1344, after William Shareshull and the other justices who had just finished sessions had left the town, a band of evil-doers went to the hall where pleas had been heard and caused proclamation to be made that Shareshull was to appear before them under penalty of £100, William Notton under penalty of £40, and many others similarly 'in mockery of the king's justices and ministers in his service'.[24] This legal system of the criminals' own devising and the use of the royal style were, of course, parodies of Plantagenet government. More significantly they were acts of a rival system of justice, one which was considered by those who concocted it as more fair and less uncertain than the king's.

An Essex gang leader, John Fitzwalter, sought not to set up his own code of law but systematically to usurp the power of the king. He had his steward William Baltrip extort sums of money 'to the abrogation of the king's law', as it was put in later indictments. He took illegal distraints to the value of forty and fifty shillings each. He sent Baltrip to Burnham, where he arrested four sacks of wool which Trusskynns of Flanders had hasted there and refused to release them until the Fleming paid him a fine. On another occasion Fitzwalter took the law into his own hands by sending two of his men after a certain Roger Byndthese, who had confessed to various felonies before the coroner of the liberty of Waltham Holy Cross, and who was on his way to Dover, intending to abjure the realm.[25] The men stopped Roger somewhere between Waltham and London: one of them, William Cannville, handed his sword to his fellow who thereupon, following Fitzwalter's instructions, cut off the abjuror's head.

[23] Middleton MS. 6/179/1 m. 3.
[24] *Select Cases in the Court of the King's Bench, Edward III*, ed. G. O. Sayles (Selden Society, 82, 1965), p. 37.
[25] P.R.O. K.B. 27/366 Rex m. 30. The account of Fitzwalter's crimes is written on six additional membranes interposed between Rex mm. 30 and 31. They contain indictments before the king's bench at Chelmsford in Michaelmas term 1351.

On several other occasions Fitzwalter interfered with the proper process of law and in a way which suggests that his authority was all important in that region. He and his men put pressure on juries, stopped the reporting of the death of a Lexden man to the coroner and, when the bailiffs of Colchester on the order of the justices of the peace attached one Wymarcus Hierde to answer, they quickly released him from the Colchester gaol.

The criminal gangs committed many types of crime. They murdered, they stole, they poached, they extorted, they kidnapped, and they cheated. A common and predictable aim was to make money, yet it was not always a design which dwarfed everything else. Sometimes money was sought as a means of revenge rather than for material gain, to recompense the band and its members for some wrong or imagined wrong once suffered. Thus most of the members of the Coterel and Folville gangs had crossed the path of Sir Richard Wylughby and perhaps been given cause to hate him prior to his kidnapping in 1332. They had met him in his judicial capacity. He had been substituted to a commission in February 1327 to hear and determine the indictments against those involved in the death of Roger Bellers. In 1328 Wylughby and a Rutland knight, who may have been murdered by the Folvilles in 1336, were entrusted with the investigation of Robert Folville's complaint that he had been plundered and assaulted by Ralph Bellers the elder of Kettleby. Wylughby was one of those commissioned to investigate the raiding, in June 1329, of the parks of Henry, earl of Lancaster, in Derbyshire and Staffordshire by the Coterels and their henchmen Roger le Sauvage and the Bradburns. He was also called on in the same capacity in January 1331 when the earl complained of the misbehaviour of the Folville brothers at Newton, Leicestershire. In October 1331 it was Wylughby again who was ordered to look into the complaint of a vicar of Bakewell, whom the Coterels had evicted from Bakewell church.[26] Sir Richard through these duties must have come to know the members of both bands well, and if in his earlier career he was as corrupt as loud complaints suggested in 1340, then the kidnapping of 1332 is easily explained. Other victims of these gangs may have suffered because they had connections with judges who were particularly disliked. A demand for £40 made of Sir Geoffrey Luttrell may have been prompted as much by his relationship to Sir Geoffrey le Scrope, the chief justice of the king's bench, as by his wealth. The

[26] *Eng. Hist. Rev.*, lxxix (1964), 708.

operations of the gang of John Fitzwalter seem to have been directed very often against the citizens of Colchester, which town he besieged so effectively in 1343 that no man there dared go to market between Easter and Whitsun. To get the siege raised several townsmen each had to pay Fitzwalter £40. A steward and tenant of Fitzwalter named Leo de Bradenham besieged Colchester in 1350 for three months with 200 armed men.[27]

There were many other crimes committed by the Fitzwalter band against the citizens of the town and their property, and they largely stemmed from a feud and the desire for revenge. Whether it was the quarrel with Bellers which turned the Folville brothers into arrant criminals, whether John Fitzwalter became a notorious robber and power for evil as a result of his quarrel with the men of Colchester, is unknown. Perhaps these were quarrels started when they were already at odds with the law, but if so it was certainly early on in their criminal careers. Obviously feuds could easily turn the gentry into the paths of crime. A knight or esquire quarrelled with his neighbour and, as often happened, each raided the other's lands. The one who was more knowledgeable about the law or with more influence in the locality could persuade a jury to indict his neighbour who, because he heard he could not expect a fair decision from the petty jury, which might also have been influenced, might decide not to appear in court. After five county courts he could be outlawed and because of this he might sometime choose to live, for a period at least, the life of a professional criminal.

Sooner or later those who were living at odds with the law turned to a type of crime which brought financial rewards. Hiring out their services to other men at feud was one obvious device. The Coterels, in August 1327, at the instigation of a canon of Lichfield, evicted Walter Can from Bakewell church and took ten shillings from the offerings. Malcolm Musard, a Worcestershire gang leader, put himself at the disposal of the evicted rector of Weston-sub-Edge, Godfrey Crombe, in August 1304. Godfrey led the gang to Weston, where it broke into the rector's house and stole grain and goods. Later the raiders shot at the manor house and the servants of the lord of the manor with their bows.[28] The next month Musard led another raid on Weston, in which the gang travelled on horseback bearing arms and pennons, and repeated the actions of August.

[27] *Cal. Pat. Rolls, 1364–1367*, pp. 54–6.
[28] R. H. Hilton, *A Medieval Society* (London, 1966), p. 257.

More popular among gang leaders were crimes which benefited themselves and their gangs directly and not at second hand. The use of threats in order to extort money or goods, which has already been mentioned, was particularly favoured. Extortion became quite a sophisticated technique. When a gang had become well known in a locality there was often no need for its leader to visit intended victims in person. A threatening letter by the hand of a messenger would suffice. In 1332 two members of the Coterel band, Roger le Sauvage and William Pymme, sent such a letter by Henry de Wynkeburn, one of their bearers (another was William's own mother, Lecia), to William Amyas, who was a Nottingham ship owner and wool merchant. Amyas had been mayor of Nottingham several times and was one of the richest men in the town. Wynkeburn demanded £20 for 'the work of the society of savage men'. The money was to be paid in Nottingham to a man who would be bearing an indented bill, one part of which had come to Amyas with the letter. The threat about non-payment was definite. Everything that he possessed outside Nottingham (he held land in the west of the county) would be burned. We do not know if William Amyas ever paid or what happened if he did not. Men similarly threatened who also possessed estates in other parts of the country must have been tempted to quit the locality. Robert Fraunceys of Hardstoft (Nottinghamshire), who was visited on 26 December 1331 by an envoy of Roger le Sauvage called William del Hethe and was asked for forty shillings, felt so threatened that he left his house and did not return for a long while.[29]

Poaching, the theft of animals and game, was a common way of filling the gang's larder, settling scores, and making a profit. In 1327–8 the Coterels and their friends raided Lancastrian estates in the north midlands and stole animals said to have been worth £5,200. This was a large sum even allowing for the probable exaggerations of the earl of Lancaster's executors who reported the loss. Malcolm Musard and his followers poached frequently on the preserves of the magnates. In an indictment of 1305 he was reported to have raided the park of the abbot of Westminster at Tiddesley and that of the earl of Warwick at Beoley.[30] A gang leader who seems to have specialized in park raiding and breaking was Richard Stafford, a Sussex knight who was known also as 'Frere Tuk'. Orders to bring him before the king's council for his entering of parks and warrens in Sussex and Surrey

---

[29] Middleton MS. 6/179/1 mm. 7, 9.
[30] R. H. Hilton, *A Medieval Society*, p. 255.

were given in 1417, but he may not have made his peace with the law until 1429.[31] Whether there was any more to such park raiding than the desire to take some revenge on the owner or to enjoy the thrills of the chase is difficult to determine. The parks and chases were certainly regarded with covetous eyes by those who did not possess them, probably for the delights of hunting rather than for the value of the animals or the desire to fill the stomach. In a few cases the gang leaders and their men may have been genuinely short of food. The grooms of William Pymme, one indictment tells us, searched for food for him and his society on one occasion. Walter Aune, the brother of one of James Coterel's allies, Sir William Aune, brought the gang rents and victuals from the manor of Stainsby. Nicholas Taddington, who guided Coterel when he and his men were trying to lie low, brought victuals to them at Bakewell.[32] The Norfolk band of Charles Nowell and Robert Ledham in the mid-fifteenth century stole sheep and cattle on a sizeable scale, some of which were salted and eaten. In many cases where gangs raided parks and chases there must have been connivance by the keepers and their underlings. The corrupt nature and criminal inclinations of the latter especially were notorious.[33]

There were several other forms of criminal activity which were favoured by the gangs because of the rewards they brought. Malcolm Musard was said to have gone habitually with his men to take seisin of land for one patron or another, and to have received payment for so doing. Homicide for money is less in evidence and, in general, killings were the result of personal quarrels or of the necessity to escape from pursuers. Thus William Beckwith's band, with its quarrel against the officials of the duchy of Lancaster, was probably involved in more killings than the Coterel gang which, apart from a dislike for Sir Richard Wylughby, had no particular feuds. If we are to judge from the deeds of John Fitzwalter, leaders of criminal bands were not averse to making money by practices which were not just illegal, but downright mean and petty. Such actions lacked the intrinsic gallantry or forthrightness of many performed by outlaws in contemporary ballads. Fitzwalter somehow managed to persuade Walter of Mocking, who was described by a jury as having less wisdom than a natural idiot, to give him his lands worth £40 a year in return for a

[31] *Cal. Pat. Rolls, 1416–1422*, p. 84.
[32] Middleton MS. 6/179/1 m. 4d; P.R.O. J.I. 1/1411b m. 6.
[33] R. H. Hilton, *A Medieval Society*, p. 256.

life rent of £22, and a robe, a tunic, and a super tunic each year. Furthermore, Fitzwalter soon kept back the rent and the clothing, allowing Walter nothing. On another occasion, at the time of an assessment for the subsidy, out of fear of Fitzwalter, the tax collectors put him down for the lowest possible sum in nine villages where he was lord of the manor.[34] Nonetheless he refused to pay, and so the villagers, out of fear of the consequences, paid for him, to their own great impoverishment.

What impact did the activities of the criminal bands have on society at large? We may surmise that there was fear mixed with a grudging admiration. The chronicler Henry of Knighton quite approved of the murder of Roger Bellers by the Folvilles and their allies. When he referred to the kidnapping of Sir Richard Wylughby he portrayed the villains as bold men taking reasonable revenge against the judges of trailbaston who had visited all parts of England the previous year.[35] Richard Folville he described not as a criminal, but as a fierce, daring, and impudent man. To have feuded, used violence, to have poached or pillaged, was not at this time held to debar any man from local or even national office. As T. F. T. Plucknett pointed out, there were a considerable number of 'seeming crooks and bandits', guilty of assaults, homicides, and housebreaking, who were elected to parliament in the earlier fourteenth century.[36] James Coterel received assistance in some form from seven men who sat at some time in the commons of parliament. In contrast, however, we know that in lawless mid-fifteenth-century Norfolk people were terrorized by criminal bands. One complaint said that the gang of Charles Nowell, who was the bailiff of Brayston, and of Robert Ledham, made such riots near Ledham's house that the men of the locality believed they might easily be murdered, and did not dare even to go about their everyday business except in groups.[37] Much depended on the number of bands operating in any one area, their size, and the length of time they were permitted to flourish. As we have seen, most gangs committed their crimes in their own backyard, so to speak, near the place where their leaders had originated or held property. To commit a crime more than about forty miles from this

---

[34] P.R.O. K.B. 27/366 Rex mm. 30 (2), 30 (3d).
[35] *Chronicon Henrici Knighton*, i, 460.
[36] *The English Government at Work, 1327–1336*, ed. J. F. Willard, W. A. Morris, and W. H. Dunham (Cambridge, Mass., 1940–50), i, 103.
[37] *Paston Letters*, ed. Gairdner, no. 179.

locality was a rarity. They preferred to capitalize on their local knowledge and felt the more secure because of their established networks of maintainers and receivers. When gangs were reported as wandering about in divers counties it usually meant they were located at a spot where two or three counties joined, probably so they could slip from one to the other when danger threatened. It did not mean they had a field of operations which stretched half-way across England. Few bands seem to have continued their criminal activities for any great length of time. Roger Godberd, a former adherent of Simon de Montfort, dissatisfied with the terms of his pardon, became an outlaw in Sherwood forest, where he apparently robbed and killed travellers for about four years. Then he was captured after a manhunt undertaken by royal command.[38] The first real reference to the Coterel gang was in August 1328, and the last probably early in 1333. Most of the band's important crimes were committed in the short period from March 1331 to September 1332. The criminal record of the Coterel brothers themselves dates seemingly from only 1328 although John and William Bradburn, two of their gang members, had taken part in a burglary in Yorkshire as far back as December 1318. Sir William Chetulton, another associate, had been committing criminal misdeeds from 1320 and had led his own gang in Lancashire in 1322. The Folvilles were first reported as criminals when they participated in the murder of Roger Bellers in January 1326. From then on they were involved fairly continuously in robbery, ransom, and murder until the end of 1332, the time when the Coterels' activities also ceased. Malcolm Musard's most notable exploits seem to have occurred in a short period of two to three years. The criminal activities of William Beckwith and his followers started at about Michaelmas 1387, and although Beckwith himself was killed in about January 1392 his adherents caused trouble until the summer of 1394. The criminal career of John Fitzwalter, in contrast, was more extended. He and his followers were reported as spreading terror and destruction throughout Essex in 1342 and they did not really have to answer for their misdeeds until ten years later. The relatively short existence of individual criminal bands comes as something of a surprise, particularly as there is little evidence to suggest that the members continued in the ways of crime by themselves or in other groups when the original gang became defunct. It points to

[38] *Cal. Pat. Rolls, 1266–1272*, pp. 633–4.

83

some success, in the fourteenth century at least, for the king and his ministers in their policies on crime.

How did the king deal with these bands of misdoers? When indicted by local juries the criminals generally made no attempt to appear in court. Therefore approximately five months after they should have made their appearance they were outlawed. For the task of hunting down outlaws the king used not only the sheriffs and their officers but also men who had a private grudge against the criminals or who wished to gain a reward. In Henry III's reign Reynold de Grey, constable of Nottingham castle, was paid 100 marks specifically to capture the bandit leader Roger Godberd. The task was in no way part of his normal duties nor the payment part of his fees. In December 1330, Roger de Wennesley, the lord of Mappleton, who nine months earlier had killed a relative of the Coterels, was given the task of arresting them and their allies the Folvilles. Setting one thief or criminal to catch another was a device the king favoured repeatedly. In November 1336, when he was on the right side of the law, James Coterel himself was commissioned to pursue and arrest a miscreant Leicestershire parson. One of Coterel's more powerful allies, Sir William Chetulton, who surrendered himself at Nottingham castle before the end of April 1332 and had been pardoned his outlawry, was on 20 July 1332 appointed with James Stafford, another notorious gang leader, to capture two robbers.[39] Despite the efforts of the sheriffs and those commissioned specifically to search out the gangs and their leaders, on most occasions little was accomplished. Not only could the criminals themselves not be found but their goods could rarely be reached for purposes of distraint. In March 1326 the Folvilles and their confederates were indicted at Leicester before a special commission of oyer and terminer for the death of Roger Bellers, but none of the principals was caught. Criminals took care to lie low for a while when they heard they had been indicted. They were usually well informed about the measures being taken against them. In the summer of 1332 James Coterel was warned of the arrival in Nottingham of the leading keeper of the peace for the purpose of hearing pleas. His informant was the prior of Lenton. Sir Robert Ingram, an ex-sheriff of Nottingham, gave a similar warning to John Coterel and Roger le Sauvage by means of a letter to William de Uston, one of their spies in Nottingham.[40] The courts which in the

---

[39] *Eng. Hist. Rev.*, lxxix (1964), 702, 709, 710, 712.
[40] P.R.O. J.I. 1/1411b mm. 6, 6d.

first instance were given the task of dealing with the Coterel band were those of justices of trailbaston and of justices of the peace, but very few of the wanted men actually appeared before them. Of those who did, William de Uston was sentenced to be hanged for robbery and Henry de Wynkeburn was remitted to gaol. A dozen or so receivers also appeared. They were acquitted but had to give pledges to appear in the king's bench to answer further charges at a later date.[41] In this court fifty or more maintainers, receivers, as well as active members of the Coterel gang, appeared between January and March 1333 and virtually all were acquitted likewise. This was not necessarily because of the fearsome reputations of many of the criminals and fears of violence among the jurors, although such a thing was not unknown. William Beckwith and his gang were said to have wandered around the Knaresborough locality bent on the murder of those who had indicted them.[42] The lack of convictions may have been the result of sympathy for the accused criminals, but most likely it was another example of the normal practice of juries of exonerating all those not of notorious record, and who were not clerics or strangers to the area where the offences were committed.

The late medieval English kings seem to have considered that one of the best ways of dealing with gangs and gang leaders, as with most felons who could not be seized immediately and who were not impoverished, was to punish them 'by the purse'. This meant allowing them to purchase a pardon. Usually pardons were obtained by cash payment although sometimes a form of service to the king was involved. When for some reason of state a general pardon was on offer, men could obtain one for only a few shillings. Most pardons were individual ones, however, and more expensive. John Fitzwalter, either because he was rich or because he was such a persistent offender, had to pay handsomely. Between 1352, when he was at last brought to book, and his death in 1361, he had to buy back his estates from the king for £847 2s. 4¼d.[43] Sometimes pardons were obtained by misdoers through the intercession of a sympathetic magnate who may have been instrumental in persuading them to desist from their activities. In November 1322, Robert de Folville was pardoned at the request of two noble scions, Edward and William de

[41] Middleton MS. 6/179/1 mm. 12, 12d, 13.
[42] Cal. Pat. Rolls, 1391–1396, p. 76.
[43] Essex Sessions of the Peace, 1351, 1377–79, ed. E. C. Furber (Colchester, 1953), pp. 64–5.

Bohun, and also of John de Grey, who all subscribed a bond of 1,000 marks as a guarantee of Robert's future good behaviour. In February 1333, William de Uston produced a pardon which he had obtained through the graces of Ralph de Nevill, steward of the king's household. The connection between these two men is not at all obvious. As well as being purchasable by the payment of what amounted to a fine, the king's pardon might on occasions be obtained by performing military service. In July 1333 Eustace Folville received a pardon in return for the service he had rendered in the Scottish war, and although no such close connection can be shown for the other members of the Folville and Coterel bands the frequency with which they participated in military expeditions between 1333 and 1340 is very suggestive. There is some indication that the king granted pardons not reluctantly but, if the criminals were troublesome enough, with considerable eagerness. Some may even have been offered an inducement to abandon their life of crime. This could take the form of an appointment to an office or a lease or gift of land, like William Wallace, then an outlaw, had sought from Edward I in 1303.[44] Sir William Aune, as well as being appointed to administrative duties, was compensated in October 1335 for his loss of a manor, which may have been a major cause of his original association with the Coterels. Nicholas Coterel was appointed Queen Philippa's bailiff of the High Peak and his brother James given the wardship of the lands of Elizabeth, the widow of Thomas Meverel. The grant to James Coterel, which was dated 23 May 1332, seems in fact to have been made during the high period of the gang's activities. This purchasing of criminal good will in order to bring back local peace, and the other seemingly desperate remedies which the king applied, have been criticized by some historians. Nonetheless they had definite merit, for the histories of the Coterel and Folville gangs show that they were largely successful.

The later careers of gang leaders like the Coterels, the Folvilles, and Malcolm Musard show two particularly interesting features. Nearly all the most prominent criminals were given local offices under the crown soon after their misdeeds had ceased. Many of the tasks were military in nature. Sir William Aune was commissioned in July 1334 to survey decaying royal castles in Wales. Sir John Legh, another of James Coterel's allies, was given in January 1335 the task of leading men-at-arms and foot from North Wales to reinforce the

[44] *Chronicle of Pierre de Langtoft*, ed. T. Wright (Rolls Series, 1866–8), ii, 351.

king in Scotland. In July 1336 Legh and Sir William Chetulton were instructed to choose hobelars and archers in Cheshire and lead them to Berwick. William de Uston, strange to relate, was commissioned in January 1341 to investigate certain homicides at Leicester thought to have been committed by the servants of his old enemy, Sir Richard Wylughby. The other notable aspect of the later lives of gang leaders was their markedly reformed character. The Coterels never rode again, and there is little to associate the Folvilles with any new wave of crime although Richard Folville, the parson of Teigh, was referred to in 1340 as being a notorious suspect and was killed resisting arrest a year later. While paying off his large fine John Fitzwalter was seemingly careful to avoid breaking the law again. Malcolm Musard in his later years was less active but his misdeeds, in contrast with the other gang leaders, never entirely ceased, even when in 1315 he was made chief forester of Feckenham and in 1321 constable of Hanley castle. His career and his ability to gain promotion by mixing service with misdeed were probably exceptional. In general, the purchased pardon, the devices of recruitment for military campaigns, and appointment to local office seem to have been effective in regard to many members of criminal gangs. Public order was in fact being upheld and local reigns of terror ended by devices which were political rather than judicial, being based on the king's prerogative of mercy instead of proper process under the law.

In conclusion, it is interesting to consider how the histories of the criminal bands compare with the stories told in ballad and metrical romance of Robin Hood, Gamelyn, and their men whose *floruit* was probably the later thirteenth or the early fourteenth century. Inspection quickly reveals that there are as many divergences as parallels. Robin Hood was a fantasy figure of the men of the lower classes, a projection of their own wishful thinking, doing the things they would never dare to do. Robin rights wrongs, rectifies delays and corruptions in the law by direct action, steals but only from the parasites of society, is ever open handed, meets his king face to face and is pardoned by him. He lives in a simple man's world where the most puzzling things are the disguises put on from time to time, where law and order are embodied in virtually one man, the sheriff, where ill-gotten wealth is synonymous with high ecclesiastics, where all outlaws are strong and resourceful, good with weapons, and conventionally pious, and all enemies are deceitful. Although we shall never know with any exactitude what went on in the minds of the

87

Coterels and the Folvilles, it seems fair to say that their deeds do not suggest a similar attitude to society. Of course there were some adventures and situations which were common to both the outlaws of legend and the historical criminal bands. The Coterels poached, ambushed, had a spy in Nottingham, ill-treated clerics, were pursued by bounty hunters and the sheriff, operated in Sherwood, entered royal service, had as an ally a member of the gentry who had lost his inheritance, were retained at one time by a local magnate and wore his livery, and were pardoned by the king. What is lacking in the Robin Hood legends in particular is the element of feud with neighbours, service in the pay of ecclesiastics (which seems to have been part of the careers of both the Folvilles and the Coterels), office-holders in league with the outlaws for purposes of profit, the employment of one criminal to catch another, and the sophisticated methods of extortion practised by men like Roger le Sauvage. Archery, a great theme in the legends, does not figure at all prominently in the misdeeds of the historical medieval bands save perhaps those of William Beckwith and his followers. Historical gang leaders used violence sometimes for purposes of intimidation and sometimes for revenge. The idea of retributive justice, it is true, may have stood behind the kidnapping of Sir Richard Wylughby, but more marked was a desire to make outlawry pay, to extort, to continue old feuds, to secure allies in the local administration, and to reacquire lost privileges. The Coterels, Folvilles, and Staffords were unlikely to become folk heroes. Those who comprised the core of their gangs were not of peasant stock, free or otherwise, but a cut above it. The activities of the bands, we may suspect, represented the will to power among the gentry, the determination to achieve a position or privilege or re-achieve an old one in county society by fair means or foul. As the ballads point out, justice was uncertain, influence and interference were to be expected, and the realization of this may have convinced gangs like the Coterels and Folvilles that to be a great nuisance to public order was the best way of helping themselves.

IV

Enforcing the Law

Those who composed the ballads about medieval outlaw life saw the sheriff as the chief enemy of the law-breaker. In the Robin Hood ballads it was the sheriff of Nottingham who was most determined on the outlaw's capture and death. To achieve that end he would resort to any ruse or treachery.[1] There was more than a grain of truth in the picture painted. In the everyday life of the later middle ages the sheriff and his staff acted as the police force and there were no real rivals. In the thirteenth century the sheriff had been not only a police officer but also one of the king's justices and a local military leader. Until the beginning of the fourteenth century a few shrievalties were still hereditary, but the remainder were filled by the joint decision of the king, the chancellor, the chief justices, the treasurer, and the barons of the exchequer.

Much of the sheriff's work centred round the county court, where small personal actions in which the property in question was worth under 40 shillings, pleas of trespass, and legal process to force the payment of rents or doing of services were dealt with. Fugitive villeins were claimed there and cases involving the illicit detention of beasts were heard. There were also cases of beating and wounding, which were not alleged to have broken the king's peace, with which a lord's court had failed to deal. Sometimes, though increasingly rarely, the county court, on the direction of the king's justices, was the scene of an inquest into the facts of a particular crime. The king's writ or the itinerant justices might authorize the sheriff in the county court to dispose of a criminal case by means of a jury, or to go through

[1] As most recently pointed out by M. H. Keen, *The Outlaws of Medieval Legend* (London, 1961), p. 149.

89

the processes which could lead to a man's outlawry, or even to deliver, that is to say bring to trial, those incarcerated in the local gaol.[2] Twice a year the sheriff made his tourn of the hundred courts to receive presentments of offences both against the king's peace and against private citizens. At one of these sessions he made view of frank-pledge. This was the old grouping together of most men into bands of about ten for purposes of public order. These were called tithings. The sheriff had to see that all able-bodied adult males, except nobles, clergy, and some categories of freemen, were in such a group. If a member of a tithing committed an offence the other nine were supposed to ensure his appearance in court when required, even by arresting him if they believed it was necessary. A fine was the penalty for failure. It was a system of anticipatory bail and at first sight wholly admirable.

The system of frank-pledge and the judicial authority of the sheriff declined at the same time. To a considerable degree their eclipse was caused by the same circumstances, namely the change in methods of justice, particularly the superseding of the general eyre. In the late thirteenth century commissions were given to justices of assize and keepers of the peace for the hearing and determination of felonies and trespasses, and the visitations of the eyre became ever rarer. Frank-pledge was geared to the production of offenders before the eyre and so lost its purpose. In the increasingly long intervals between eyres, or between the committing of a crime and the next eyre, membership of a tithing group could alter radically. Offences could be dealt with by other justices in the intervening period, the use of gaols and a more limited system of bail serving to produce the misdoers in court rather than the tithing system. Only the leader, the tithingman, was still found useful: he became an assistant to the constable of the hundred. The first statute of Westminster (1275), in defining who was entitled to mainprise and who not, demonstrated the narrower use being made of bail. Possibly as a result of the long-lasting agrarian expansion which only ceased at the end of the thirteenth century, society was becoming less rigid and status and domicile had come to change more rapidly. Edward I recognized the effect of the new-found freedoms, in 1293, by making the men of the whole

[2] The exaction on five separate occasions of fugitive suspects prior to outlawry became one of the most important functions of the county court. However, the process could only be initiated on proper instruction from the king or his justices: see *Munimenta Gildhallae Londoniensis*, ed. H. T. Riley (Rolls Series, 1859–62), II, i, 336–7.

township responsible for damages incurred by robbery when they did not produce the criminal.[3] It was no longer the responsibility of a mere ten men.

As the frank-pledge system declined and the judicial competence of the sheriff grew less, so also did the importance of the county court. There was a decrease in its popularity, probably on account of its adherence to the older methods of trial. It still favoured compurgation, which was the use of men who vouched for the accused's good character on oath, instead of the newer modes of trial involving the use of a petty jury. By the end of the thirteenth century trial by jury was dominant in the courts of the justices of assize, the great central courts which were usually resident at Westminster, and in the sessions of the keepers of the peace. With the decline of judicial business in the county court the sheriff lost many opportunities to demonstrate his authority and his prestige locally must have diminished.

The sheriff was a loser because he had a finger in too many pies and cannot have been as competent a justice as the king required. The later thirteenth century was a period when English common law was being refined and defined. The age of judicial expertise was at hand and the sheriff, one of the local landholding gentry, could not be expected to know a satisfactory amount of law, considering his many other commitments. The same was true of the keepers and justices of the peace in the fourteenth century, but they did not usually sit alone, and it became the custom to have present at least one man with a legal training.

The duties remaining with the sheriff in the later middle ages were still multifarious. As before, they were largely connected with justice, but now in an executive capacity. Any suggested extension of his purely judicial powers was unpopular.[4] Possibly the commonest task which faced the sheriff and his servants, for he had a household of clerks, was the execution of writs, both those emanating from the

---

[3] This was in fact a moderation of a new practice. In 1285 the first chapter of the statute of Winchester had made the men of each hundred and franchise responsible for robberies and damages resulting from their failure to present misdoers: *Statutes of the Realm*, i, 96.

[4] The sheriff seems always to have been regarded at large as a minion of the king despite the fact that the position was always held by a member of the squirarchy. The justice of the peace, who could be the same man as had been sheriff the previous year, was not viewed in the same light at all. It may have been the executive nature of the sheriff's tasks with the opportunities to extort illicit fees and the necessary unpleasantness to the recipient which caused the general dislike.

king and those obtained by private persons in chancery. The sheriff also took pledges for the prosecution of the case and summoned the defendant. On the king's or the justices' command or occasionally on his own responsibility the sheriff would make an arrest, but in civil cases his normal duty was to attach those required in court. This involved taking custody of the body of the accused or his pledge. Before the justices could hold sessions the sheriff had to summon a panel of jurors. When the court was sitting he might have to hold a number of inquests, which were enquiries into specific facts arising out of the cases and undertaken by special juries. If a defendant failed to appear in court the sheriff had to distrain him, that is, to deprive the wanted man of the enjoyment of his lands and chattels in order to compel his attendance on a suitable day. The services of the sheriff were in this way at the command of the visiting justices. Between their visits it was the sheriff's responsibility to decide whom to hold in gaol and whom to free on bail. He alone decided whether an appeal of felony was made in malice. If he believed it was, then the accusation did not lie. On the instructions of the justices of the king's bench he executed writs of *certiorari*, which moved cases before them from lower courts, and also sent prisoners and men who knew the facts. On the orders of the king's council, or of the chancellor, he dispatched to them complainants, defendants, and the findings of inquests, thereby assisting jurisdictions which did not operate under the English common law.

Executive duties which were administrative rather than judicial were just as numerous. They ranged from the taking and giving of seisin of land and chattels and the collection of the farm of the shire and exchequer debts, to the maintenance of highways, the enforcement of commerce and coinage regulations, and making extents of lands. The sheriff also had the less acceptable tasks of keeping the county gaol and supervising the execution of convicted felons, although his physical presence at the gallows was not essential. The office of sheriff also carried executive duties of a military nature, such as producing armed men for military service in wartime. In this field, as in the others, the sheriff found his duties being usurped in the later thirteenth century by new classes of officials, each more specialized and therefore more competent in his task.

There is very little evidence to support the thesis that the reduction of the sheriff's functions was caused by a fear that one man might become all important in a county, and thereby a danger to the central government. From our position of advantage we can see that such a development might have been a blessing. Had the sheriff's powers been allowed to accumulate, had the permitted term of office been more than a single year at a time, the magnates of the region would have found their authority undermined and been unable to dominate both the law and society as they did through maintenance and the giving of livery. As it was, the sheriff was nothing more than a local knight or esquire temporarily vested with office, and in the fifteenth century, at least, under the influence of the nobleman whose badges he might wear. Because of the duties of his office the sheriff may have been hated or feared by criminals and outlaws. It is unlikely to have been on account of the sheriffs themselves, for there was no sheriff 'type'. A member of the gentry became sheriff because the office gave status to the holder and was a recognized stage in the local *cursus honorum*. Sheriff one year, knight of the shire in parliament another, justice of the peace after that, such was the pattern of many an ambitious knight's career. It is commonly argued that in the fifteenth century there came a change. The shrieval office became less attractive because sheriffs found it difficult to collect the required farms and to account satisfactorily at the exchequer; the position was therefore filled increasingly by members of the royal household in the line of duty. Equally persuasive, however, is the argument that rewards paid by the crown made the office profitable rather than expensive.

The medieval constable was a local police officer and the official with whom most criminals came into contact in the first instance. There were constables of the township and constables of the hundred. Both types were elected to office yearly. Constables of the township, either two or three in number, had to make the arrest when hue and cry had been raised. This was usually when a life had been endangered, a house broken into, or an injury threatened, and the normal action taken if the miscreant was not pursued on sight was to search houses and woods. In the fifteenth century there was a definite reluctance on the part of the local inhabitants to participate.[5] When the township constable had captured the miscreant (who was nearly always more than a suspect, having usually been seen committing the act or carrying away his loot) he kept him in custody until he could be handed over to the sheriff or his bailiff. The constable was expected to arrest

---

[5] By the sixteenth century men were wont to say 'God restore your losses, I have other businesse at this time': Holinshed, *Chronicles of England, Scotland, and Ireland* (London, 1807), i, 314.

those who carried weapons at fairs and markets and the misdoers whom the statute of Winchester (1285) called 'roberdesmen and draw-latches'. On the orders of the sheriff or the coroner, the constable arrested men who had been appealed or indicted. Sometimes he was set to guard men arrested by the sheriff's bailiff or the bailiff of a franchise. For this purpose he might use the stocks. He was also expected to maintain a watch on the property of fugitive felons and of those men who were in custody. Township constables were men of relatively lowly station, and, unfortunately for the maintenance of public order, were often unsuited for the task, being without the requisite knowledge or authoritative manner.

The constable of the hundred, in contrast, very nearly had histori-cal importance thrust upon him. The office had a semi-military character, for the hundred constables were the permanent captains of the hundred posses. They were expected to see that the statutory requirements about the arms to be possessed by each man were obeyed, and in addition they had to present before the justices any failure to keep watch, to clear the highway, or to follow the hue and cry. There were occasions when they received indictments concerning breaches in the statute of Winchester, but they were never empowered to enquire into felonies, or trespasses in general. Eventually, having for a period in the early fourteenth century been unconscious rivals with the keepers of the peace for the prize of being local justiciar, they passed into oblivion.

Both types of constable received many of their instructions from the sheriff, but his closest servants were the men who executed royal writs, the itinerant bailiff and the hundred bailiff. Since both were normally appointed by the king, royal approval was necessary if they were to be replaced. Their duties included making attachments, arrests, and distraints, but, in addition to such shrieval business, they purveyed food and animals for royal use, and even helped to collect subsidies. In some places they held the hundred court and the sheriff's tourn. The hundred bailiff acquired a reputation for extor-tion by threatening to arrest people arbitrarily, impounding beasts wrongfully, and letting men off army and jury service.

The natural enemy of the late medieval criminal was less the sheriff than the justice of the peace. The forerunner of these justices was the keeper of the peace, who first emerged in the guise of a local military lieutenant during the civil war of 1263–5. Edward I on two occasions appointed keepers of the peace in each county to assist the sheriff, but it was his son who first issued regular commissions to them. Until 1329 the keepers had power only to record breaches of the peace, but in that year and then intermittently until 1389 when the duty was made permanent, the keepers and their successors, the justices of the peace, were empowered to determine felonies and trespasses.[6] Before this time local peace commissions had often sent the indictments to the justices of assize. From 1350, except for a few years, the keepers and justices of the peace had the power to determine offences against the labour laws. When the keepers were made justices in 1361 they were given the power to arrest summarily certain types of suspects, and in 1362 were told to take sureties from men who were threatening bodily harm and arson to others.

The reluctance of the king to give the keepers of the peace the power to act as justices probably stemmed from doubts about the depth of their legal knowledge. These fears were largely stilled by the practice, which dated from 1344, of putting on the peace commission men with legal training, one or two of whom had to be present when a felony or trespass, according to the rule for that year, was being tried. The commons of parliament, apparently reflecting popular dislike for commissions operated by important men and with wide powers, pressed continuously for an increase in the authority of the keepers. Perhaps they believed this was to their own advantage, since, being members of the local gentry, they were likely to be appointed to the peace commission. The king's desire for popular support in the war with France was probably equally efficacious in winning the day for the knights and esquires. There were nonetheless periodic withdrawals of the power to determine, which arose from a doubt as to the ability of the justices of the peace to handle lawlessness of major proportions. Thus one period of diminished judicial power occurred after the Peasants' Revolt of 1381 and lasted from December 1382 to November 1389. In the suppression of the revolt itself the king relied not on the justices of the peace but on powerful commissions of oyer and terminer which contained a high proportion of nobles and judges of the two benches. The same thing happened after Jack Cade's revolt in 1450. Despite these setbacks the powers of the justices of the peace continued to grow, even if B. H. Putnam's point that in the early

[6] A. Harding points out that the popularity of the new action of trespass played a considerable part in the rise of the keeper of the peace. Many of these actions were aimed at arbitrary officials: 'The Origins and Early History of the Keeper of the Peace', *Transactions of the Royal Historical Society*, 5th Series (1960), 109.

fifteenth century the operation of new statutes concerning such matters as counterfeiting, the giving of livery, and Lollardy was entrusted to the justices of assize who were professional lawyers is correct.[7] By the end of the fourteenth century the justices of the peace were being commissioned regularly to deliver gaols. In 1461 they gained another function when the king ordered that all indictments taken at the sheriff's tourn should be handed to them, and in 1484 they acquired the power to admit to bail prisoners taken on suspicion of felony. Hitherto this also had been the sheriff's task.

During the fifteenth century forcible entry and riot began to bulk very large in the work of the justices of the peace, but the cases were not always dealt with at the quarter sessions. By certain statutes they were given the power to act in a manner quite foreign to the English law. In cases of forcible entry one justice, when ordered to act by royal writ, could hold an inquest at the session, or, and this was the novelty, he might convict summarily and punish by fine. This process would never have been permitted by public opinion had life or limb been endangered. The rule for riot was similar. When two justices of the peace, and the sheriff with the county posse, had made an arrest they could punish forthwith, or one of the justices hold an inquest within a month.[8] A second way of dealing with rioters was for a justice to send a certificate which had the force of a presentment, to chancery or the council. The matter was dealt with there unless the accused objected to the justice's version of events. In that case it was moved into the king's bench. Only a very few other crimes, as for example the labour offences mentioned in the statute of 1414 (2 Henry V st. 1 c. 4), were handled in the same summary fashion.

The sessions of the peace were held quarterly. Sometimes there were two separate sessions in succession, one for labour offences and the second for other crimes. The justices' rate of progress through the pleas varied greatly. Sometimes only one indictment might be heard in a day, yet on other occasions there might be twenty or thirty. There is even reference to more than fifty. The justices of the peace were almost invariably selected by the chancellor and the treasurer at a meeting of the king's council, but no doubt they were influenced

---

[7] B. H. Putnam, *Proceedings before the Justices of the Peace, Edward III to Richard III* (London, 1938), p. li.

[8] This was really a revolution in common law practice and suggests desperate remedies for dangerous circumstances. The new procedures originated in 1391 (forcible entry), and 1411 (riot), and the reasons for their adoption deserve investigation: 15 Richard II c. 2; 13 Henry IV c. 7.

in their choice by pressure from the magnates, who wished to have their own supporters in office in the regions where they had extensive landed interests. Even with the biographies of the justices of the peace before us it is often difficult to tell which particular pressure was paramount at any one time, although when a magnate was as important as for example was John of Gaunt in Richard II's reign, the peace commissions of several midland counties for many years contained a considerable number of knights and esquires with a definite Lancastrian connection. At certain periods starting in the late fourteenth century the great nobles were themselves appointed to the peace commission, although their personal appearances on the bench cannot have been many. Justices of the higher courts were also nominated. Since their commissions were sometimes to as many as ten counties at once they must have been absent as often as the magnates. To serve as a justice of the peace when nominated was in theory compulsory. Whether in their earlier years the justices were paid we are not sure. Possibly they were allowed by the king to take money from the fines they collected. In Richard II's reign payment at last became official and regular at four shillings a day up to a maximum of twelve days a year, although any lords on the commission were expected to serve gratuitously.[9] From the end of the fourteenth century justices had to be resident in their counties, but noblemen and justices of assize were excluded from the rule. From 1439 justices of the peace had to possess lands and tenements worth £20 a year unless they served in towns or there were insufficient men in the county who were learned in law and of that wealth. Being an official of another sort did not automatically bar a man from the peace commission: sheriffs, constables, and bailiffs, all seem to have served on it although infrequently. From the beginning of the reign of Henry VI ecclesiastics were also appointed. Whether they dared to play any part in the trying of felonies, which might involve judgments of blood, is uncertain. One of the justices of the peace was given the title of chief justice, and although the commission was delivered to him it did not necessarily make him the chairman of the sessions. It was usual for a fifteenth-century commission of the peace, like commissions of oyer and terminer, to instruct that authority should only be exercised when there were two or more members present of whom one was

[9] In the mid-fourteenth century commissioners of oyer and terminer were sometimes appointed for life and granted a third of the fines and amercements : *Rotuli Parliamentorum* (Record Commission, 1767–77), ii, 286.

named on a shorter list commonly known as the quorum. This select group seems to have comprised gentry with a knowledge of law. Much of the court's administrative work was done by the clerk of the peace, who was usually a man of some wealth and local importance. From the mid-fourteenth century his was a life appointment. One of his duties was to act as attorney for the king, an important task when the crown was unable to initiate legal proceedings against a criminal itself but must rely on the accusations of a man's neighbours.

At the end of the fourteenth century there were usually about eight justices appointed to each peace commission. The number grew until, in Tudor times, there were nearer forty. The more ambitious gentry must have vied with each other to secure appointment. There is no suggestion that being a justice of the peace was an unwanted duty. By giving judicial authority it must have made a man feel his property was secure, and, just as important, it caused him to be courted or at least held in respect by the local nobility. To have a justice of the peace on one's side must have seemed to a magnate as useful as having corrupted the jury when important interests were in legal jeopardy. Thus by the fifteenth century the justice of the peace was often a local 'boss' in his own right, a man whose friendship was well worth cultivating and whose connections with men in his own district were stronger than any desire to serve the king. Nonetheless, holding the office seems to have restricted the gentry in its everyday behaviour since only rarely were they brought to answer for violent deeds committed when in office or, and this is more likely, those men with a predilection for settling quarrels by violence were often excluded. The fracas at the Bedfordshire sessions in 1438 when the justices and their supporters were divided into two armed groups ready for a battle must have been uncommon.[10]

Although most criminals appeared in court before a justice of the peace, a few whose offences were of a rarer, more important, or an exotic nature might find the justices in charge were those of assize or oyer and terminer. The justices of assize were professional lawyers, usually justices of the two benches or king's serjeants, and were mainly concerned with the possessory assizes. They also received commissions of gaol delivery, especially until the justices of the peace were given the power to determine the indictments they had taken.

[10] J. F. Baldwin, *The King's Council in England during the Middle Ages* (Oxford, 1913), pp. 298–9, 529–31; *Proceedings and Ordinances of the Privy Council of England*, ed. H. Nicholas (London, 1834–7), v, 35, 39, 57.

The justices of oyer and terminer were the judges of the king's bench and common pleas, together with an admixture of noblemen, royal servants, and notable gentry. The noblemen were more in evidence when the main business had a political flavour, such as in cases of treason. In the fifteenth century the percentage of noblemen grew steadily. The commission usually directed any two or three of its nominees to enquire into crimes committed in one or a number of counties and to determine them. Sometimes the whole number of offences committed in one area were to be investigated, and at others it was only one special offence or category of crime, such as the giving of livery or the causing of an insurrection. The commission of trail-baston, which originated in 1304 in an enquiry into those who disturbed the peace, maintained malefactors, and abused jurors was, like the first of these types, the general commission of oyer and terminer. L. O. Pike and W. S. Holdsworth have argued that the trailbaston commission gave an additional power, that of deciding suits between parties.[11] The oyer and terminer commission was the most powerful instrument the king possessed, and it was invariably used when public order was in serious peril. Although not popular, it was accepted as being the surest medicine, as the commons of parliament acknowledged on one occasion in 1409 when they asked for a permanent commission of this sort to be set up beyond the Trent.[12] Often the oyer and terminer commissioners held their own inquests rather than receiving the indictments presented before others.

The most prestigious of common law courts dealing with criminal causes was the king's bench. Although it was essentially a central court, it spent a considerable amount of time in the fourteenth century away from Westminster in the counties. In the first twelve years of Edward III's reign it was absent from the capital, according to one estimate, for about two-thirds of the time.[13] Between 1339 and 1350 it was away about a third of the time, but then settled more firmly at Westminster until it began to move again during the later years of Richard II. In the fifteenth century movement was rarer and it ceased entirely after 1421. The chief justice seems to have decided whether it was to travel about or to remain in one place. When the king's bench

---

[11] W. S. Holdsworth, *A History of English Law* (London, 1956), i, 273; *Year Books, 14–15 Edward III*, ed. L. O. Pike (Rolls Series, 1889), p. xxxvi.

[12] *Rot. Parl.*, iii, 624.

[13] B. H. Putnam, *Proceedings before the Justices of the Peace Edward III to Richard III*, p. lix.

arrived in any county all local courts were supposed to cease their jurisdiction, and all justices appointed to hear and determine felonies and trespasses sent in any indictments not yet determined. The king's bench also busied itself delivering the prisoners in the local gaol. Sometimes it might hear and determine presentments made by its own juries. This it also did at Westminster, together with receiving cases from inferior courts by writs of error, *certiorari*, or *terminari*. If the defendant claimed error it was usually on the grounds that there had been a mistake in the form of the indictment. The jurors' names, or the year or the place of the offence, might have been omitted, or the description and valuation of the chattels taken. Sometimes the man accused was only an accessory, and the principal offenders had not yet been convicted or outlawed as they should have been. Writ of *certiorari* was intended to draw attention to a difficult point of law in a case. The justices of the king's bench, having sent for the indictment, could hear the case themselves or remit it to the justices of the peace, or to *nisi prius* justices, that is to justices of assize who would be visiting the county before the next meeting of the king's bench. Until the middle of the fourteenth century the king's bench received few indictments from the keepers or justices of the peace, but after 1350 there was a rapid increase. According to B. H. Putnam, about ninety per cent of the king's bench *rex* rolls of the reigns of Henry VI and Edward IV consist of cases removed from the peace sessions.[14] Another important feature of the court was the production of pardons. By the fifteenth century, if not before, these could be purchased for most crimes at a relatively low fee. Usually they were offered by the purchaser when he had been outlawed and had surrendered to the marshalsea prison, or had appeared to answer an indictment moved into the king's bench by writ of *terminari*.

Only a select band of criminals came into contact with the king's council. In the later middle ages it dealt mainly with matters such as counterfeiting, heresy, the spreading of rumours against the nobility, serious riots, cases which originated outside the realm, and cases which held a natural interest for the king. Some historians have argued that the exclusion from conciliar jurisdiction in 1352 of matters involving freehold meant the exclusion by implication of treasons and felonies. In fact the council acted as a clearing house for treason cases, directing them to other judicial organs for determination. Occasionally it appointed a number of its own members to act as

[14] *Ibid.*, p. lxiv.

the requisite commission of oyer and terminer. This was necessary because the council was unable to inflict punishments of the severity of those awarded under the common law. It could pillory, imprison, and fine but not decree judgment of life or limb. Conciliar jurisdiction developed during the fourteenth century as the council received petitions that justice could not be obtained in the common law courts, or that the courts' decisions were not being enforced. Sometimes the implication was that the great power of one of the parties was corrupting justice. In Edward III's reign (1346) new types of writ originated by which men could be summoned before the council under threat of penalty for disobeying. Usually they were issued under the privy seal. They gave the defendant no warning of the charges against him, and thereby caused a great deal of bitterness. In the early fifteenth century (1415) the king was asked to consent to the inclusion of the cause of the summons, but refused and continued to use them as before. In 1453 parliament agreed to a royal request to legitimize the writs for a period of seven years, but for riot cases only. Edward IV seems to have continued making use of the writs regardless of the fact that the statutory period had expired. By that time they were such an essential part of government the king could not do without them. It was always difficult to persuade men to receive the writs. There are several reports of messengers receiving bodily hurt, or having to eat the document they had come to deliver.

The sanctions which could be imposed on those who ignored the *sub poena*, or *quibusdam certis de causis* writs as they were known, were limited. A mandate might be given for the arrest of the offender, or a proclamation issued for his appearance on pain of forfeiture, but there could be no outlawry. If the man still refused to appear his lands could not be taken as forfeit and the king accepted this.[15] If the miscreant did appear before the council the procedure differed very much from that employed in the common law courts. Before the trial began questions of fact had been decided by inquests held on the council's instructions and the evidence was thus in writing. If sufficient information was not available by this method, recourse was had to inquisitorial examination in which accused and accuser were each separately required to answer questions, which were often based on facts in the original complaint. There is no real evidence that in the

---

[15] *American Journal of Legal History*, ix (1965), 150. There were, in the 1450s, some efforts to make forfeiture the penalty in fact as well as theory but there is no evidence they were successful.

late middle ages the methods of the council ever came near to superseding those of the common law, or that the council itself was anything more than an important auxiliary in the fight against crime. Men knew their rights too well for any extension of the royal prerogative by conciliar means to be contemplated. Anything which conflicted with the principles of the common law was regarded as impugning Magna Carta and detrimental to the traditions of English justice.

Before a criminal could be put on trial he must have surrendered to a law officer or have been captured. The rules governing the arrest of a man who had already been indicted were simple compared with those obtaining before any indictment or other legal accusation had been made. Originally, as we have seen, the tithing and later the township had been responsible for the arrest of men who had committed homicide. At this time arrest was very closely connected with the hue and cry and was a prime duty of the constables of the vill, who were expected to lead the pursuit. As long as there was manifest proof through the miscreant's being observed in the committing of the offence, or carrying his loot, everything was relatively straightforward. Difficulty arose when a man fell under suspicion who had not been noticed behaving in a provocative manner, and was not a member of a tithing or the vill. In the later thirteenth century, as the population grew and became more mobile and the importance of the tithing group declined, this became increasingly common. Some guidance was given by the statute of Winchester, which decreed that strangers could be arrested if they behaved suspiciously at nighttime, and the Northampton statute of 1332 ordered the arrest at any hour of armed men or others suspected of evil-doing who should pass through the townships. A moderate degree of suspicion now sufficed instead of the virtual certainty required before.

The power to arrest such suspects was carefully limited. Constables, bailiffs, and mayors in towns must have been able to do it if they were to prevent breaches of the peace, but their action had to be based on their own knowledge of the misdeed. The justices of the peace only received the power in 1361 and for a period of eighteen months. In March 1364 they were given instead the power to take sureties for good behaviour from those who threatened bodily harm or arson. For the arrest of notorious suspects by the justices a special commission was usually necessary. The powers of arrest possessed by the ordinary citizen were, like today, ill-defined. Even F. W. Maitland could make little of them.[16] An ordinary man, one who held no official commission, could apparently make a lawful arrest if there was good cause for his suspicion. A fair reason was the raising of the hue and cry. A year-book case from the reign of Edward IV suggests that in the later fifteenth century the citizen's duty of arrest was giving rise to discussion. It was agreed that a man must make an arrest if he knew a felony had been committed, or even if a trespass had been committed which might lead to a felony. If, however, he only suspected a felony had been committed, but had good grounds for his suspicion, he could make an arrest but was not obliged to do so. Anyone who broke open a door in order to effect an arrest was not protected from a lawsuit on the part of the suspect if it was later found he had not in fact committed the offence.[17] In general, suspicion had to be grounded on good evidence, unless the one who suspected was the constable, when the grounds could be less certain.

What was to be done with a man taken into custody until he was put on trial? The king, who ordered a great many arrests as a result of information he had received, might keep men in gaol for a considerable time before allowing them to appear in court. John Bildeston, a chaplain who was suspected of counterfeiting the great seal, was put in the Tower of London on the king's writ and stayed there for over two years before Edward III let him be brought to trial.[18] In the parliament which met in January 1315 William Gentilcorps petitioned the king for delivery from gaol in Rochester castle, where for more than two years he had been detained on the king's writ, so as to be able to answer those who accused him of the rape and death of Alice de Beauchamp. The judges of the king's bench to whom the matter was eventually referred were unable to find any record of proper accusation before a court and seem to have persuaded the king to release William late in 1318.[19] At the other end of the judicial structure constables of the vill could, by the end of the fifteenth century, keep suspects in custody, perhaps in the stocks, until they were examined before a justice of the peace. In the sixteenth century,

---

[16] See F. Pollock and F. W. Maitland, *The History of English Law before the Time of Edward I* (Cambridge, 1923), ii, 582–4.
[17] *Year Books, Les Reports del Cases en Ley* (London, 1678–9), 10 Edward IV, Mich. pl. 20; 11 Edward IV, Trin. pl. 8; 13 Edward IV, Pasch. pl. 4.
[18] *Select Cases in the Court of the King's Bench, Edward III*, ed. G. O. Sayles (Selden Society, 82, 1965), p. 31.
[19] *Rot. Parl.*, i, 321–2; *Select Cases in the Court of the King's Bench, Edward II*, ed. G. O. Sayles (Selden Society, 74, 1955), p. 84.

if no indictment was forthcoming but the justice of the peace still viewed the man with suspicion, an announcement was made in court asking for anyone who could say anything against him to speak forth. If no one did so he was acquitted by proclamation. There were occasions when men sued for false arrest and imprisonment, but the chances of winning were not good. If the defendant could show a royal commission and that the plaintiff had been guilty of a serious offence, it was held sufficient justification.

If one man killed another accidentally, he was not supposed to wait until the constable arrested him, or took surety, but was expected to seek out the constable and surrender to him. When an arrest had been made the question of release on bail often followed. Edward I's first statute of Westminster listed the categories where bail was allowable and where it was not. It was not to be permitted before indictment in cases where a man was captured carrying loot, when a man turned approver, that is to say when an accused appealed others of also being responsible for the misdeed, and when men who were appealed by approvers who were still living were not of good reputation. It was also denied to those who had broken out of prison, to those who had been arrested for felonious house burning, uttering false money, or counterfeiting the king's seal, or when, as it was put, men were taken for manifest offences or treason touching the king himself. Each of these offenders had either committed a crime which was heinous, or there were exceptionally strong grounds for believing he was guilty.

Under the common law a man could not usually be tried on a criminal charge in his absence. There exists on record a case of 1282 in which John de Clifford was appealed of the rape of Rose le Savage. The appeal failed on a technicality, but the king's attorney then prosecuted Clifford at the king's suit, and although he was absent the jury found him guilty.[20] This case is, however, the only one so far discovered. Very often men were found guilty in their absence, but it was by outlawry, not trial. Whether the accusation against the misdoer was by personal appeal or by indictment of a jury, the process of outlawry was very similar. Writs of *capias*, often three in number, successively ordered the sheriff to seize the wanted man. If each time he returned that the accused was not to be found in his bailiwick then

---

[20] *Select Cases in the Court of the King's Bench, Edward I*, ed. G. O. Sayles (Selden Society, 55, 1936), i, 102.

the exigent, or demand for his appearance in the county court, was made. After five such exactions, each in a different county court, the man was outlawed. His goods and his chattels were forfeited to the king when the first exigent was awarded, and when he was finally outlawed his land was escheated to his immediate lord. If he was captured, the outlaw was usually brought straight before a court, the indictment and proof of exaction read out, and execution ordered by the justices. In the twelfth and thirteenth centuries an outlaw could be captured by any man, and if he resisted he could be slain like the wolf whose head he was said to bear. W. S. Holdsworth believed this practice continued until 1329, when Edward III's judges decided the justices alone could put to death a man outlawed for felony.[21] This did not mean the practice disappeared completely: men with no official position still dealt with outlaws in summary fashion. In March 1397 William Speke of Spalding, Lincolnshire, and a number of his associates were pardoned for arresting and beheading, some five years previously, an outlawed felon in the belief that it was lawful.[22] Men who were exacted often found ways of defeating impending outlawry. An obvious device was to flee to another county, having before exaction made over one's moveable goods to a friend, but a safer recourse was to enter the king's service. Then one's person and possessions were under royal protection. A man could not be outlawed if he was already captured and in custody. Although very often it did little to improve his hopes and condition, many a miscreant was able to show that he could not possibly have answered to exaction in one county since he was in gaol in another at the time. There was little exchange of information about wanted and captured men among those who administered justice.

By the later fifteenth century to be outlawed was much less of a calamity than it had been even a century before. There was less inclination to flee blindly, or take to the woods and become a professional robber. Instead men lay low with their friends and waited until a pardon could be obtained, or they moved a fair distance from their homes and continued to practise their trade. So secure did many of these migrants feel that they did not bother to purchase a pardon even when these could be easily acquired and at a low fee. We know of one outlaw who plied his trade in London for twenty-two years before he bought one. A Sussex labourer who murdered his wife in

---

[21] W. S. Holdsworth, *History of English Law* (Boston, 1923), iii, 605.
[22] *Calendar Patent Rolls, 1396–1399* (Record Commission), p. 92.

1431 and was outlawed for it, purchased a pardon only in 1446.[23] Securing a pardon did not restore a man to the exact state existing before outlawry. He might get back his lands but not his goods and chattels. Outlawry was also the extreme form of mesne process in civil suits. It appeared first at the time of Bracton in cases of trespass, but later on in actions of account (1285), debt detinue and replevin (1352), and actions of case (1504). In contrast with criminal cases, where it rarely took more than five months to complete, outlawry in private suits, because of the room allowed for legal manoeuvring and delays, could take years to complete. It involved no danger to life or limb, or even to lands held.

Most homicides and assaults were committed in a moment of uncontrollable rage. The offender, as we have seen, was supposed to surrender to the constable of the vill, but if the relatives and friends of the victim were on hand they often wished to revenge blood with blood and to act, if death had occurred, as a lynching party. If the man who had inflicted the injury chose not to surrender he would very likely try to flee the neighbourhood. If pursuit was immediate, and the hunters drew ever closer, the fugitive might decide to seek the protection of a sanctuary. The privilege of affording sanctuary was possessed in some degree by all consecrated buildings and land, as well as by certain secular liberties on the Welsh marches and in northern England. Every parish church could give it, even the churchyard. Churches which held a charter mentioning sanctuary in specific terms, such as Durham cathedral, St John of Beverley, the abbeys of Westminster, Glastonbury, and Beaulieu, might offer the fugitive an immunity from pursuit and capture up to a mile from the actual ecclesiastical buildings. In some cases stone crosses were set alongside the highway to mark the limits of the protective area, and there were gradations of fine which the church authorities could impose on pursuers according to how far within the perimeter they dared to penetrate. As well as notable churches there were areas of particular lay jurisdiction which offered a most superior type of sanctuary. This was where the lord had royal rights and the king's writ did not run. Thus in the earldom of Chester, Hoole Heath, Overmarsh, and Rudhealth offered protection to fleeing criminals for an unlimited period. To live there was as effective as fleeing to a foreign land. Other lay franchises which were very attractive to sanctuary seekers were Tynedale, Redesdale, the marcher lordships of Wales and the county palatine of

[23] R. L. Storey, *The End of the House of Lancaster* (London, 1966), p. 215.

Lancaster. A rule which suggests earlier medieval practice was that during his flight no man was supposed to be hindered or obstructed by neutral parties, provided he announced his intention of taking sanctuary. If, however, the hue and cry had been raised there were, of course, no neutral parties and it was everyone's duty to stop the fugitive.

Not every type of criminal was permitted to go into sanctuary or, if they got in, allowed to remain. Those excluded from the privilege were common or notorious offenders (men in modern parlance with a criminal record), suspected or indicted traitors, heretics, those who dabbled in sorcery, clerks, those who were believed to have committed a felony in a church, and those originally caught in the act. Nor were men who had committed only a minor offence against the king's peace, which did not involve the danger of loss of life or limb, afforded any protection. No man could have sanctuary if he had already been convicted of the offence, either by judgment in court or by outlawry. As the middle ages drew to a close an increasing number of debtors tried to gain entry into sanctuary despite several laws designed to dissuade them. A statute of Edward I (1278) allowed the seizure of goods and property of fraudulent debtors seeking sanctuary, and an act of 1379 said more precisely that debtors who had made feigned conveyances of goods or lands to their friends and then fled to a chartered sanctuary were to be summoned weekly for five weeks by the local sheriff to appear before the king's justices. If they failed to appear judgment was to be given against them with execution on their goods and lands. A petition in the parliament of 1402 pointed out that in the sanctuary of St Martin's-le-Grand, London, were to be found not only a great number of debtors but also apprentices who had stolen their masters' goods, and men who forged bills, indentures, and acquittances and made a practice of ordering victuals and merchandise to be delivered there and then refused to pay.[24]

On arriving safely within the precincts of a chartered sanctuary the fugitive was expected to make a confession of his misdeeds to the ecclesiastical officials, to surrender any weapons, and to put himself under the supervision of the religious head. He had to swear to observe the sanctuary's internal rules and then he was enregistered. His name, his normal place of domicile, his occupation, his confession of the crime, the weapon he used, the name of the victim, were all set down, and the new arrival paid a small fee to the bailiff of the liberty

[24] *Rot. Parl.*, iii, 503–4.

and another to the clerk whose pen noted the information. Those who were admitted to Beverley promised to be faithful and true to the archbishop of York, to bear good heart to the bailiff, the governor, the burgesses, and citizens of the town, never to carry a weapon, and to hold themselves ready in case there was any debate, strife, or sudden fire in the town. Within the sanctuary they had to ring the church bells at the proper hour and attend mass. They were well lodged and fed, although they were not allowed, as they were in some Cistercian abbeys, to put on the religious habit. For the man who had sought sanctuary in a parish church conditions might be very different. He could obtain food only through the good offices of the priest, and sometimes the watch kept on the sanctuary by local men was so strict that, as a statute of 1315 put it, 'they [the fugitives] cannot depart from the hallowed ground to empty their belly and cannot be suffered to have necessaries brought unto them for their living'.

Watch was kept on a sanctuary which was known to be harbouring a fugitive by the men of the four nearest townships. This was their duty and if the fugitive escaped they were liable for a fine to the king. They were expected to inform the coroner about the man in sanctuary, and he was supposed to come and hear the confession if there was one. The evidence suggests that the coroner did not come at once, perhaps in order to allow the fugitive time to reflect on his plight, and thereby be the more ready to confess when the opportunity offered. Usually he arrived in three or four days, but he might take as long as a fortnight. The confession took place before the coroner, the representatives of the four townships, and other witnesses. There followed, after an interval whose length varied, an oath by the criminal at the door of the church that he would abjure the realm for ever. From the time of his entry into sanctuary he had forty days to take the oath, although he could, of course, decide to surrender himself and stand trial. According to Bracton, if the fugitive did not forswear the realm or surrender within the allotted period, he was to be held convicted, but in the fourteenth and fifteenth centuries it is more likely that a man who was forcibly removed or starved out was given a normal trial.[25]

Starvation was the usual method of bringing a sanctuary seeker from his bolt-hole. Sometimes the watchers went as far as to set the church on fire. Very occasionally the anger of the pursuers was so

---

[25] Bracton, *De Legibus et Consuetudinibus Angliae*, ed. G. E. Woodbine, translated and revised by S. E. Thorne (Cambridge, Mass., 1968), ii, 383.

great that they entered the sanctuary and removed the fugitive by force, braving, or momentarily forgetful of, the anathemas of the church authorities. There was a notable case in 1378. An esquire called Robert Haulay, who had sought sanctuary on breaking out of captivity in the Tower of London, was slain together with a sacristan in the abbey church at Westminster.[26] The offence seemed the more outrageous for being committed in front of the prior's stall, by a large number of armed men led by the constable of the Tower, when high mass was being celebrated at the high altar. The case aroused great public interest and undermined the authority of the government. Those who committed the murders were excommunicated and had to pay a large fine to the abbey. The abbey church was closed for several months and had to be reconsecrated.

If sanctuary was invaded successfully and those seeking refuge removed, it was usually on the orders of the king or the church authorities themselves. In 1322 Isabella Bury killed the clerk of All Saints-by-London-wall and placed herself in sanctuary in the same church.[27] The bishop of London decided she could claim no immunity and ordered her to be seized. She was later hanged. In the fifteenth century kings commanded a number of their political enemies who had fled to sanctuary to be removed. In 1454 the duke of Exeter was taken by force from Westminster Abbey despite the protest of the abbot. After the battle of Tewkesbury Edward IV had the duke of Somerset and a score of other notable Lancastrians dragged from Tewkesbury abbey and beheaded. In 1486 Sir Humphrey Stafford was forcibly moved from Culham church near Abingdon on Henry VII's instructions.[28] In each of the three cases where the king intervened it could be argued that the fugitives had committed manifest treason, were indicted of treason, or were notoriously suspect of that crime. Since treason and a felony committed in a church were not supposed to be protected by sanctuary, it seems that both the king and his bishops acted with right on their side. No king chose wilfully to disregard proven privilege of sanctuary.

[26] *Thomae Walsingham Historia Anglicana*, ed. H. T. Riley (Rolls Series, 1863–4), i, 376–9.

[27] *Chroniques de London*, ed. G. J. Augnier (Camden Society, xxviii, 1844), p. 42.

[28] *Chronicles of London*, ed. C. L. Kingsford (Oxford, 1905), p. 164; J. Warkworth, *A Chronicle of the First Thirteen Years of the Reign of Edward IV*, ed. J. O. Halliwell (Camden Society, x, 1839), pp. 18–19; *Year Books, Les Reports del Cases en Ley* (London, 1678–9), 1 Henry VII, Pasch. pl. 15, Trin. pl. 1.

Not all sanctuary seekers were docile and ready to abjure the realm, surrender for trial, or meekly await their fate. A few escaped to other refuges, and a number of bolder spirits used the sanctuary as a base for raiding the homes of those who lived nearby. The sanctuary men of St Martin's-le-Grand, who were particularly infamous, raided the city of London in 1455–6 and participated in riots against alien merchants. In 1440 a soldier named Knight was rescued by four men from that place, when being taken from Newgate prison to the Guildhall for trial. In 1487, when a false report had it that Henry VII was defeated at Stoke field, the sanctuary men of Westminster went out to rob the houses of those who were known to have gone with the king.[29]

Sanctuary seekers, like many other types of medieval criminals, are difficult to appraise as a class since biographical detail is difficult to discover. Fortunately the registers of the two northern sanctuaries of Durham and Beverley supply one or two valuable pieces of information on this obscure subject.[30] Of considerable interest and not easily explainable, save as the result of a witness's or accomplice's death-bed confession, is the arrival in sanctuary of men and women who had committed their offences many years previously, in one case twenty-six years before. One man sought sanctuary as a result of the theft of an ox seventeen years before. Of the 500 names in the Beverley register in the period 1478–1539, 200 were associated with crimes of violence and 208 with debt. The Durham register, which records sanctuary seekers between 1464 and 1524, shows 195 men fleeing from some sort of homicide out of a total of 243 crimes recorded. There were also sixteen cases of debt, nine of cattle stealing, seven of theft, and four each of escaping from prison, horse stealing, and house-breaking, and one each of thief-harbouring, petty larceny, rape, and failing to prosecute. The Beverley register shows tailors as the most common perpetrators of violence, whereas the most frequent debtor was the builder. Overall, the largest percentage of sanctuary seekers came from the farmer and the agricultural labouring classes, which tells us very little since most men earned their living from the land. There were a few gentlemen and above, and the occasional woman. We may fairly infer that most of the crimes of violence were the result of men drawing their swords, or daggers, or making use of

[29] *Calendar of Letter Books of the City of London, K*, ed. R. R. Sharpe (London, 1911), pp. 241–6; *Calendar of State Papers, Venice, 1202–1509* (Record Commission), no. 519.

[30] See *Sanctuarium Dunelmense et Sanctuarium Beverlacence*, ed. J. Raine (Surtees Society, v, 1837), especially pp. vii and viii.

clubs or staffs which happened to be handy, at the time of a verbal altercation. At Beverley 500 men sought sanctuary in the sixty-one years covered by the register, and at Durham there were 243 in fifty-six years; but since men must have travelled considerable distances to avail themselves of the extensive privileges which these churches offered, the figures cannot be used to assess the general incidence of sanctuary seekers per county per year. One relevant figure we do possess, but no more. It is that in the first year of Edward I's reign (1272–3), in Staffordshire, twenty people sought sanctuary. Whether the figure is accurate and typical is very doubtful.

Sanctuary privileges remained virtually intact until the earlier Tudors ascended the throne. There was legislation against various abuses of sanctuary from 1376 onwards, but it did not deal with the crux of the matter. During the fifteenth century, before the reign of Henry VII, the church could usually count on royal support when attacks were mounted by parliament and town councils, but more and more often the sanctuaries' charters were examined critically for proof of privilege during the argument. Thus the sanctuary authorities were forced onto the defensive. The royal judges viewed sanctuaries as liberties where the king's writ did not run, and therefore as something to be gradually eroded. In 1399 they said there should be no new sanctuaries. In 1486 they argued that the king alone could no longer grant sanctuary for treason, although they admitted he had done so in the past. The reign of Henry VII saw the acts against fraudulent debtors rigorously administered, and even extended, and there were some notable encroachments on sanctuaries in cases of suspected treason. Henry VIII virtually extinguished the sanctuaries. Rape, murder, burglary, arson were all excluded from the privilege, and another decisive blow was struck by the dissolution of the monasteries. As a replacement the king founded eight so-called cities of refuge, but they were abandoned during the reign of his son.[31]

A considerable proportion of those who fled into sanctuary did not surrender because of starvation, did not escape, or were not lucky enough in their choice of a refuge to be able to settle down to a life in confinement. They decided to abjure the realm. In theory the oath of

---

[31] About sanctuaries in general see N. M. Trenholme, *Right of Sanctuary in England*, University of Missouri Studies, vol. i, part 5 (1903), pp. 298–403, and I. D. Thornley, 'The Destruction of Sanctuary' in *Tudor Studies presented to . . . A. F. Pollard*, ed. R. W. Seton Watson (London, 1924), pp. 182–207. The information about sanctuary seekers in Staffordshire in 1272–3 is to be found in T. J. Mazzinghi, *Sanctuaries* (Stafford, 1887), p. 41.

abjuration was taken at the door of the church within forty days of entry, and following confession of the crime to the coroner. The oath-taker swore never to return except with the king's licence. According to the late thirteenth-century legal writer *Britton*, after forty days in sanctuary a man was deemed a convicted felon automatically and debarred from abjuration. Bracton, writing a little earlier, suggested that the origins of abjuration were to be discovered in the assize of Clarendon (1166) which decreed that the indicted criminal who purged himself successfully by ordeal must quit the realm within a few days. The types of malefactor which were excluded from the privilege of abjuration were very similar to those forbidden sanctuary, but there were two additions. Clerks in sanctuary who claimed bene-fit of clergy could not be made to abjure the kingdom, nor could lay-men who had abjured once already and been allowed to return. When a man had sworn the abjuration oath he might yet remain in sanctuary until the forty days had expired. Watch was still kept by the men of the nearby townships, although the sanctuary seeker was probably allowed a number of comforts. Then he must set out for the port where he must take ship, or a town from which he could cross into Scotland. Usually this was chosen for him by the coroner. His chattels were forfeit to the king and his lands escheated to his immediate lord.

A man who abjured the kingdom had his movements and behaviour between the sanctuary and the town of exit carefully regulated. By the end of the fifteenth century, before he set out he was branded on the brawn of the thumb with the letter 'A'. He had to go barefooted and bareheaded, wearing white sackcloth which bore a red cross upon it, and carrying a wooden cross in his hand. His original clothing he supposedly gave to a church official, but since in the fourteenth century there is mention of shirt and breeches being worn the earlier rules cannot always have been enforced rigidly. At all times during his journey the abjuror had to keep to the highway and might not make use of the footpaths which ran alongside the great roads. Nor could he use the roads and hospices in the manner of a pilgrim, which presumably meant to travel in company. It was forbidden for any man to molest an abjuror as he passed on his way, and in order to protect him from an enemy in ambush, as well as to make sure he reached his destination, men from the four townships nearest to where the crime had been committed gave him an escort. If the mis-doer left the highway, except to find a bed for the night, he might be summarily beheaded on capture. According to Bracton, no abjuror could stay in one place for two nights together, but there are in fact examples of men being permitted a day's rest on the way. Coroners very often were quite specific in their instructions about the journey, fixing halting places, and giving a definite time for its completion. Different abjurors were given different schedules. One man was allowed three days to reach Yarmouth from Mildenhall, Suffolk, while another, who was a horse stealer like the first, was given six days for the same journey. Sometimes abjurors were given what appears an excessively long time to reach their destination. In 1295 a Norwich coroner assigned Portsmouth as the port of embarkation, and allowed three weeks for a journey of about 180 miles. In contrast, John Kipernol, from Gayton church near Lynn, was ordered to travel to Sandwich, a distance of 170 miles, in a mere four days.[32] Possibly the coroner took account of the age and health of the abjuror, or the season of the year; otherwise it is hard to explain why one man should be expected to average over forty miles a day but another only ten. The port assigned was often Dover, sometimes Hull or Berwick, and occasionally Rochester, Orwell, Sandwich, Lancaster, Boston, Tynemouth, Portsmouth, Padstow, Looe, Ilfracombe, and similar towns of lesser standing. When the abjuror arrived at the place from which he was to quit England he was supposed, as he had promised in his oath to the coroner, to seek diligently for a boat to carry him overseas. If the search was successful he must not delay more than a single tide. If there was no ship available he must go into the sea up to his knees once a day as a token of his desire to leave the realm. If after forty days he had still not succeeded, the abjuror must return into sanctuary, presumably the one he had left, to await a suitable opportunity.

Abjuration of the realm, like the seeking of sanctuary, was no proof that the man or woman involved was actually guilty of any crime. Sometimes men fled into sanctuary merely to escape the wrath of their personal enemies, and they might even have to quit the kingdom for the same reason. *Britton* was aware of such cases. He wrote that a man who abjured the realm, although innocent, in order to

[32] *Britton*, ed. F. M. Nichols (Washington, 1901), i, 55; *Bracton, De Legibus et Consuetudinibus Angliae*, ed. G. E. Woodbine (trans. S. E. Thorne), ii, 382–4; J. C. Cox, *The Sanctuaries and Sanctuary Seekers of Medieval England* (London, 1911), pp. 28–30. The author of *A Relation of the Island of England*, ed. C. A. Sneyd (Camden Society, xxxvii, 1847), pp. 36–7, remarks on how the English (*c.* 1500) considered abjuration to be as bad a fate as death.

save his life, might later obtain a pardon from the king.[33] Then his lands would be returned, but his goods and chattels would remain forfeit. Legal writers usually had a particular case or cases in mind when they made a generalization, but *Britton's* example of this type of pardon has escaped detection, as has any later instance. Generally when abjurors had left the realm they were never heard of again, even if, like Thomas Wayland, the chief justice of common pleas who went into exile in 1290, they had been men of substance and rank in England. Although the lack of coroners' rolls for the fifteenth century does not allow us to be certain if abjurors diminished in number as the middle ages closed, the guarded opinion of R. F. Hunnisett is that they probably did not. Abjuration of the realm was ended by Henry VIII who, by a measure we have already noted, substituted confinement in a number of recognized sanctuary places which were to be always under guard.

Apart from the king's council and chancery, all the institutions and the procedures emanating from them concerned with the administration of justice operated under the common law. Occasionally the king, by virtue of his prerogative, used devices which were in contrast ancillary to the common law. These appeared mainly in the mid-fifteenth century and probably originated in governmental despair at the low level of public order. They were directed less against criminals of lower rank, although ultimately the conduct of such men was bound to be affected, than against the misdeeds of the gentry and nobility. One device was for a commission of local knights to give a list to the sheriff of all those persons whom they thought should take an oath not to maintain men known or suspected of breaking the peace. This was first tried in 1434. Those whose names were given were landholders whose social rank was knight, esquire, or mere gentleman.[34] In 1434 they totalled roughly between 100 and 400 for each shire. There is evidence that the king attempted to keep men to their oath, for there were a number of prosecutions in the following years which made a direct reference to the recent statute against maintainers of quarrels. Apart from this there is no way of testing the efficacy of such methods for improving public order and we may suspect that men soon forgot their oath. Nonetheless, on his accession in 1461, Edward IV, who later on showed great shrewdness in dealing with the lawlessness he had inherited, decided the method

[33] *Britton*, i, 55.
[34] *Rot. Parl.*, iv, 455–7, 422; *Cal. Pat. Rolls, 1429–1436*, p. 370.

was worth using again. Thus in parliament the lords promised to aid all men seeking to capture evil-doers, even if the latter were in their own entourage.[35] There was another example in the reign of Henry VII. Soon after seizing the throne the king arranged for the knights, esquires, and commonalty of each shire to take an oath of allegiance, promising to do no treason, to reveal traitors, and not to retain other men or be retained by them except according to the law. The reason for the restriction on retaining was shown in a commission issued in January 1486. Those appointed were to take an oath from knights, esquires, gentlemen, yeomen, and any others who gave liveries and retainers, that they would not retain, aid, or comfort any man knowing him to be a murderer, a felon, or an outlaw.[36] Again there is no evidence that the oaths taken inhibited the would-be lawbreaker. Perhaps lack of experience of kingship at the time gave Edward IV and Henry VII a faith in men's words which the realities of government soon took away: perhaps Henry VII merely copied his Yorkist predecessor.

Another instrument which operated outside the common law was the writ of proclamation. To a certain degree it was an extension of conciliar jurisdiction in that proclamations were often ordinances of council publicly proclaimed. In March 1456 the sheriffs of Devon and Somerset were told to proclaim against the holding of gatherings or assemblies without the king's assent on pain of forfeiture. The mandate pointed out that if every Englishman was to call or attend gatherings no one could be sure of his personal safety, and there would be no king's peace. In April 1457 the sheriff of Worcester was told to proclaim that no man should give badges or liveries contrary to the statutes under threat of pains and forfeitures provided by the king and council. It was also by no means uncommon for sheriffs to be ordered to proclaim in every hundred court, and at markets and fairs, and all other places where people were wont to assemble, one or a number of statutes dealing with the keeping of the peace. In one case in October 1426 it was the statute of Winchester of 1285 and the act of 7 Richard II which confirmed and extended it.[37] There was another group of proclamations, which were issued at the request of parliament, where a private petition for a proclamation had been successfully made. The petitioners commonly desired the appearance of

[35] *Rot. Parl.*, v, 488a.   [36] *Cal. Pat. Rolls, 1485–1494*, pp. 39, 71.
[37] *Cal. Pat. Rolls, 1452–1461*, p. 304; *Calendar of Close Rolls, 1454–1461* (Record Commission), p. 205; *ibid., 1422–1429*, p. 316.

some rival or malefactor in the king's bench, before the council, or before the chancellor. Because men ignored outlawry and other sanctions of the common law, the injured party, in order to enforce appearance, sought through parliament penalties of a type more severe than the king's council or chancery could apply. They hoped for, and often obtained, the forfeiture of the wanted party's lands, goods, and chattels to the king, his loss of royal protection, or his conviction and attaint, as if he had already been tried and found guilty. Some of these parliamentary petitions even proposed punishment for the sheriff who failed to handle the proclamation in the proper manner.

One of the earliest examples of this procedure occurred in the parliament of 1415. John Brompton of Beverley petitioned for the Yorkshire sheriff to be ordered to proclaim that John Hayton and his covin who had ambushed him should appear before the chancellor, on an appointed day, to give surety for their good behaviour in the future. The chancellor was to have the legal power to hear and determine the case. If those whom Brompton named did not appear at the proper time, they were each to be liable for a fine of 100 marks. The penalties suggested in this and a similar case in the parliament of 1432 were very moderate, but a petition in the 1420 parliament against a number of Westmorland malefactors, who were said to have withdrawn to the woods and other solitary places, demanded that if they did not surrender to the sheriff within eight weeks preparatory to appearing before the council, they should be put out of the king's protection and forfeit lands, goods, and chattels to the king. There was another very similar petition, also granted, in the same session.[38]

The most striking example of the use of parliamentary sanctions to compel the appearance of malefactors in court occurred in the parliament of 1450, and concerned the murder by ambush of William Tresham, a speaker of the house of commons. His wife Isabella, in her petition, explained why she resorted to this method of obtaining satisfaction. If, as many widows did, she had appealed the culprit at common law in the normal way, no sheriff or other officer would have dared to arrest the evil-doers or execute writs against them. She wanted the Northamptonshire sheriff to proclaim the criminals to appear in the king's bench the following Hilary term to answer her bill of appeal. She stipulated that they should not be allowed bail, and,

[38] *Rot. Parl.*, iv, 83b, 124b, 416b.

that if they asked for trial by jury, the jurors were each to be men worth £20 a year and living in Northamptonshire. In case it was necessary to compel their appearance in court she set the size of the distress. She tried to ensure the success of the appeal by asking parliament to forbid any unreasonable challenge of it in court; to legislate that the names of the misdoers, which she gave, would be sufficient; that the appeal should be effective against receivers of the criminals, even if the principal murderer was not named; and that if she herself died or was unable to sue then the next heir should have the benefit of all these provisions.[39] Far from being the product of an over-stimulated imagination each of the demands was eminently sensible. Isabella obviously knew of the weaknesses of proceeding by appeal and how the accused might take advantage. By this time judges seem to have regarded appellants with positive disapproval. Lastly she asked that, if the supposed felons failed to appear, they were to be convicted and attainted of the felony, apparently without any process of outlawry.

There were only a small number of petitions of this sort, and they cannot, despite the supplicants' pleas that they were one of the few certain ways to make an example of exceptional offenders, have had any great impact on the level of crime or the condition of public order. Their importance lay in the exemplification of defective legal processes and the futility of normal procedure. The sheriff, quite rightly, was noted as being particularly likely to be corrupt. Outlawry was shown to be held in contempt. The sanctions which could be imposed by the council and chancery were ridiculed. The insistence in the common law courts of the exact name of the accused, the rule whereby principals must be accused if their followers were to be tried, the subterfuges in pleading, and the abuses common in the empanelling of jurors were all pointed out.

The desire to avoid common law civil procedures with their interminable delays and uncertainties was frequently apparent among families which were engaged in open feuding. Rather than undertake or continue unceasing and unsatisfactory litigation, a fair number of men sought to settle differences by means of arbitration. By the mid-fifteenth century litigation, like the use of force, was often no more than a tactical instrument in an unending campaign against a foe of many years' standing. Court decisions about property were sometimes valueless because they could not be enforced. Many disputes ended

[39] *Ibid.*, v, 169a.

only because the parties were bored, exhausted, or dead. Arbitration allowed men to break off long-lasting feuds and cut their losses without suffering the stigma of defeat. In arbitration there was no plaintiff and defendant and, in contrast with the courts of law, those who rendered judgment were unlikely to reach a verdict which was wholly favourable to one side. There is no evidence that the king disapproved of the device. He probably welcomed it, since it was often when a quarrel had gone before the chancellor or the council that one or a number of arbitrators were appointed with the consent of the parties. Thus in chancery in July 1387 two disputants, Gilbert Tyler and Giles Laurence, submitted themselves to abide by the award of Thomas Garwenton and John Frenyngham.[40] If these two were unable to make a final agreement between the parties, Chief Justice Robert Bealknap was to undertake the task and complete it without, as it was put, thwarting either party. As was the custom in most cases of arbitration each party made a bond, in this instance of £200, which was forfeited if it hindered or infringed the agreement. Choice of arbitrators probably lay with the two parties. In 1435, in a quarrel between the earl and countess of Westmorland, each chose three lords and two justices to mediate. To settle the dispute between the bishop of Norwich and the prior of Norwich the former, in 1395, chose the prior of Christ Church, Canterbury, Guy Mone, clerk, and Michael Sergeaux, dean of the Arches, London, on his side.[41] If there was no agreement among the arbitrators by a predetermined date, the case would probably go to the award of an umpire named by the king. Although arbitrators were reluctant, through the conditions of their appointment, to find that right was wholly on one side, there was at least one example of the blame for starting the quarrel being placed firmly on one party. Sir Thomas Harrington, who in 1447 was called on to settle the differences between the Threlkelds and Thornburghs in Cumberland and Westmorland, concluded that the evidence showed that the original fault lay with the Thornburghs, who owed a rent for one of their properties.[42] Of course, there was much more likely to be a finding like this when there was but a single arbitrator. Those entrusted with arbitration sometimes attempted to deal not only with contested titles to land and other property but also

[40] *Cal. Close Rolls, 1385–1389*, pp. 437–8.
[41] *Proceedings and Ordinances of the Privy Council*, iv, 289.
[42] F. W. Ragg, 'De Threlkeld', *Transactions of the Cumberland and Westmorland Antiquarian and Archaeological Society*, xxiii (1923), 198–9.

with injuries inflicted in open conflict. In one interesting case in 1455, when the duke of Buckingham arbitrated at the instigation of the council in a dispute between Sir John Gresley and Roger Vernon, a tariff of payments was established for the various types of injuries received in the quarrel. For the murder of a woman twenty marks was to be paid, for inflicting a head wound one mark, and for breaking a leg 40s. A blow on the foot was rated at 20s., but if it caused permanent injury the fine was to rise to 100s.[43]

These devices, owing so little to the common law, which were adopted to prevent feud and open violence in the fifteenth century show the inventiveness to which men were driven, but they were not a permanent solution. The private use of parliamentary sanctions soon disappeared although arbitration in suits about property was still common in the later sixteenth century. The deficiency here was that the awards of the arbitrators, though cheaper to obtain than a common law judgment, were probably less respected and sooner challenged and overthrown. In the matter of public order Henry VII (who seems to have followed Edward IV) and Henry VIII after him, put their trust largely in the procedures and the courts of the common law, supplemented by a judicially active council. This acted as supervisor of the system and as a clearing house for all difficult cases, inquiring into the circumstances and then directing each matter to the court where it could best be handled.

The late medieval English kings had neither a proper police force nor a professional judiciary of sufficient number. The machinery which was supposed to apprehend and try the suspected misdoer was staffed by a few professionals at the centre and a much larger number of amateurs based locally. The professionals were the ten or so judges of the two benches, the justices of assize, the clerks of chancery, who wrote down the king's instructions, the king's attorney, and the sergeants at arms. The amateurs were the sheriffs, constables, and justices of the peace; they had other ways of making a living as well as administering the law. The extension of royal justice in the twelfth and early thirteenth centuries had provided quicker remedies for quarrels, readier access to the king's courts and for more classes of men, better methods of accusation and trial, and had probably instilled greater respect for due process of law. What it had not produced was an efficient method of noting offences as they occurred, an effective way of taking and holding suspects, and a smoothly

---

[43] *William Salt Archaeological Society*, New Series, ii (1899), 57–8.

119

functioning system of local royal courts which had the competence to try virtually any category of offence and the ability to do so soon after the crime had been committed. In the fourteenth century the problem of the courts was provided with an acceptable solution, but no satisfactory way was found of dealing with the suspect who took to flight. Because of change in the manor, the decline of the manor court, new systems of farming, alterations in social status, and new lords, there could be no reliance on the community policing itself as in centuries past, since the community was in a state of flux. Nonetheless, the king tried to work with as much of the old system as possible. In the fifteenth century, when public order seems at times to have been even less well kept, attempts were made to improve the administration of the law by devices which were quite novel and outside the common law. These met with only mixed success. The real trouble was that economic trends, politics, and the development of social institutions were each working in a way which was particularly disruptive to public order and they were doing so simultaneously.

V

◇◇

Accusation and Trial

◇◇

Most men and women who were arraigned in the courts of late medieval England were there because they had been indicted by a jury. There were other reasons why men should have to appear, such as being captured while in possession of goods they had just stolen, or being appealed (that is formally accused by a single man or woman) but these were less common. Indictment or presentment, the term which had been more common in the thirteenth and early fourteenth centuries and which was virtually synonymous, can be traced back to the assize of Clarendon of 1166 under which twelve men in each hundred where the crime had been committed or where the criminals resided, together with four men of each township therein, were required to report suspected robbers, murderers, thieves, and their receivers, each time the king's justices visited. This was probably the most important single method of indictment. Presentments were also made by frank-pledge tithings to the sheriff when he made his tourn. Usually this was when a general eyre was anticipated. Since visitations of the eyre had virtually ceased by the third decade of the fourteenth century this method was of less and less importance. Another form of indictment, one which became increasingly popular in the fourteenth and fifteenth centuries, stemmed from the custom of lodging bills with justices, who in turn offered them to presenting juries to supplement their other information and charges. The jurors then decided if they were true, should be endorsed, and men made to answer to the charges in them. To report offenders to authority was the duty of all men even after the frank-pledge system and decayed. The statute of Winchester made the men of the hundred and of franchises responsible for any robbery and any damage arising from their failure to present offenders.

The indicting juries of the fourteenth and fifteenth centuries usually contained twelve jurors, although as few as nine and as many as twenty-nine have been noted. They were all men of substance and many had at some time held offices in local government. Except in cases touching Lollardy, there was no qualification of property but clergy, women, and aliens were excluded. From the time when the jury of presentment had its origins, its members had been elected rather than chosen directly by the officers of the king. At the coming of the justices they were chosen by two men who had been nominated in each hundred or borough by the bailiffs. Usually juries told of the crimes in a single hundred, the one where they themselves had property, but on occasion they were drawn from several hundreds and reported the misdeeds in a whole county. There are also a number of references to hundred juries which reported suspects outside their own hundreds as well as within.

Presenting juries got their information about misdoers and misdeeds in a variety of ways. They received it by word of mouth from the constable or reeve and the men of the townships in their hundred. No doubt they had their own bits of information, the result of local gossip, personal enquiry, or even personal injury, for there were instances of jurors indicting men whose mischief had been directed against themselves. In addition the justices must have told them about crimes they had witnessed or of which they had good knowledge. It was the justices also who passed on to the jurors bills or petitions for relief or redress which had come into their hands. If the jury felt the charges in these were genuine and sufficient it added its own support by stating the petition was a 'true bill'. It has been argued that this last method of gaining information was responsible for the formula *inquiratur pro rege* which found its way increasingly into legal records in the fifteenth century. William Lambarde, the Tudor legal historian, reckoned that such endorsed bills were indictments proper and that all other accusations by jury were to be called presentments. In the thirteenth century, when the judicial eyres were at their zenith, the word indictment or *privata* referred to accusations founded on the jurors' own suspicions, and presentments was the name given to the answers to the articles which the justices put to the jurors. The former were secret, the latter overt. The confusion was long-lasting. A late medieval Hampshire justices' roll assumes that a presentment deals with trespasses and an indictment with felonies.[1] In other records indictments are mainly larcenies, and presentments deal with deaths. Whether the distinction had any fundamental significance is a question to which historians as yet have no good answer.

The shape which the indictment or presentment finally assumed was determined not just by the sources of information available to the jurors and their views on the veracity of each but also by the instructions which juries received from the visiting justices. Each judicial session, whether of general eyre, trailbaston, oyer and terminer, or of the peace, was ordered by the king to investigate particular rather than general flaws in public order; at the lowest level the sheriff's tourn and the court leet both operated under articles of enquiry. Jurors sometimes referred to the delineated areas of investigation as the 'points' of the particular commission. Instructions of this type were no doubt intended to prevent the justices from being engulfed in a sea of trivial offences which could be dealt with in other ways. The articles might perhaps ask for information on homicides, larcenies, rapes, highway robberies, riots, interference with officials, forcible entries, the regrating or forestalling of food, offences against the statute of labourers; at other times the command might be for investigation of only two or three of these categories, and occasionally it might be all the above and a dozen more in addition. From about the middle of the fourteenth century articles were based where possible on the statutes which were thought to have been broken, even if the exact words of the act were sometimes avoided. Evidence from the fifteenth and sixteenth centuries suggests that the questions put to the indicting jurors became more and more precise, especially when infamous misdeeds and misdoers were to be investigated. In this way the king was making up for his inability to prosecute directly. He was accusing the suspects, as it were, by proxy, the questions to the jurors being carefully arranged so that they covered all possible aspects of the crimes and revealed clearly the intent of the perpetrators. The same result could also be achieved by a royal servant

---

[1] W. Lambarde, *Eirenarcha; or of the Office of the Justices of the Peace* (London, 1602), pp. 458–9; *Crown Pleas of the Wiltshire Eyre, 1249*, ed. C. A. F. Meekings (Wiltshire Archaeological and Natural History Society, Records Branch, xvi, 1960), pp. 93–5; P.R.O. J.I. 1/795 mm. 1, 1d, 2, 2d (printed in B. H. Putnam, *Proceedings before the Justices of the Peace, Edward III to Richard III* (London, 1938), pp. 200–8).

lodging a well-drafted and detailed bill with the justices, providing of course the jurors approved it a *billa vera* when asked.

Another procedural factor which must have affected the shape of the indictment was the putting of information received orally from the representatives of the townships into written Latin. The presenting jurors must have acted in concert on this, no doubt with a clerk to assist them. The clerks' expertise must have varied, for although indictments taken preparatory to the case being heard in a court operated by professional judges, like the king's bench, were quite precise and arranged logically, those which went to the justices of the peace were often cast in nothing more than narrative form. They might fail to give a technical name to the crime and to say which facts were criminal. Most drafters of indictments could manage, as the law required, to insert the names of the jurors, the year, day, and place of the misdeeds, a description of any chattels involved and their value, and the adverb *felonice* if the crime was a felony. There was a tendency in the fourteenth century for juries and those who wrote on their behalf to try to suggest the greater gravity of some crimes by adding, for example, adverbial phrases such as 'stealthily by night' to an indictment for larceny, or by making many crimes out of a single offence. The king condoned these vagaries, being more anxious that jurors should speak freely than that their charges should be technically accurate. There may be some truth in the argument that this proliferation of offences and aggravation was the result of a desire to make it more difficult for the grave offender to obtain a pardon.[2]

Although trial juries were reluctant to convict, juries of presentment were by no means loth to indict. The behaviour of the juries which refused to name names after the Alton pass robbery and after the collapse of the Peasants' Revolt in St Albans was probably exceptional.[3] The very willingness to indict may have been promoted by the unlikelihood that petty juries would find the arraigned persons guilty. Only in cases involving treason, misdoers whose record was bad and whose misdeeds were quite notorious, men accused of felony who on pleading claimed benefit of clergy, and some trespasses of an economic nature, was there as great a chance of conviction as acquittal.

[2] As argued by T. F. T. Plucknett in B. H. Putnam, *Proceedings before the Justices of the Peace, Edward III to Richard III*, p. cxl.
[3] The incident at St Albans is described by Thomas Walsingham, *Historia Anglicana*, ii, 22–36.

Presenting jurors could also console themselves with the thought that they were not saying that they themselves suspected a man's involvement in crime but rather that the men of the locality suspected such a connection. We do not therefore hear of men being punished by the king for failure to indict, although threats were occasionally made against the jurors by those they had indicted. As we have seen, William Beckwith and his Yorkshire band in 1389 were reported as planning to kill those responsible for their indictment; in February 1373 two Derbyshire brothers Geoffrey and Thomas de Redich, who had been outlawed for not appearing to answer to an indictment for the rape of Margaret Forster, were said to be planning to kill their indictors or do them evil, either in body or by burning their houses.[4] The most sinister practice involving juries of presentment was the procuring of the indictment of their enemies by magnates and by criminal gangs. The duke of Clarence got Ankarette Twynho indicted as he wished, although his position on the Warwickshire bench must have been an assistance. In Suffolk in 1348 a gang of criminals extorted money by threatening that if a certain sum was not paid them the victim would be indicted at the next visitation of the justices. The history of this particular band suggests that the threat was not an idle one.[5] In mid-fifteenth-century Norfolk the gang of Charles Nowell and Robert Ledham used false indictment as a cover for their own offences. Having through Roger Church, one of their number, stirred up an insurrection in the hundred of Blofield, they accused, by means of a bill delivered to the justices, gentlemen and yeomen of good reputation as being responsible.[6]

An older method of accusation than indictment by jury was appeal. Verbally, until the thirteenth century relying only on his memory but later probably having the assistance of a written schedule, the appellant in formal manner accused one or several persons of committing a felony or a trespass against the peace. If the supposed crime was either larceny or rape, which could be in either category of offence, it was up to the appellant to decide how it rated. As soon as the misdeed had been committed the would-be appellant was supposed to seek out the hundred bailiff and the men of the four neighbouring townships and then the coroner. It was the particular task of the coroner to make a record of the events, to take sureties from the

[4] *Calendar of Patent Rolls, 1370–1374* (Record Commission), p. 307.
[5] L. O. Pike, *A History of Crime in England* (London, 1873–6), i, 271.
[6] *Paston Letters*, ed. J. Gairdner (Edinburgh, 1910), no. 179.

appellor to prosecute his appeal at the next county court, and sometimes to attach the accused. When the county court met, the appellor made his charge in the prescribed form, relating the deed itself, the time, the day, the year, the place, the weapons used, the injuries inflicted, and any chattels taken. Then he offered to prove the veracity of the accusation on his body, that is by armed combat. The charge was taken down verbatim so that the appellor should not change his story at a later date. The person appealed had to appear at one of the next four county courts and, if he wished to deny the accusation, he was supposed to offer to prove his case by battle. Usually the appellee first objected to some detail of the appeal by raising exceptions. In the king's bench at Michaelmas term 1312 Anastasia Spychefat of St Albans appealed Richard de Capele and two other men of causing her husband's death, reading out her appeal from a schedule.[7] Richard denied the charge and claimed there was a discrepancy between Anastasia's appeal and her writ to have him attached. In the writ his name was spelt 'Capele', in the appeal it was 'Caples', one name being three syllables long, the other two. Furthermore, he was called 'knight' and 'of St Albans' in the appeal but not in the writ. Richard then put himself on a jury, as was allowed in appeals on payment or with the consent of the other party, and was acquitted. One way of traversing, that is to say objecting to, an appeal, which grew increasingly popular during the thirteenth century, was for the appellee to claim it was motivated by spite and hatred. This also would put the case before an inquest jury.

In the fourteenth and fifteenth centuries appeal was perhaps more a woman's action than a man's, despite the association with trial by battle. In theory a woman was only allowed to appeal if the crime was rape or if her husband, having been mortally wounded, died in her arms. In practice the king's justices allowed appeals by women for other offences as well, such as the killing of a son, a brother, or nephew, and even for robbery. This was in contrast with the stricter rules governing men's appeals, for an appeal against the murderer of a father, if not brought by his wife, must be by the eldest son, the closest in blood, and not by a younger son. Women seem often to have made appeals from a consuming desire for revenge. Appeal was the most direct means available and, even if it failed to avenge blood with blood, as most did, it had good nuisance value. In 1333 Mar-

[7] *Select Cases in the Court of the King's Bench, Edward II*, ed. G. O. Sayles (Selden Society, 74, 1955), p. 44.

garet, the widow of Robert Esnyngton, appealed John, son of Roger de Swynnerton, and seventeen other men of the death of her husband.[8] The appeal displays well the nature of this form of procedure and Margaret's great determination. John Swynnerton, she said, approached her husband feloniously as a felon, holding in his left hand a bow of Spanish yew two ells in length and of the thickness of four men's thumbs, and with a barbed arrow called a cloth-arrow which he held in his right hand, and shot Robert through the heart. Of this wound he died in his wife's arms. She then said, in proper form, that she had raised the hue and cry and that she was prepared to prove the homicide against him as a woman and as the court should think fit. She next appealed all of John's accomplices in turn, attributing to each a different wound in her husband's body. She said that if Robert had not died from the wound inflicted by John then he died from the wound given by B, if not by B's then by C's, if not by C's then by D's, and so forth. Margaret must have allowed her imagination full rein since the appeal claimed her husband had been killed by being shot through the heart by an arrow, stabbed to the heart with a dagger, shot in the back, shot in the stomach below the navel, struck on the head with a staff, having his left foot cut off, and by suffering several other substantial injuries. Rarely did women pursue these appeals through to the end despite the penalties for abandoning them. The appeal of Margaret Esnyngton went into the king's bench and continued there for two years until one day she failed to appear. Margaret, like many other women, was hoping to cause the appellees apprehension and expense; perhaps also she was trying to limit the opportunities of their purchasing a pardon, which were more easily come by if accusation was by indictment. There was also the chance that once the appeal had been made the king would decide to investigate the matter himself.

Few appeals led to judicial combat. Those which did had usually been made by approvers, indicted men of bad record, offering accusation of their accomplices in return for a further lease of life. Periodically we read of duels being waged but that merely meant the two parties had given sureties and undertaken to fight on a day fixed by the court. When the day of the duel actually arrived the parties had often made a concord and put themselves on the king's mercy, or the appellor had withdrawn the appeal. However, it was not all bluff. There were some duels in the fourteenth and fifteenth centuries which were not instigated by approvers, but most were the result of accusations of treason and all were between men. The king was probably against trial by combat. The chronicler Higden states that after the battle between Walshe and Martigo on an appeal of treason in 1383, the king had the loser executed so as to stop the multiplication of such appeals.[9] Contemporaries were well aware that youth and strength were likely to prevail and that justice might easily fail to be done. Townsmen were very keen that the privileges of their borough should protect them from the chanciness of trial by battle. The nearest a woman came to participating in judicial combat was in the reign of Henry IV.[10] A chronicler tells us that the king suggested that a woman and the clerk whom she had accused of treason should fight together but with the clerk having one hand tied behind his back. However, no fight took place in the end.

The most frequent participants in judicial duels were approvers and those they had appealed. Approvers, unlike appellors, had of necessity to have been indicted of felony or treason or caught committing those offences. They might have been arraigned in court but they had not yet been convicted. No woman, child, or man aged over seventy or unsound in limb, could become an approver since they could not fight a duel, which was a very possible outcome. Men decided to become approvers when in gaol. If there were justices on hand the appeal was made before them: if there were not, it was made before a coroner. Such appeals gave the king information about the approver's accomplices and they also provided him with details about other criminals and their misdeeds. Both were particularly valuable to a king who had no proper police force. Since the chances of acquittal in a jury trial were great, those who became approvers must have been men with long criminal records or been captured in circumstances which virtually proved their guilt. Another possibility, indeed distinct probability, is that duress of some sort within the gaol, or a bargain with the gaoler or the sheriff, persuaded the suspect to become an approver. Suggestion of these practices is to be found in legislation and instructions to commissions of enquiry. Article 26 in the Hundred inquest of 1274 was for the investigation of those who had compelled men in prison to appeal honest, decent persons: an act of 1327, which sprang from a commons' petition, ordered the

[9] *Polychronicon Ranulphi Higden, Monachi Cestrensis*, ed. C. Babington and J. R. Lumby (Rolls Series, 1865–86), ix, 53.
[10] *Eulogium Historiarum*, ed. F. S. Haydon (Rolls Series, 1858–63), iii, 389.

king's justices to discover which sheriffs and gaolers had compelled prisoners to become approvers. To limit these undesirable practices Edward II had enacted that the time during which approvers could make their appeals was the three days following their first accusation of that sort.[11] They were not to be held indefinitely without trial while other names and misdeeds were extracted from them. Gaolers, it seems, were less interested in the maintenance of law and order than in extorting money from those whom the approvers desperately, yet often falsely, appealed. Approvers frequently got the names of their appellees and details of their crimes from gossip in gaol. In 1291 Hugh Kirton, who had been imprisoned in Nottingham gaol, said he did not really know Richard de Thistleton, John Bozun, and others whom he had appealed, but had learned their names from other prisoners and visitors.[12] He appealed them, he added, because of the hunger and the hardship he sustained in his confinement. Known approvers were sometimes supplied with additional information by ordinary citizens bent on doing mischief to their private enemies. In March 1294 Henry de Heapham of Lincoln, then in the Tower of London, who had admitted to forging the king's seal, was visited and bribed by John de Ramsey, parson of St Andrew's, London, and three other Londoners, to appeal Nicholas de Thornton, a clerk, of harbouring an accomplice of his.[13] They did this in retaliation for Nicholas's suit of conspiracy and trespass against them.

To postpone their impending trial approvers would sometimes appeal not one man but many, and they would provide a mass of supporting detail. In 1405 John Veyse, a sawyer and notorious thief, appealed no fewer than fifty-nine abbots and priors of aiding the rebel Owen Glendower by means of financial support. Despite the unlikelihood of the accusations the ecclesiastics were all summoned to Huntingdon.[14] Veyse was then asked to identify each of them but was quite unable to do so. The abbots and priors were therefore acquitted, since the law required that any appellor must be able to recognize those he accused, and Veyse was executed. There are other

---

[11] *Statutes of the Realm*, i, 253–4 (1 Edward III c. 7). There was another act concerned with duress by gaolers in 1340: *ibid.*, i, 284. The three-day rule is in *ibid.*, i, 165–6 (5 Edward II c. 34).
[12] *Select Cases in the Court of the King's Bench, Edward I*, ed. G. O. Sayles (Selden Society, 55, 1936), ii, 55.
[13] *Ibid.*, iii, 34.
[14] *Johannis de Trokelowe et Henrici de Blaneforde Chronica et Annales*, ed. H. T. Riley (Rolls Series, 1865), pp. 415–16.

examples of one approver accusing a large number. In 1294, 1348, and 1365 we hear of seventy, forty-one and forty-six men respectively being so appealed. The best example of the great circumstantial detail which was often provided is to be found in the appeal of Robert Goodgroom in January 1440.[15] No fewer than 3,500 words in length, it described how he had gone mole catching in Graveney parish in Kent and found in a cheese house the arm and hand of a dead man. Through this discovery Robert had become privy, so he said, to a traitorous plot to poison the dukes of Gloucester and Norfolk and the king. Proof of the power of the intended poison, which he was told had been distilled from herbs and human flesh, was given him in a most positive way. Three drops were put on the back of a dog and resulted in its immediate death. Goodgroom also accused one of the conspirators, John Sinclair of Faversham, of poisoning John Martin, a justice of common pleas in 1436, and of plotting to poison Edward Guildford, the sheriff of Kent. Meetings, conversations, dates, times of day, localities, and names were all precisely given and there must have been an element of truth in many things the approver said. John Martin, the judge, had died in 1436 although by no means aged, and there was treason afoot in Kent in 1438–9. However, the jury was not convinced by the tale which Goodgroom told and it acquitted those he accused. The approver, as the law demanded, was therefore executed.

To become an approver meant, in practice, to confess to the crime of which one had been indicted and then to appeal one's accomplices. Thereby the approver became the agent of the king in preserving public order. Because of this the king would pay him a penny or three halfpence a day whilst he was in custody. Success in securing a conviction, either by the verdict of a jury or by battle, might mean an increase in this payment: defeat of the accusation by either means usually meant immediate execution.[16] It has been pointed out that many approvers seem to have died soon after making their appeals and before any combat or jury trial, but for lack of sufficient evidence we may attribute this to the virulent gaol fever which visited periodically. It is still more difficult to explain a reference to the 'doing of

[15] Printed by M. Aston in the *Bulletin of the Institute of Historical Research*, xxxvi (1963), 86–90, and by R. L. Storey (with modern spelling and dating) in *The End of the House of Lancaster* (London, 1966), pp. 199–209.
[16] Pike, *A History of Crime in England*, i, 481. The controlment roll 22 Edward III records the deaths of no fewer than fifty approvers in the prison of York castle (mm. 59–61d).

justice' on forty-one approvers on one occasion in Edward II's reign. The reward to an approver for a successful appeal which convicted the appellee was in theory either prison for life or permission to quit the realm. In practice there was sometimes a royal pardon, although on at least one occasion the king said the killing of the appellee was manslaughter and therefore the approver's life was forfeit. If he had appealed not one man but several the approver had to convict the greater part of them to avoid execution. He did, however, have the opportunity to select the order in which he fought them, that is, if they foolhardily opted for trial by battle rather than trial by jury.

Trials by battle, whether they involved approvers or not, continued to occur well into the fifteenth century but were uncommon enough to impress contemporaries and to cause the details of several to be fully recorded. A high percentage involved charges of treason, the reason being that appellees realized juries were less likely to acquit in such cases and felt obliged to put their trust in battle. There was no hiring of champions, as had been allowed until the thirteenth century in suits involving land. For the most part the judges of the two benches were against the continuation of trial by battle and did what they could to make its most common form, which was between approver and appellee, a spectacle involving disgrace and degradation. The combatants were armed with shields and a special type of club. According to a fifteenth-century source these were three feet long, fashioned from green ash with the bark still on, and bearing at one end a sharp iron hook made like a ram's horn. A drawing, which represents one such combat fought after the visitation of an eyre in Henry III's reign, shows the contestants bearing weapons shaped rather like picks.[17] They were in no way like the normal weapons of war. The appearance of the two protagonists must have been quite striking. The approver fought with shaven head and both he and his opponent were clad in leather, which was sometimes white but at others red. The defendant entered the area marked out for the combat first and denied the accusation word for word. The approver repeated his charge, swearing it was true, and then, when silence had been proclaimed, the fighting began. The duel continued until one contestant was killed, or being wounded or merely exhausted had been forced to cry 'craven'. This was held a confession of guilt and the beaten man was executed. If the approver had won, and there were other

[17] To be found in a separated membrane (K.B. 26/223) which is exhibited in the Public Record Office Museum, case ix, number 3.

appellees who had chosen battle, a day was set for the next contest. If he lost, his opponent was released on bail, but the appeals he had made against others were continued although obviously there could be no additional battles.

The duel between approver and appellee is perhaps portrayed best in the description by the London chronicler, Gregory, of the combat at Winchester in 1456 between a thief, Thomas Whitehorne, and James Fisher.[18] Whitehorne had been kept in gaol by the king for three years, receiving three halfpence a day and continuously making appeals, no man apparently daring to resort to combat against him until Fisher did so. The battle took place on 'the most sorry and wretched green that might be found about the town'. The combatants were instructed that if their weapons broke they must fight with their hands, fists, nails, teeth, feet, and legs. The defendant, to add to his troubles, was warned that if he slew the approver, whose accusations had been so useful to the king, he might be hanged. If he was a man of good reputation there was a chance, no more, of a pardon; he would receive it of the king's grace, not by right. He was also told that, if killed in the duel or executed, he would not be buried in consecrated ground. Before the duel began juries were asked about the reputations of both men. Fisher was said to be the 'truest labourer in all that country'. Whitehorne was found to be a wanderer and of low repute. On the day of the duel the defendant entered the arena weeping, with beads in his hands. He knelt down and begged the forgiveness of every person present. When the battle began he struck the appellor with his weapon, which broke. The appellor struck back and then had his weapon taken from him by the supervising officers. The two men then fought for a long time with their fists, then rested, then fought again. The battle next turned into a form of wrestling match on the ground with both men using their teeth 'so that their leather clothing and their flesh was torn in many places'. At another stage the approver turned to kicking his opponent, with some success. The duel was finally brought to a close when Fisher seized Whitehorne by the nose with his teeth and put his thumb in his eye, making him cry for mercy and admit his appeal was false. The judge declared the fight over and the approver admitted to wrongfully accusing eighteen men in all. He was hanged and the defendant pardoned.

---

[18] *The Historical Collections of a Citizen of London in the Fifteenth Century*, ed. J. Gairdner (Camden Society, New Series, xvii, 1876), pp. 199–202.

Trial by battle on appeal made by a man not already suspect or indicted and not against accomplices was rare by the fourteenth century, being largely confined to crimes which touched on treason.[19] Proceedings in these cases usually began in the courts of common law but the duel itself often took place under the jurisdiction of the constable: the stigma which the justices of the two benches tried to attach to it was lacking. The participants were provided with instruction in the handling of weapons, with suitable harness and clothing, and even with tents or pavilions. John Hill, an armourer of Henry IV and Henry V, wrote a treatise called *The Battle of Treason*, which referred to such elaborate ceremonial as the duellist's counsel watching over him the night before the battle, and his equipment being laid out overnight before a church altar and the Gospel read over it. The site of the battle was no muddy meadow or rubbish tip but proper lists, forty paces by sixty and surrounded by barriers, as one account tells us. The combatants went there, not alone but accompanied by their confessors, counsellors, their armourers, and their servants. So sensational was such a duel by the fifteenth century that, as well as the constable and the marshal, even the king might be present. The appellant took up his position in front of his tent to await the appellee and when he came 'took heed . . . of his countenance that he might take comfort of it'. The weapons, which were proper weapons of war, usually lances and swords and certainly not pointed staves, were examined, and both appellant and defendant reaffirmed their oaths three times. They also had to swear there were no additional weapons concealed about their persons nor magic stone or herb. The spectators were warned not to intervene or cry out or even talk. The several examples of these trials to be found in the earlier part of the fifteenth century are to be explained by the knightly and therefore prestigious nature of the proceedings. Men of the middle classes of society not only watched such trials but might take part. There was a case in 1446 when an armourer, who had been accused of treason by his servant, chose trial of this sort. His decision was most foolish, for although juries were more likely to find one guilty in cases of treason than in other crimes, the chances of acquittal were high.[20] Even more foolishly the armourer, who no doubt by his trade

---

[19] A late example of one concerned not with treason but larceny is to be found in *Select Cases in the Court of the King's Bench, Edward III*, ed. G. O. Sayles (Selden Society, 82, 1965), p. 119.

[20] Pike, i, 391; *Proceedings and Ordinances of the Privy Council*, vi, 55, 59; J. Stow, *Annales or A Generall Chronicle of England* (London, 1631), p. 385.

was skilled in the use of weapons, drank so much Malmsey wine and aqua vitae before the battle that he was vanquished and killed.

Appeal and indictment were the usual methods of accusation, yet in the thirteenth and early fourteenth centuries men were sometimes arraigned merely on account of their suspicious deeds and known bad character. At one early stage suspicion, albeit strong suspicion, as when a man of known criminal tendencies was seen leaving someone else's house carrying loot or was captured bearing stolen goods, sufficed to convict him without any trial at all. Execution in such cases often followed immediately on arrest. By the mid-fourteenth century a suspect taken with property in his possession was assured of a trial, but one deferred until a local jury had pronounced on his repute. Public opinion at this time demanded that a man should not be tried if he did not have a definite charge laid against him; that is, indictments must be specific and not general. The king was not too sure about this. In February 1308 a Northamptonshire jury said that William Aleyn of Melton was a common obstructor of the peace. The king said that since he was indicted without mention of a definite obstruction of the peace or trespass he should be freed *sine die*.[21] Yet the indictment, he added, was good in substance and William must behave himself in future and give sureties to answer anyone who spoke against him about the trespass. The use of the general as against the particular in indictments was condemned by the judges in 1313, 1348, and 1355, yet it continued. Juries of presentment felt there were known evil-doers who must be put on trial even if, because of the careful way they had covered their tracks, a definite crime with time and place could not be given. Nonetheless, by the end of the fourteenth century phrases like 'notorious robber' and 'common thief' were being used only to aggravate other charges which were more specific. Ill fame, which had once worked immediate conviction and then later on had taken the place of a precise indictment, served only to attest to the charge being more serious than usual within its own category. It must have been one way in which a presenting jury could inform a petty jury that conviction in a particular instance would be well deserved.

Another form of trial where indictment or appeal was lacking was the one involving 'record'. In such instances certain royal officers or the king himself simply proclaimed the misdoer convicted of a particular offence. In the thirteenth century and for most of the fourteenth

---

[21] *Select Cases in the Court of the King's Bench, Edward II*, p. 6.

this practice was confined to the crime of treason, but in 1391 the justices of the peace were authorized to pronounce convicted those they found holding any place forcibly, and in 1411 they were given similar powers with regard to those they encountered causing riots. Later statutes confirmed and extended these powers.

'Information' was yet another way of bringing a misdoer to trial. It usually took the form of an accusatory piece of writing in the shape of a letter, although it might also be given by word of mouth. The charges concerned infractions of the peace. 'Information' was less formal than a bill or petition, which in turn was less formal than an indictment or appeal. The 'information' was not offered to a jury for confirmation as were indictments. Nor did the misdeeds listed necessarily touch the informant. Virtually anyone could lay information and it could concern all types of offence. Information was sent in April 1297 by letter to the king by two canons of Chichester, accusing a certain William de la Hoke of homicides, thefts, and the harbouring of criminals. On this account William was seized on the king's orders and imprisoned until acquitted by justices of gaol delivery. The lodging of information became noticeably more common in the later fifteenth century when it was popularized, for example, by Edward IV as a method of curbing the illicit giving of livery. 'Every person', said an act of 1468, 'that will sue or complain against any persons offending . . . against . . . this ordinance (on liveries) . . . shall be admitted at the discretion of the judges . . . to give information for the king therein . . . ; and this information shall stand . . . instead of a bill or original writ.'[22] All the informer had to do was to take an oath on the Bible before a judge that his complaint was rightful. Then the judge either allowed the accused trial by jury or he convicted him summarily after his own examination of him. To encourage informing, the original complainant was to be given a half of any possessions forfeited by the accused. From 1496 to 1509, because of the failure of the juries involved to present offenders, informing was extended to crimes which often accompanied the giving of livery, such as retaining men, causing riots, maintenance, and embracery. Thus, as the middle ages drew to a close, it seemed as if informing had a golden future and was likely to become a most popular way of bringing suspects to trial.

So far we have considered only what may be called common law methods of making charges against misdoers. As well as the courts of common law, the king's council and even chancery were concerned

[22] 8 Edward IV c. 2; *Statutes of the Realm*, ii, 42.

with the upkeep of public order. The act of 1352, which seems to have barred it from matters involving freehold, did not prevent the council from interfering in serious crimes which the king felt were especially grievous and of particular concern to himself, like counterfeiting, rioting, necromancy, heresy, falsification of records, and offences originating outside the realm, but, as we have seen, the penalties it could impose were only fines or imprisonment which did not involve shedding of blood. Usually the council investigated the accusations and then, if necessary, a commission of oyer and terminer was appointed to hold the trials. The council and chancery, whose staple fare was less serious riots, received allegations of misdeeds either in the form of petitions or as information; there seems little doubt that sometimes the complaints had been induced by the king, but nonetheless he asked the accusers to give sureties that their charges were not groundless. If they were in written form these complaints (which claimed, seemingly as a matter of form, that the injured party could not get justice elsewhere) were delivered to the clerk of the council, to individual councillors, or to the king in person. Then those against whom the charges were laid were summoned to answer by means of subpoena writs. Before the council, as before the courts of common law, prosecution was hardly ever the work of the crown; it was a task which was left to the king's subjects themselves. Only in the late fifteenth century, and then merely in committees of council and the courts of chivalry and admiralty, can we recognize something like crown prosecution proper as distinct from the attaint of jurors who gave illogical verdicts, approvers appealing for reward or from duress, and jurors who had been told what misdeeds they should present.[23]

On a number of occasions during the fourteenth century and fairly frequently during the fifteenth, the crown investigated misdeeds by examination pending trial. Those examined were not merely the witnesses to the offence but chiefly the principals. The king's council is known to have resorted to inquisitorial examination fairly often. On reading complaints made by plaintiffs the council concocted series of questions based on the accusations. The men accused, having

[23] For example, there was reference in 1482 to the office of king's promoter of all causes civil and criminal or concerning crimes of lese majesty before the king's judges of the constableship and admiralty of England: *Cal. Pat. Rolls, 1476–1485*, p. 343. See also *Select Cases in the Council of Henry VII*, ed. C. G. Bayne and W. H. Dunham (Selden Society, 75, 1955), pp. cxxix–cxxxv, where the topic is government prosecution for riot.

sworn to give truthful answers, were examined separately, each being unaware, at least at the outset, of the exact misdeeds laid against him. Anyone else who had knowledge of the facts might also be examined, though perhaps by an inquest jury rather than by the council itself. Whether there was any questioning in the strict sense of the word is doubtful. Most likely the defendant, having been sworn, simply went on to make a statement which the clerk of the council took down. The council made its decision when the evidence had been weighed. It must have been from either the council or the ecclesiastical courts that the practice of examination spread into the common law. One other possible origin was the procedure used by the coroner, who questioned both jurors and other knowledgeable persons about the circumstances surrounding sudden death. That those who operated the common law were favouring examination processes by the fifteenth century there can be no doubt. There were even references to it in the fourteenth century. When in 1326 an oyer and terminer commission was investigating the Staffordshire feud between Thomas de Brumpton and William de Ipstones and their followers, Sir William Stafford and James Stafford, both partisans of Brumpton, were reported as being questioned by the judges separately during the hearing of pleas. In May 1331 Master Robert de la Marche of Canterbury and two London goldsmiths were taken by the sheriffs of London on the orders of council to Newgate prison;[24] then they were brought to the king's bench where each was examined in turn. Their suspected crime was necromancy, but because no one had actually been killed they were never indicted. In 1345 a clerk accused of forging a writ was brought before the king's bench where, having taken the oath, he was examined 'secretly' by the justices. In the fourteenth century, examination, except when conducted by a coroner, was perhaps only used when the offence was of a type which was novel or with great consequences for the maintenance of public order. If justices of the peace were wont at this time to make examination of suspects the evidence of it has not survived.

From the early fifteenth century quite a different tendency is found. Statutes demonstrate that examination sometimes stood as a form of trial alternative to that by jury. Two acts made definite reference to examination on oath: one was Henry V's statute of labourers (2 Henry V st. 1 c. 4) and the other was the statute of Henry VII on

---

[24] *Wiillam Salt Arch. Soc.*, x (1889), 66; *Select Cases in the Court of the King's Bench, Edward III*, ed. G. O. Sayles (Selden Society, 82, 1957), p. 53.

retaining (19 Henry VII c. 14). Other acts of the period which allowed interrogation concerned the tanning trade (2 Henry VI c. 7), apparel (8 Henry VI c. 5), weights and measures (11 Henry VI c. 8), alien merchants (18 Henry VI c. 4), practices of employers in the clothing industry (4 Edward IV c. 1), and the making of tiles (17 Edward IV c. 4). Those who performed the task were usually the justices of the peace. The answers they obtained were recorded so that they might, if necessary, be certified to the king's bench or the council. It was possible for a commission of oyer and terminer to be appointed with instructions not only to enquire through juries but to examine as well. In November 1482 Earl Rivers and others were ordered to summon William Lumnor and his enemies Thomas Brygge of Manington (Norfolk) and his wife Margaret before them for purposes of examination. The results were to be put in writing and then the commissioners were to enquire by jury inquest into felonies, murders, trespasses, and other offences supposedly committed by the Brygges and to send the findings to council.[25] By the mid-sixteenth century, when a man was committed to gaol or brought into court, prior examination by a justice of the peace was taken for granted. The sequence of events was normally this. The king's council sent to the justices articles of examination in which were suggested questions and lines of interrogation. The justices examined the suspect, and from the answers received concocted a bill or several bills (according to the number of suspects) of articles, which were then put before a jury to be endorsed as true. Thus arose the indictment.

For the prisoner, examination meant making statements in answer to a list of articles: at the worst it was verbal interrogation with perhaps some hectoring. It was not supposed to involve physical duress. Admittedly some gaolers put their prisoners in the vilest of dungeons, loaded with chains, and may have starved them of food, but the king usually did his best to stamp out such practices, even if they meant confessions and therefore convictions. Departures from this laudable principle were few and stand out sharply. The only physical duress which the common law allowed was connected with pleading. A man who refused to make a plea of 'guilty' or 'not guilty' could be put in prison, loaded with chains, and allowed only a little stale bread one day and a cup of water the next until he decided to offer a plea. This penalty, known as *peine forte et dure*, was not a torture proper, for no confession or information was demanded, but

[25] *Cal. Pat. Rolls, 1476–1485*, p. 343.

merely the consent of the accused to be tried by a jury. Torture *per se* on the orders of the king was practised in England in the later middle ages on only two or three occasions at most. It was never administered under the common law. Chief Justice Fortescue in his *De Laudibus Legum Anglie*, when on the subject of common law practices, wrote: 'an innocent man cannot suffer in body or members' and he 'will not fear the calumny of his enemies because he will not be tortured at their pleasure. Under this law therefore life is quiet and secure.'[26] Sir Edward Coke thought that it was the Lancastrian kings who first used torture in England. He held that the rack or brake was introduced by John Holland, first duke of Exeter and constable of the Tower of London under Henry VI, as part of a scheme concocted in conjunction with William, duke of Suffolk, for bringing the imperial civil law to England.[27] For this reason, said Coke, 'the rack is called the duke of Exeter's daughter'. Whatever the truth about these fifteenth-century innovations, torture had been used in England before. J. F. Baldwin argued it had been used in 1441 when the sorcerer, Roger Bolingbroke, was reported as being first held in the Tower and then brought forth to be exhibited to the people with his instruments hung about him: he was then led before the lords of council to be examined. Baldwin was wrong. The instruments referred to were not tools of torment but of necromancy, being a painted chair, four swords, and four copper images;[28] they were the accoutrements of a magician. The earliest and perhaps the only official use of torture proper before the reign of Edward IV was in 1310. Those suspected of grave crimes were not ordinary criminals but the whole order of Templars, and the offences were heresy, idolatry, and moral corruption. Papal inquisitors came to England and, sitting with the bishops, interrogated the knights one at a time. Failing to get confessions, the inquisitors asked Edward II for permission to do with the Templars' bodies what they wished, in accordance with ecclesiastical law. The king agreed at the time but eight months later, in August 1310, Pope Clement complained he had heard that Edward had prohibited the use of torture as being contrary to the laws of his kingdom: as a result the inquisitors were powerless. The king once

[26] J. Fortescue, *De Laudibus Legum Anglie*, ed. S. B. Chrimes (Cambridge, 1942), p. 65.

[27] E. Coke, *The Third Part of the Institutes of the Laws of England* (London, 1797), pp. 34–5.

[28] Baldwin, *The King's Council*, p. 298; Stow, *Annales or A Generall Chronicle of England*, p. 381.

more told the inquisitors to proceed and this time, despite the bishops' initial complaint that they could find no one to inflict the torment since it was unknown in England and their request to import experts from abroad, torture was eventually used and confessions gained.[29]

Not for a century and a half did the king order torture to be used again and then it was in quite different circumstances. In 1468 Cornelius 'Sutor', a servant of Sir Robert Whittingham, was captured when carrying secret letters from Queen Margaret to Lancastrian supporters in England. Having been taken before King Edward at Stratford Langthorne, so the chronicler tells us, Cornelius was committed to the Tower of London and persuaded to confess by being burned in the feet. According to Stow, one of those he accused, John Hawkins, a servant of Lord Wenlock, was also incarcerated in the Tower where 'he was brought to the brake called the duke of Exeter's daughter'.[30] There are no further mentions of torture, apart from one unsubstantiated accusation against Richard III, until the reign of Henry VIII, when the rack began to be used fairly frequently. In both Yorkist and Tudor times the torture was applied before trial, even before indictment or appeal, and so cannot be regarded as part of the trial. The answers extracted from the suspect were used as a basis for an indictment, or the duress used to make him appeal others.

In late medieval England most of the criminals who were captured by the king were eventually tried in courts of common law and before petty juries. Trial by battle and even the waging of law (compurgation) continued to exist, but were resorted to infrequently. Most of those who had been indicted objected not at all to trial by jury, being perhaps aware of local sympathy in their own favour or mindful of the incidence of acquittals in general. A few men, perhaps strangers to the region where they were supposed to have committed their offence or knowing of the influence of their enemies with the jurors, resolutely refused, when asked by the judge to plead guilty or not guilty, to make any plea at all. In the early thirteenth century if a man did this, and if other things such as the accused's reputation or the circumstances of his misdeeds seemed particularly sinister, the justices

---

[29] H. C. Lea, *A History of the Inquisition* (London, 1888), iii, 298–301; *Archbishop Greenfield's Register*, ed. W. Brown and A. Hamilton Thompson (Surtees Society, cxlv–cliii, 1931–40), v, xxxiii–xl; *Chronicle of Walter of Guisborough*, ed. H. Rothwell (Camden Society, 1957), p. 392.

[30] *Letters and Papers Illustrative of the Wars in France*, ed. J. Stevenson (Rolls Series, 1864), ii, ii, 789–90; Stow, *Annales or A Generall Chronicle of England*, p. 420.

might declare him convicted without more ado. What happened if he bore a good character but refused to plead we do not know. Perhaps the trial proceeded and the jury gave a verdict regardless. By the mid-thirteenth century it had been decided that standing mute was not tantamount to a confession and that no man could be tried by a jury without his consent. It was therefore necessary to force men to plead. The first statute of Westminster (1275) said that notorious felons who refused to plead should be put in strong and hard imprisonment as refusing the common law of England. However, this was not to apply to those against whom there was little suspicion. None the less, by the fourteenth century the rule came to apply to all who would not put themselves on a jury. Initially the imprisonment was not quite the ritualized form of execution which it was to become later, although it was very severe. The prisoner, perhaps enchained, was to be left 'barefooted, bare-headed and ungirt' on the bare ground in the worst place in the prison. The diet was a limited number of morsels of bread (made of barley or bran) one day and a few sips of stagnant water the next. Evidence from late in the reign of Edward I shows by that time a new punishment had been introduced. The prisoner was being laden with 'as much iron as he could bear'. By the beginning of the fifteenth century the notion was no longer of severe imprisonment but of severe pains. In 1406 Chief Justice Gascoigne ordered that on two suspects there should be placed as great a weight of iron as they could bear *and more*. In the reign of Edward IV a judge instructed that an appellee should be put naked in a cell with his arms and legs each tied by cord to a corner. By the mid-sixteenth century it had become the practice at quarter sessions to put those who would not plead on a table and then to place another table on top laden with stones and lead. The chronicler Holinshed stated that men who stood mute at their arraignment were pressed to death by huge weights laid upon a board on their chests and that a sharp stone was laid underneath them so the load would break their backs.[31] By 1662 a new device was being used on those who would not plead. The man's thumbs were tied together with whipcord and this apparently was so painful that he was very quickly persuaded to change his mind and offer a plea.

The last example suggests that the intention behind these cruel

---

[31] *Year Books, Les Reports del Cases en Ley* (London, 1678–9), 8 Henry IV, Mich., pl. 2, 4 Edward IV, Pasch., pl. 18 ; R. Holinshed, *Chronicles of England, Scotland and Ireland*, i, 312–13.

practices was not to kill the prisoner by degrees. Very possibly he could stop the torment at any time by offering to plead, but the evidence on this is not unequivocal. In a case in August 1394 the justices adjudged a man for his dumbness 'to die . . . and [be] put to his pain'. However, the king ordered him to be set free from his suffering although retained in custody. In another case Nicholas Durdent of Fisherwick, Staffordshire, on his refusal to plead, was committed to gaol for what was called 'perpetual penitance'.[32] The resolution of many of those condemned to *peine forte et dure* was remarkable. Bold men, said Sir Thomas Smith, were wont to choose it in order to save their lands and goods. By this he meant that felons who realized they would probably be convicted by jury trial and so forfeit all their possessions sometimes chose to die by 'the press', as it was called, so that their families would not starve. Holinshed said exactly the same. Those who were put to *peine forte et dure* might survive for several weeks, though hardly for six months as one man was reputed to have done in Stafford gaol. In that particular case suspicion soon attached itself to the sheriff. There are references to some remarkable feats of endurance. In February 1384 John atte Puttes of Bishopsdon was pardoned after enduring *peine forte et dure* for so long that it seemed a miracle he remained alive. In 1359 Cecilia Rygeway, indicted for the death of her husband, was adjudged to her penance and survived without food or drink for forty days 'after the manner of a miracle and contrary to human nature'. The king 'moved by piety, to the praise of God and of the glorious Virgin his mother from whom as is believed this miracle has proceeded' granted her pardon of the execution of the judgment and her freedom.[33]

Trial by oath, commonly called compurgation, was characterized by the use of oath helpers to rebut accusations. In the later middle ages it was in obvious decline. Its last strongholds were the antiquated customs of certain boroughs. The accused had to produce in court a number of neighbours and friends, even relatives until the thirteenth century, who would swear to the truthfulness of his oath of denial. In time this became an oath affirming the belief in his general veracity rather than his innocence of the particular crime in question. These oath helpers did not necessarily have to be witnesses or even have

---

[32] *Calendar of Close Rolls, 1392–1396* (Record Commission), p. 309; *William Salt Arch. Soc.*, xvi (1895), 7.

[33] *Cal. Pat. Rolls, 1381–1385*, p. 373. The Rygeway case is quoted by Pike from the Patent Rolls (31 Edward III Pt. i, m. 11).

knowledge of the facts. In the king's courts compurgation disappeared in criminal cases after the assize of Clarendon (1166), but it continued for a long while in suits between parties which did not concern the king's peace, such as detinue and debt. In the court of common pleas at Michaelmas term 1482 there were as many as twenty-eight examples of compurgation. In each case it was permitted because the plaintiff had nothing with which to support the charge but his own affirmation. Trial by oath also remained popular in local and particularly in urban courts, where it was used for both offences against the king's peace and disputes between parties. The actual method of compurgation varied considerably from place to place. Crown pleas in London during the thirteenth century were usually determined by six, eighteen, or thirty-six purgators, according to the gravity of the misdeed. In thirteenth-century Ipswich, a defendant who denied a debt used only five men's oaths, but in parts of Wales until at least the early fifteenth century the accused needed 300 oath-takers to clear himself. Arranging for the assistance of compurgators was not left entirely to the accused person: his choice was not a completely free one. All the oath helpers had to be men of good repute; this was standard practice. In Ipswich the accused seem to have offered to those who were entrusted with the maintenance of public order a list of ten names. These men came to court and were divided into two groups of five. A knife was thrown down between the groups and the five towards whom it eventually pointed were told to make their oaths.[34] In fourteenth-century Leicester the borough court decided the number of oath-takers required in each case; in London the compurgators were elected by the mayor and citizens, although they could be challenged by the accused on the grounds of personal enmity. Very possibly townsmen showed this desire for an outmoded form of trial out of fear of the perils of trial by combat. They knew their occupations and upbringing provided them with little experience in the handling of weapons. Yet, as the middle ages drew to a close, despite the reservations of some of the inhabitants, trial by jury slowly began to supersede compurgation. First it was used in pleas of debt and trespass, and later with more serious crimes. Perhaps the townsmen were won over by the appointment of their own justices of the peace at the end of the fourteenth century.

[34] C. Gross, 'Modes of Trial in the Medieval Boroughs of England,' *Harvard Law Review*, xv (1901–2), 695–701; *Borough Customs*, ed. M. Bateson (Selden Society, xviii, xxi, 1904–6), i, 36–42.

As it declined in use in the courts of common law, compurgation, rather remarkably, took on a new popularity in the proceedings of parliament and the king's council. On a number of occasions it was a device used by men of importance to clear themselves of suspicion without accepting the chances of a proper trial. Ralph, Lord Cromwell, in 1453 cleared himself before the council of the accusations of Master Robert Colynson by his own oath. Henry Beaufort, bishop of Winchester, repelled the insinuations of his enemies in the same manner in the parliament of 1425. John Maltravers, a probable murderer of Edward II, offered trial by oath in parliament in 1345 but the king would not accept. By the mid-fourteenth century any form of trial by oath was considered an easy option, but the king acknowledged it had its uses. It was a way of dealing with unwelcome accusations and also with an over-large number of captured misdoers. Thus in 1382 Richard II, as a measure to relieve the mass of litigation over damage done in the recent insurrection, allowed people charged with trespass to purge themselves with the assistance of a modest three or four fellow swearers.[35] Finally, we must bear in mind that a great many suspected or convicted felons, who when on trial in the king's courts successfully claimed benefit of clergy, were required at a later date to purge themselves by oaths in ecclesiastical courts.

In contrast with judicial practices in many continental countries, the trial of criminals in England under the common law was open to public view. There was nothing secret about the doing of justice except perhaps for the examination of suspects before the trial and the deliberations of the petty jury. From 1362 the language of the courtroom was English, the popular tongue. The court records, that is to say the summary of each case on the justices' rolls, continued to be in Latin. Apart from the accused, those in attendance at any trial were the petty jurors and the justices and their clerks. There might also be a number of witnesses but they were by no means essential. From the many reports of violence within the courtroom we may assume that it was not uncommon for the friends and supporters of the accused to be in attendance.[36] The English criminal trial differed

---

[35] 6 Richard II c. 5. In 1410 the commons of parliament wanted those who were arrested for Lollardy to be allowed to clear themselves in this way: *Rotuli Parliamentorum* (Record Commission), iii, 626b.

[36] Those accused by jury of presentment of breaking the king's peace were seemingly not allowed legal counsel who might answer on their behalf. Some did retain legal advisers however.

most noticeably from its continental counterpart in the fourteenth and fifteenth centuries in the employment of juries. In England petty juries were virtually essential, whereas on the continent inquest by jury was in decline and employed but rarely. Before 1391 the only frequent form of trial under the common law, excluding trial by battle or oath, where petty jurors could be dispensed with was that before the antiquated court leet; there presentment itself, as long as the case did not involve freehold, was tantamount to conviction. From 1391 conviction for forcible entry and riot were permitted merely on the record of the justices of the peace. In all other cases jurors were essential and a panel was assembled before the sessions began.

In the thirteenth century petty juries were often chosen from the jurors who had made the presentments. In some cases the presenting jury may have been turned immediately into a trial jury although, if it was, the indictment would perhaps also be offered to a jury from another hundred for a second verdict. There were some occasions when the petty jury was recruited from the personnel of several accusing juries: at other times it was obtained by adding a presenting jury to one specially elected for the purposes of trial. During the fourteenth century the tendency was towards a petty jury, drawn at least in part from the hundred where the crime was committed and the neighbouring townships, whose members had not served on the juries which presented the crime. The king was not at all pleased by this for he felt the chances of conviction were reduced. Maybe he believed that petty jurors who were meeting the case for the first time might, through their lack of knowledge about it, be lacking in sympathy for the party injured. Despite the increasing use of the testimony of witnesses this fear may not have been unfounded. Nonetheless, in 1352 Edward III had to give in to popular pressure and agree that no indictor should be put on a petty jury if challenged by the accused. The jurors on the elected panel often totalled twenty-four but there were instances of two or three times that number. Often those who actually sat on the jury numbered either twelve or thirteen but as few as nine and as many as sixteen have been noted. They were all men of substance and had frequently served in the same capacity before. There was no property qualification until 1414, but thereafter the jurors had each to be 'free and lawful' men and have lands worth at least 40s. a year. No doubt this was so they should be less susceptible to bribes and pressures. Another rule was that no juror should be directly related to the prisoner. According to Fortescue writing *circa* 1470 the accused could, and sometimes did, challenge up to thirty-five jurors without giving any reason.[37] It is often forgotten that medieval petty jurors were more than mere passive hearers of statements in court. Their task began before the defendants were arraigned. They had to set about enquiring for themselves into the facts of cases with which they were concerned. They were virtual detectives as well as deciders of guilt. Since the role of the jurors was so decisive there were many attempts to influence their decisions and even their selection. The sheriffs who made the jury panels were often under considerable pressure to select men known to favour a particular party. Those guilty of this embracery, as it was called, were very numerous indeed. Even the king might interfere. In 1451 King Henry asked the sheriff of Norfolk to make such a panel as would acquit Lord Molyns, his favourite.[38]

In the middle of the thirteenth century it was customary to bring the accused into court with their hands free, although sometimes with their legs in irons. Towards the end of that century they were being led in bare-headed but without irons of any sort. According to the treatise writer, *Britton*, this was so 'they should not be deprived of their reason', presumably through the pain which could be caused. In the sixteenth century prisoners were described as standing in the courtroom chained together. Proceedings began when one was called to the bar and told to raise his hand: then the indictment was read out. The accused man was told either to confess his guilt or to plead not guilty. Some lucky ones might instead plead their clergy or offer a pardon, but there could be only one plea: 'guilty but in self-defence' was not acceptable. The judge, who was no passive hearer of evidence but an active protagonist for the crown, would often urge the accused to confess, suggesting falsely that to tell the truth would more readily secure mercy. An appellee who asked to be tried by battle might be wheedled or tricked into putting himself on a jury. To attain this end judges were not above saying, quite untruthfully, that since they themselves believed in the prisoner's innocence surely a jury would. There can be little doubt that the questioning of the accused by the judge was the most important part of many trials, especially if there had been no prior examination of the accused by a justice of the peace and there was no record of a previous appearance

[37] Fortescue, *De Laudibus Legum Anglie*, p. 71.
[38] *Paston Letters*, ed. Gairdner, no. 155.

in another court for the same offence.[39] If no confession could be extracted from the suspect a judge would often turn to a confrontation between the party injured and the accused. He might ask the victim to look at the prisoner and say if he knew him. Then an argument would often ensue with the suspect denying he had ever seen the man he had allegedly robbed or injured. Very likely it was at this stage that witnesses were introduced in order to substantiate the facts, although we must remember that according to records their appearances were infrequent before the fifteenth century.

In the England of the fourteenth and the fifteenth centuries all witnesses were supposed to be reluctant. Medieval men had a great distrust of the person who, without invitation, appeared in court to say what he knew about the matter in hand. To do so was held as maintenance, that is assisting a man in his suit when it did not concern one personally. If, however, the visitor said he knew the truth of the matter and was in court to tell it at either the plaintiff's or the defendant's behest, that was quite acceptable. Jurors might of course pay a visit to the house of a man or woman who was known to have been on hand when the offence was committed. The evidence the witness gave in those circumstances was also quite valid. In the courtroom witnesses were allowed to say only what they had seen or heard themselves: hearsay was not permitted. Only in private suits was their testimony given on oath, yet in no case could it be challenged. The criminal received no notice of a witness who would appear against him nor could he arrange for any to appear on his own behalf. Although the statements of the witnesses, which could be in writing as well as verbal, were not directed specifically at the jury, the latter had the opportunity if it wished of examining each testifier individually. In a case of trespass which reached the king's bench at Trinity term 1318, where the validity of a written deed was in question, the counsel of the accused offered to prove his case by witnesses as well as by jury. Thereupon the jury examined four witnesses separately, and then the justices did the same.

Since in all criminal cases, with the exception of those started by appeals, the king was a party, crown witnesses might be expected to figure fairly frequently in the records. This was not so; their appearances were rare. A case at Michaelmas term 1320 shows a certain

---

[39] The tract *Placita Corone* suggests this: *Placita Corone*, ed. J. M. Kaye (Selden Society, Supplementary Series, 1966), pp. 15–22. Maitland had little to say on this aspect of the medieval trial.

Bertram le Munk testifying in the king's bench 'on the king's behalf in order to aid the king's prosecution' in a charge of forging money.[40] The reason why a witness was used in this instance may have been that the matter touched on treason and was therefore more an offence against the king than virtually any other crime. Another example of men testifying on the king's behalf again concerned counterfeiting, but of seals instead of money. 'Several trustworthy men', runs the record of the king's bench of Easter term 1325, 'have given the court to understand that Philip Burdon [a Hampshire chaplain] and others of his covin have among them a counterfeit impression of the king's seal in metal for sealing writs.'[41] The very choice of words used to describe the appearance and testimony of the witnesses reflects their uncommonness. There was no concise verbal formula available of the type beloved by medieval clerks of court. A witness was as open to corruption as any man who participated in the carrying out of justice; indeed since his appearance was perhaps the most fleeting he was the most vulnerable of all. As the use of witnesses grew more popular so did efforts to influence their testimony, and there must have been many occasions when men lamented, like a correspondent of Sir John Paston, that against them were likely to appear testifiers who knew nothing about the matter at issue beyond that which they had been told to say.[42]

Priming a jury with information, on the other hand, was quite in order. In personal actions the jurors' names were supposedly given by the sheriff to the parties so they might supply them with information. According to a statute of 1361 the information should have been passed in open court, but a statute of 1427 suggests it had become the practice to supply it before the trial took place.[43] 'Labouring', which

[40] *Select Cases in the Court of the King's Bench, Edward II*, pp. 81, 103.
[41] *Ibid.*, p. 158.
[42] *Paston Letters*, ed. Gairdner, no. 591. Trial by witnesses in contrast with trial by jury was probably unknown to the common law. F. W. Maitland noticed the rather odd process used by the king to discover who had murdered Henry Clement in 1235, but it may have been nothing more than the separate examination of witnesses subsequent to indictment or appeal and prior to trial by jury: see 'The Murder of Henry Clement,' *English Historical Review*, x (1895), 294–7. Another mysterious trial procedure which involved witnesses led to the execution of the London cordwainer John Constantyn on 11 February 1384. Because he had persuaded people to riot he was seized, arraigned, and by witnesses sworn and examined adjudged to death: *Cal. Pat. Rolls, 1381–1385*, p. 391.
[43] As argued by T. F. T. Plucknett in *The English Trial and Comparative Law* (Cambridge, 1952), p. 44.

in the fifteenth century meant trying to make a jury appreciate particular arguments or sets of facts which were likely to bulk large in the forthcoming trial, was not a word with a necessarily sinister connotation. The influencing might be no more than a request that the jurors should follow their consciences and avoid perjury. The prior of Snoring, who in 1459 was engaged in a quarrel with Lord Scales, told the jurors that 'if they had dread of God and hurt of their souls they would accept instruction from one party as well as another'.[44] It has been suggested that juries welcomed the 'labouring' as it provided them with the circumstantial detail which they so badly needed. If they had any sense and concern for their own safety the jurors would keep the information laid before them to themselves, particularly when one of the parties in the case was the king. In January 1343 a Cirencester jury appearing before the king in chancery was itself investigated to discover which of its members had revealed to the defendants the secrets told them before the council about those who were usurping the king's rights.[45] In the normal way of things the suspected criminal would rarely have the opportunity to labour the jurors, but his friends might and no doubt did, although usually if they were men with records in crime they used more direct methods to secure the prisoner's acquittal.

In contrast with labouring, which was permissible, to 'embrace' a jury was a crime. Embracery was to try to influence a jury to favour one side or the other by means of threats, bribes, or other illegal methods of persuasion. Judging by the numerous and repeated complaints in parliament and elsewhere it was commonplace. In 1478 the duke of Clarence, as we have seen, frightened a jury into convicting Ankarette Twynho against its conscience. The indictment of Robert, son of Robert de Bulwick, who was arraigned before the king's bench at Lincoln in July 1331, said that he had stated in the presence of many folk that if he was found guilty the jurors would be punished with burnings or in some other way.[46] A petition of the men of the town of Swaffham in 1451 said that a jury of that neighbourhood employed in a case of novel disseisin dare not 'out of dread of the horrible menaces of Sir Thomas Tudenham do otherwise than be forsworn in giving its verdict'.[47] The giving and taking of bribes was

[44] *Paston Letters*, ed. Gairdner, no. 341.
[45] *Cal. Pat. Rolls, 1343–1345*, p. 66.
[46] *Select Cases in the Court of the King's Bench, Edward III* (1957), p. 63.
[47] *Paston Letters*, ed. Gairdner, no. 151.

probably just as prevalent, at least when the accused and the injured were men of some substance. There were petitions by the commons in parliament which asked for severe penalties on jurors who received money from the parties. It was suggested they should forfeit ten times the sum they had taken or suffer a year in gaol. On another occasion the demand was for each juror to say on oath if he accepted any gift. The king might himself sue jurors suspected of the practice and there is at least one example of their being exhibited to public ridicule. 'This yeere', said the chronicler Stow, referring to 1468, 'divers persons being common jurors (such as at assises) were sworn for rewards or favour of parties, were judged to ride from Newgate to the pillory of Cornehill with miters of paper on their heads and then againe to Newgate.' Men knew well that, because of the frailties of the jurors, verdicts often went to the party with the deeper pocket. In 1381 Robert Cliveden, at odds with Sir William Cogan, sought trial by battle rather than by jury, saying that he had no chance of a fair verdict from jurors because of his enemy's wealth.[48]

When the testimony of the principals and the witnesses before the court had been brought to a close the jurors retired to consider their verdict. Very probably they took with them into their separate room nothing in writing but the indictment itself. By Tudor times it had become customary for the court bailiff to wait on them and to see that no one tried to speak with them. The hectic nature of the court day, and the great amount of judicial business to complete, apparently caused justices to send out the jury to make its decision during the lunch hour. In the room to which they had retired the jurors were not supposed to receive any food or drink or even be allowed the comfort of a fire. Sir Thomas Smith said that if they wished to hear any witness a second time or question him again more fully it would be arranged. Until the fourteenth century the verdict of the jurors did not necessarily have to be unanimous. When, around the turn of the thirteenth century, the writer *Britton* referred to trial of felony, he stated that if the jurors could not agree they should be separated and asked the reason. If there was no hope of a common verdict the decision should be that favoured by the majority. As late as the reign of Edward III there is evidence that in personal actions, if the alleged crime was no more than trespass, a majority of eleven to one might be sufficient for conviction. When they retired, juries were often expected to consider the guilt of two or three persons rather than of one. To

[48] *Rot. Parl.*, iii, 105–6.

more than three they were wont to object since it was too taxing on the memory. If three persons were tried simultaneously they had probably all been involved as either principals or accessories in the same crimes. It is of course not impossible that they were arraigned one at a time, the jury only withdrawing after the third accused had been heard. Juries reached their verdicts not so much on the basis of the accusations and answers made before them in court, since they were only called in when defendants asked for a decision on the general issue, but on their own knowledge of the facts. If the jurors had been in court during the earlier proceedings, and many must have been, they would have acquired additional information, but their presence was not demanded. A jury which acquitted in defiance of reason was liable to punishment by the king, usually by means of disciplinary action before his council. If the case was one of murder, the jurors, when they returned their verdict, might be asked by the justices who in fact was the guilty party if not the accused. When men were arraigned at the suit of the king there could be no attaint of the jury later on as in a personal action, neither could an appeal be made to another court. The trial closed with the justices declaring the verdict of the jury, and they did this in a form which often must have followed the indictment exactly. If the accused had been found not guilty he was discharged. If found guilty he was probably asked what he could say for himself.[49] Not infrequently the answer took the form of a claim for benefit of clergy, that is to say a demand as from one in holy orders to be handed over to the bishop's officer for trial in an ecclesiastical court.

Benefit of clergy did not operate for all crimes. Treasons and minor transgressions did not qualify their perpetrators for the privilege, and those who had committed trespasses against the king's peace, since the offences were punishable by relatively light penalties, were not always inclined to make the claim. The suspected felon was the criminal who found the device most attractive, since it promised escape from the threat of the gallows and the institution of a punishment at its worst no more severe than imprisonment and penance. Any *clericus* could claim benefit of clergy, which meant all men in

---

[49] *Rot. Parl.*, ii, 259b, 266a; T. Smith, *De Republica Anglorum*, ed. L. Alston (Cambridge, 1906), pp. 100–2; *Britton*, ed. F. M. Nichols (Washington, 1901), i, 26; *Year Books, Les Reports del Cases en Ley*, 41 Edward III, Mich., pl. 36; B. H. Putnam, *Proceedings before the Justices of the Peace, Edward III to Richard III*, p. clii.

holy orders, that is all who had had the first tonsure. Tonsures of sorts were easily acquired in gaol before trial, as justices had cause to complain. Thus there developed in the reign of Edward I the reading test as a method of ascertaining literacy, which was the new criterion for being in holy orders. Until the fifteenth century and the rise of a numerous educated laity this was a reasonable way of separating clerk from layman. The test, or examination as it was called, was made immediately on the lodging of the claim to benefit of clergy. This could be when the accused was asked to plead or it could be at any later point in the trial. When it was the former the prisoner sometimes coupled a plea of 'not guilty' with the proviso 'saving his clerical privilege if convicted'. In the thirteenth and fourteenth centuries suspects more frequently made the claim when asked to plead, but from the reign of Henry VI the tendency was to wait until after conviction. When benefit of clergy had been requested, the accredited bishop's officer who represented his master at each sessions, or the court officials with the officer observing, conducted the reading test.

The prisoner would usually be given a book, perhaps a psalter, and told to read several lines. The bishop's representative was then required to say either 'he reads' or 'he does not read'. Since their lives depended on it many prisoners claimed to be able to read when they could not, hoping that a few memorized words would see them through. John, son of Thomas Dennyson Trotter, the elder, tried to pass the test in this way but the judge, who was suspicious, then gave him a book turned upside down and, unknowing, he read as he had before. Men desperately sought to become literate while they were in gaol before they were put on trial. John Trotter, who was apparently a layman and illiterate at the time of his arrest, had been taught what letters he knew when in Carlisle gaol by two boys from Appleby who had been admitted through the good offices of the gaoler. In the reign of Edward III judges instructed that this sort of practice should be investigated but it seems to have continued: Sir Matthew Hale thought it became permissible. It was not always easy to be sure a man could read. In a case in 1344 William Pernill, who was accused of robbery before the justices delivering Colchester gaol, failed to read at his first attempt and the bishop's officer would not claim him as a clerk. Before the sentence of hanging was carried out the officer appeared before the justices again saying that William could read and was therefore being claimed.[50] Whether it was a change of decision on

[50] The Trotter and Pernill examples are given in L. C. Gabel *Benefit of*

the basis of his later reflections on the test, or whether William was able to show him on another occasion a proper ability to read, is unknown. Although his verdict was usually accepted the bishop's officer was not the supreme arbiter of the reading test. A judge who disagreed with his decision could overrule him. Sometimes the reading test must have been the only method of checking clerical status which was used but the more careful officer may also have made enquiries about the supposed clerk's letters of ordination and even have tried to ascertain if he was a bigamist. Unsatisfactory answers to either of these two investigations would bar the accused from gaining the privilege.

The reason why many accused misdoers delayed claiming their clergy until they had been convicted was largely so they would have the chance of being acquitted by the king's court first. Any man who claimed his clergy before trial was virtually certain to be found guilty by the jurors, who seem to have been very jealous of the privilege. Since the accused person was quite likely to escape the death penalty they had no compunction about giving a verdict which carried it. After the completion of their trial in secular court those who were claimed by the clerical representative would be taken to the bishop's gaol. The prisoner then petitioned to be admitted to purgation. A day for this process was duly proclaimed so that anyone who chose to oppose the purgation would be able to appear with his objection. Such persons would most likely be those who had suffered personally from the prisoner's misdeeds. Purgation was not an automatic provision. It was completely denied to misdoers who had been outlawed or who had once abjured the realm. Whether it should be refused in other cases was largely up to the secular justices, but unless the prisoner possessed a notorious criminal record or he had confessed to felonies before a lay court they rarely exercised their veto. To do so was to condemn the man to incarceration in the bishop's prison for life. There were restrictions from the ecclesiastical side as well. Before the process of purgation was begun the bishop ordered an inquest to be made into the career and reputation of the prisoner, including the veracity of accusations made against him in the lay court. This task was usually assigned to twelve rectors or vicars. The nature of their deposition decided whether the bishop allowed the prisoner to proceed to purgation.

The purging itself took the form of a declaration of innocence

Clergy in England in the Later Middle Ages (Smith College Studies in History, 1928–9), pp. 72–3.

sworn before an ecclesiastical judge and a jury of clerks, and was accompanied by the taking of an oath by a dozen or so compurgators.[51] As in compurgation in the towns, their oath was that they believed in the prisoner's truthfulness, not in the actual fact of his innocence. Not all the compurgators had to be in holy orders: sometimes as many as three-quarters were laymen. It should not be thought that prisoners who attempted purgation were automatically successful. There is indication that public opinion kept back some men from making the oath on the prisoner's behalf and that a fair number of would-be purgers could not muster the required number of helpers. One archiepiscopal register shows sixteen failures in twenty-nine cases, but such a high percentage was exceptional.[52] Very noticeably, purgation did not follow immediately after it was claimed by the ordinary. Sometimes there was a delay of three or four years, and in one case the prisoner waited fourteen years. This was most probably deliberate policy. The bishop, knowing the man's criminal record, feared his successful purgation and therefore delayed giving him the opportunity. It might also have been an attempt to gain a confession. The price of failure to purge on the proper occasion was degradation, by which the prisoner was deprived of his holy orders, together with penance and remand to the bishop's prison for a period of up to life. The successful purgator was restored to good fame and, when chancery received the certificate of purgation, the king returned his goods and chattels. It seems unlikely he was allowed to purge himself later of a second offence.

Legal records show that those who in the later middle ages claimed benefit of clergy were drawn from a wide variety of occupations and classes. There were, as we might expect, a good proportion of artisans and tradesmen but there were also a fair number of labourers. The evidence suggests that it was indeed a loop-hole for criminals who could read. Particularly dangerous to public order was the high percentage of highway robbers who were able to plead their clergy and who returned to their particular form of crime at a later date. There is no sense in the argument that men entered holy orders before embarking on a criminal career merely to preserve life and limb on subsequent capture, but there is the possibility that they were tempted into crime years after that occasion by among other things the know-

[51] *Ibid.*, pp. 93–102.
[52] *Register of John le Romeyn, Archbishop of York 1286–1296, and of Henry of Newark, 1296–1299*, ed. W. Brown (Surtees Society, cxxii, cxxviii, 1913–17).

ledge of the mildness of any punishment which might come their way. Some miscreants must have successfully claimed benefit of clergy more than once, but it was only in the sixteenth century that the king devised an answer to the cleric who was a persistent criminal. He who claimed his clergy was branded by hot iron in the justice's presence to show the letter 'T' for thief or 'M' for manslaughter on the brawn of his hand. Then if he was taken for a criminal offence a second time he was executed.

A type of misdeed which was handled in its entirety by the church and never at any stage of the proceedings appeared before a lay court was the moral offence, such as fornication and adultery. Acting apparently on information received and gossip, rather than on formal accusation, the ruridecanal courts, whose records are unfortunately scanty, dealt with the sexual misdeeds of peasants, and the more important ecclesiastical courts with those of the upper classes. Forms of immorality which did not involve sexual behaviour were of much less concern. Of 107 persons from fifteen different parishes in Droitwich rural deanery who were cited in deanery chapters in the year 1300, only one, a husband accused of wife beating, was not involved in allegations of fornication or adultery. Most of those cited made an appearance in court but several fled the locality and were excommunicated, as were those who at first stood their ground and refused to accept the court's jurisdiction. Some of those who appeared were allowed to try to purgate themselves by oath: a fair number failed. Most of the convicted suffered a beating rather than imprisonment, which in these cases was rare. The offenders were whipped round or through the market place either once or twice, according to the degree of their guilt. In one case tried at Dodderhill in the reign of Edward I, Henry le Cooper of Birmingham was said to have fornicated several times with Isabella, the daughter of Richard le Potter.[53] The punishment was for both to be beaten twice: once for fornication and once for contumacy. Allegations of immorality concerned the upper as well as the lower classes. It has been suggested that the knight who was thought by his neighbours to have committed adultery was unlikely to suffer punishment. Certainly there was little chance of his being whipped, but excommunication and then a fine when he was contrite were definite possibilities. Throughout the fourteenth and fifteenth centuries the ecclesiastical courts, like the king's courts, seem to have encountered increasing difficulty in mak-

[53] R. H. Hilton, *A Medieval Society* (London, 1966), pp. 265–6.

155

ing men appear before them. In July 1449 the bishop of Coventry and Lichfield petitioned the king that there were many adulterers and fornicators and other misdoers in the county and city of Chester whom his officers dare not cite on account of the maintenance the miscreants received from powerful lords.[54] He therefore requested the power to cite men living in those areas to answer in matters concerning the law of the church in some other place in his diocese. Good lordship, we may reflect, extended its influence even into the ecclesiastical field of moral discipline.

In contrast with adultery and fornication, prostitution was the preserve of urban rather than ecclesiastical courts and what rules there were governing it existed in local police regulations. The church might deal with the fornication of the clerical client but the whore, though expelled periodically from towns of profit like London, Oxford, and Cambridge, was unlikely to have to appear in either the ecclesiastical or the king's courts. There was a similar and perhaps a surprising lack of interest on the part of the church in witchcraft and sorcery. Which courts should try these offences was never finally settled in the period under review. Secular courts were wont to try only those whose sorceries resulted in the committing of a definite felony or trespass. The magical practices were not illegal on their own. The view of the church was probably not dissimilar. If the sorcery did not lead to an actual crime, yet the king thought it dangerous because in some way it threatened his safety or that of his people, then the council was the proper body to investigate.

No examination of the English judicial processes would be complete without some estimate, however conjectural, of their effectiveness. Sir John Fortescue, the ex-chief justice of the king's bench, writing when in exile in France, in the later fifteenth century, eulogized the English trial but was obviously aware that trial by jury, which was its distinguishing feature, failed to produce as many convictions as the methods used in continental Europe. He defended the English practice by saying it was better for twenty guilty to escape than a single innocent to be condemned. At the same time he refused to admit that the English system was likely to acquit a man who was guilty, arguing that if a criminal was allowed to go free by verdict of a jury, the jurors, presumably like other men of the locality, were going to suffer from his future wrongdoing. The logic of this argument is hardly compelling. F. W. Maitland, writing some seventy years ago,

[54] *Proceedings and Ordinances of the Privy Council*, vi, 75.

held that the criminal law of medieval England was exceedingly inefficient. He pointed out that when the justices in eyre visited Gloucester in 1221 'they heard an appalling tale of crime which comprised some 330 acts of homicide'. Yet as a result of their visit only 14 men were hanged and 100 orders of outlawry were given. Seventy-seven murders were dealt with by the justices in Northumberland in 1256 but 72 accused had to be outlawed and only 4 murderers were hanged. 'Even in quiet times', contended Maitland, 'few out of many criminals came to their appointed end.' Court records of the fourteenth and fifteenth centuries show a pattern similar to that of the thirteenth century which Maitland described. Few of the accused appeared in court, there were very few convictions for some types of crimes, and a large number of non-appearers were outlawed. According to the rolls of the Shropshire justices of the peace for the period 1400–14, 178 felonies were reported and 251 felons named in indictments; 156 were summoned into the king's bench, which in this instance was the first court, yet only 14 actually stood trial and not one was convicted. When the king's bench came to Lincoln at Easter term 1396 it attempted to try those whose indictments on the Lincolnshire peace rolls were yet unheard. Summonses were issued to 224 felons; 54 appeared, of whom 42 were acquitted by trial and 11 produced pardons. The other 170 were outlawed, and not one was convicted.[55]

These examples show the treatment of felony by the courts at its most ineffectual. Slightly more effective and perhaps more typical of the later middle ages are the figures to be discovered in the rolls of the Warwickshire justices of the peace of the period 1377–97. In that shire and in the town of Coventry it has been calculated that 231 people were indicted of felony. Of the 169 of them whose subsequent fate is known, 86 were outlawed, 44 acquitted, 16 pardoned, and 13 sentenced to hang.[56] Much more impressive is the Hampshire peace session roll of 1475–6 in which 29 people were indicted of felony. Ten were tried before the justices of the peace, one was acquitted, one allowed benefit of clergy, and eight were convicted and sentenced to be hanged; four others were kept in prison to await the justices of

---

[55] These figures were calculated by E. G. Kimball in *The Shropshire Peace Roll, 1400–1414*, p. 41, and in *Records of Some Sessions of the Peace in Lincolnshire, 1381–1396* (Lincoln Record Society, xix, 1955), pp. liii–liv.
[56] *Rolls of the Warwickshire and Coventry Sessions of the Peace*, ed. E. G. Kimball (Dugdale Society, xvi, 1939).

gaol delivery.[57] The Hampshire figures, like those for Shropshire above, were hardly typical. The norm, as far as one can judge, was closer to those calculated for Warwickshire. One big problem which the English kings faced continuously was that of getting the suspect before the court. In some sessions as many as eighty per cent failed to appear and the absence of half of those who had been indicted of felony was quite common. The justices of gaol delivery alone were likely to be able to arraign all the suspects, that is, as long as the gaoler was an efficient one. We should therefore expect to find a higher percentage of convictions in sessions of this type. Investigation reveals that there was an increase but not a great one. At the delivery of Canterbury gaol in 1317, 76 cases, mostly felonies, were tried; 43 prisoners were found not guilty of the crimes whereof indicted, 7 were found guilty. At the delivery of Worcester gaol in 1304, 36 persons were indicted of felonies, including 18 murderers, and 5 were hanged. It has been calculated that out of 337 persons accused of felony or trespass who were in 17 gaols delivered in 1348, 83 were convicted.[58] A very rough estimate would be that of those tried by justices of gaol delivery in this period, somewhere between 10 and 30 per cent were convicted.

Wherever we look we find that few of those suspected of felony were convicted. In contrast, there can be no doubt that jurors found guilty a considerable proportion of those accused of trespass, particularly of trespass against economic regulations. This severity was probably connected with the punishment which the different types of crime carried. To be found guilty of felony meant the death sentence, and jurors hesitated to condemn their neighbours to that, but to be guilty of trespass often meant only the payment of a fine. The king's bench, when it visited Lincoln in 1396 to act as a court of the first instance, convicted, as we have seen, few felons, but the percentage of those accused of trespass who were found guilty was much greater. The court summoned before it all those indicted of trespass in 1395–6 in Holland and Kesteven and all but 11 in Lindsey; the total was 273 persons. Of these, only 28 were acquitted while 92 were put in exigend and presumably outlawed, and 153 had to pay fines. An analysis of the proceedings before the Bedfordshire justices of the peace of 1356–

[57] Putnam, *Proceedings before the Justices of the Peace, Edward III to Richard III*, pp. 237–74.

[58] B. H. Putnam, *Kent Keepers of the Peace* (Kent Archaeological Society, Records Branch, xiii, 1933), pp. xxxv–xxxvi; Hilton, *A Medieval Society*, p. 250; Pike, *A History of Crime in England*, i, 480.

1359 shows 207 persons indicted of trespass. Of these, 200 were dealt with totally at the peace sessions, 8 were acquitted, 24 outlawed, and 168 fined. The rolls of the Warwickshire and Coventry sessions of the peace for 1377–97 reveal that, of 244 men and women accused of trespasses not of an economic nature, 38 were outlawed, 5 pardoned, 171 fined, and only 23 acquitted. In the later fourteenth century and the early fifteenth, justices of the peace often had the burden of hearing pleas concerned with infractions of the labour laws, such as paying or receiving excessive wages, departing from one's master before the period of service had expired, and refusing to work at the legal wages. All these offences were, strictly speaking, trespasses, but by their nature they can be, and have been, treated separately by legal historians. The records show that the proportion of 'economic' offenders found guilty was higher even than that for other forms of trespass. The rolls of the Warwickshire and Coventry peace sessions mentioned above show 300 people accused of these crimes. Of the 201 whose subsequent fate is known to us, no fewer than 192 were fined, three put in exigend, only one pardoned, and none acquitted. Even in the Shropshire roll of 1400–14, which shows the doing of justice at its most ineffectual, there were 28 men fined for economic misdeeds out of 118 summoned for trial for trespass. This was, in fact, the total of convictions for all offences, since no one was found guilty of felony or of another type of trespass.[59]

Another factor which must be considered in any estimation of the efficiency of medieval English justice is the prejudice of the jurors. Juries, we have noted, were probably loth to find a man guilty of felony because of the punishment he would incur. Their decisions may also have been influenced by the fact that the man on trial was usually their neighbour or at least from their own locality. Robert Bulwick, appearing on 1 July 1331 before the justices of the king's bench then at Lincoln, boasted that if anyone had indicted him of felony, conspiracy, or confederacy, he would be acquitted by his neighbours.[60] There was one way in which a jury could acquit a man of one type of felony in the face of the most damning evidence, and it

[59] Putnam, *Proceedings before the Justices of the Peace, Edward III to Richard III*, pp. 43–61; *Rolls of the Warwickshire and Coventry Sessions of the Peace, 1377–1399*, ed. E. G. Kimball, p. lxvii; *The Shropshire Peace Roll, 1400–1414*, ed. E. G. Kimball, pp. 41–2; *Records of Some Sessions of the Peace in Lincolnshire, 1381–1396*, ed. E. G. Kimball (Lincoln Record Society, xix, 1955), pp. liii–liv.
[60] *Select Cases in the Court of the King's Bench, Edward III* (1957), p. 63.

was adopted not infrequently. In a charge of larceny the jurors would find the value of the goods stolen to be under twelve pence, even if in fact they were of much greater worth. This meant that if the indictment was for felony the accused was quit, since a man could only be a felon if the goods were worth over a shilling. Relying on his general impressions rather than any set of statistics, the historian must conclude that the types of misdoer most likely to be convicted were these: those taken with loot in their possession or while actually committing a crime; men whose misdeeds were notorious in the region and who had possibly been convicted or taken in most suspicious circumstances before but who had survived; and thirdly, those who were strangers in the place where the crime had been committed and who may have been named by juries of presentment and found guilty by petty juries as sacrificial victims. Those suspected only of trespass the jurors would convict more frequently, and those indicted of an offence under the economic legislation of 1351 were more likely to be found guilty than innocent. Misdeeds connected with wages and prices seem to have been regarded as despicable rather than grave—as cheating one's neighbours rather than grieving the king. He who had been taking high wages or had offered them, it was no doubt argued, could well afford to pay the fines inflicted by the courts.

The crisis in public order which afflicted England in the fourteenth and fifteenth centuries has sometimes been blamed on the inefficiency of the courts but it should be apparent that to do so is unfair. There can be no doubt that procedural weaknesses existed, but they were to be expected in an age of legal change and experimentation. The important thing was they were not disastrous. The most troublesome were probably the loop-hole of benefit of clergy, which with the better opportunities for education was ever widening, and the susceptibility of the jury system to embracery. Labouring was necessary since witnesses appeared in court in criminal cases only infrequently and were denied to the accused altogether. The king as yet lacked the control over accusations which he undoubtedly desired, but he found a way to interfere and influence through the increased judicial activities of his council, the old weapon of approvers, and the new weapon of examination, which at first was viewed by the nation at large with much suspicion. The petty jury could cause the king and his judges much exasperation but it was a crucial element in the judicial process and never in danger of being superseded. It is nowadays rather fashionable to play down the petty jury's importance and eschew the once popular title of 'pillar of English liberties', yet there is much to be said for the view that the existence of the petty jury served to ensure that the body of the English population should not become alienated from the justice of the king. The middle classes at least were always an integral part of that justice. The tendency to acquit felons was, in the long run, a small price to pay for this benefit.

VI

◇◇

Prison, Punishment, and Pardon

◇◇

Prisons of one sort or another have existed in England since Saxon times and by the later middle ages were an important instrument in the maintenance of public order. Most kings preferred to fine or execute immediately all those found guilty, but even if this was possible there was still the period between the surrender or capture of a suspect and his trial when confinement in custody was essential. If such a control was not exercised, and the suspect was allowed to be at large, no one could be sure that he would put in an appearance when the justices held their sessions. Bail and attachment, which had been popular with the kings of the eleventh and twelfth centuries, failed to produce the desired results in the thirteenth as society became more fluid and as the frank-pledge system decayed. Thus, in certain circumstances, imprisonment on suspicion became the rule, and thereby the need for greater prison space grew. These irrepleviable charges were listed in the statute of Westminster of 1275. There was to be no bail when a man was captured with the *mainour* in his possession, when the crime touched on treason, when a man was suspected of arson or breaking out of gaol, when the accusation had been made by way of an appeal, or when the capture had been made on the orders of the king or his chief justice. Bail was denied not so much on account of the heinousness of the particular crime as because of the nature of the arrest and the procedure of accusation. In the fourteenth and fifteenth centuries a number of statutes were promulgated, such as those which were directed against recalcitrant labourers, which expressly forbade persons arrested for certain new offences from having bail. The natural consequence of these developments was an increase in the number and size of gaols and greater royal interest in them.

Many of those who languished in later medieval gaols were there not awaiting trial but having already been tried and sentenced to imprisonment, either as their sole punishment or as part of it. Condemnation to a term of incarceration in gaol was not a particularly common form of punishment. This was because there were other penalties available which provided the king with reward rather than expense; in many cases a fine was much to be preferred. The king and his legal advisers had no objection to imprisonment on principle. The use which the church made of it to punish unpurged clerks was a constant reminder of the favour it enjoyed in other quarters, and the king must have been aware of the argument that it might effect a change of heart through the time it gave the misdoer to reflect on his crime and his predicament. The duration of punitive imprisonment varied from weeks to a lifetime. By the end of the reign of Edward I petty larceny, so it has been deduced, was sometimes punished by imprisonment at a rate of a week for every pennyworth stolen and three days per ha'p'orth.[1] Life imprisonment was infrequent but there are clear references to it. In 1266 the king promised to Gerard de Furnival he should not suffer, for what were called his trespasses, either loss of life or limb or perpetual imprisonment. In 1345 Richard de Carlisle, a tailor, who had on his own admission threatened and injured jurors at Westminster, was sentenced to have his right hand cut off and to suffer imprisonment in the Tower of London for life. Usually sentences were for a period of one year or two.[2] As long as the offence was not in contravention of a statute which laid down exactly the term of incarceration, it was up to the king and his justices to decide for how long the offender should go to gaol. That there were more sentences of imprisonment in the later middle ages than in preceding centuries cannot be doubted. One reason seems to have been the popularity, from the later thirteenth century, of the action of trespass following misdeeds like assault or petty larceny which men claimed had broken the king's peace. When the courts found a man guilty on this count he was liable both to the payment of damages and to a period in gaol. Another reason was the increased promulgation of

[1] T. F. T. Plucknett, *A Concise History of the Common Law* (London, 1956), p. 457.
[2] *Calendar of Patent Rolls, 1258–1266* (Record Commission), p. 559; *Select Cases in the Court of the King's Bench, Edward III*, ed. G. O. Sayles (Selden Society, 82, 1965), p. 41.

laws which contained clauses imposing imprisonment, often precisely defined as to duration, on those who broke them. These laws, as for example the Forest Charter (1217) and the statute of Merton (1236), first appear in the first half of the thirteenth century and suggest popular support for their penal provisions in that they were fabricated with the consent of the whole community.

The statutes of the thirteenth, fourteenth, and fifteenth centuries which enjoined imprisonment for offenders on conviction covered a large range of crimes. The misbehaviour of officials who were concerned with justice or tax collection, such as sheriffs, justices, bailiffs, and custom officials, figured in a good number of these. So did attempting to corrupt the course of justice, riots, forcible entry, disseisin, and livery and maintenance offences, all of which were likely to lead to prolonged feuding. A number of economic crimes were also involved, such as fraudulent mercantile and manufacturing practices and especially offences by employees and empoyers against the statutes of labourers. What these different types of misdeeds had in common seems in part to have been their novelty. Of course no law, not even a statute, was regarded as new law, but rather as the discovery and affirmation of some rule of previous centuries, yet these crimes to a notable degree would have been unknown to Norman kings. Another common element may have been that they touched the king directly, being matters crucial to the efficient upkeep of public order, as distinct from private quarrels and their subsequent injuries. Statutes did not always lay down exactly the length of the term of imprisonment to be inflicted on those found guilty. When they did, it varied from forty days to two or three years, but it was rarely longer. Sometimes imprisonment was accompanied by a fine, sometimes by an order to perform a definite deed. There was always a tendency to pardon a man his imprisonment when the accompanying fine had been paid or when he had completed a required deed. By imprisoning to gain compliance, the later medieval kings were copying both the Angevins, who made use of imprisonment to compel officials to make payments and restitutions, and the thirteenth-century monarchs, who used it to make reluctant accusers prosecute appeals and to persuade prisoners at the bar to allow petty jurors to decide their guilt.

Coercive imprisonment, as it may be called, was used before trial as well as upon conviction. There were no hard and fast rules which the king must obey and this was reflected in his arbitrary treatment of prisoners from time to time. Sir John Mortimer of Bishop's Hatfield, Hertfordshire, who claimed to be the heir of the earl of March and therefore Richard II's lawful successor, was arrested at the beginning of December 1418, indicted before the steward and the marshal of the king's household for treasons, felonies, and trespasses in the subsequent April, and then imprisoned on the instructions of King Henry. There was no semblance of a trial until just before the knight was executed in 1424. A petition in parliament referred to his being held 'hard and grievously . . . in iron' which 'is not bearable'; another, to the council, said he was lodged in the Tower underground without light or air and 'could not long exist.'[3] In May 1350 Edward III ordered four prisoners in the Tower of London to be examined in order to discover how long they had been in prison there and on what grounds each had been arrested.[4] One had languished for seven and a half years, another for four years. About the causes of their arrest and imprisonment they said they knew little. One had received gold from the treasury in order to make profit for the king by alchemy and had presumably failed, another had been involved in the straightforward forging of coin. There was no reference to any of the four being indicted, much less tried, even after the investigation into the causes of imprisonment. Only one is known to have been released, and he was not formally discharged until eleven years later. Here the arbitrary nature of one type of medieval imprisonment is clearly demonstrated. The king, who had imprisoned solely on his own whim, did not know who was in custody or, because there was no proper accusation and therefore no legal record, why they were there. To give them their due the judges of the two benches seem to have disapproved of such confinement. Less arbitrary, and less likely to arouse judicial concern, were cases of imprisonment on the orders of the king and his council. In October 1421 Henry V summoned Nicholas Thorley, an esquire who had married the countess of Oxford without royal licence, before council, and when he admitted the fact he was committed to the Tower where he languished in irons until February 1424, when he paid a fine to be pardoned.[5] Sentences to imprisonment by the king's council which were not intended simply to gain compliance were rare but not unknown. In 1348 Sir

---

[3] P.R.O. K.B. 9/218/2; K.B. 9/222/2; *Rotuli Parliamentorum* (Record Commission), iv, 160b; *Proceedings and Ordinances of the Privy Council*, ii, 311.
[4] *Select Cases in the Court of the King's Bench, Edward III* (1965), p. 73.
[5] *Proceedings and Ordinances of the Privy Council*, ii, 303.

William Rothyng, who had been accused before Edward III and his council of trespass, was sentenced to perpetual imprisonment.[6]

There is little evidence that the mass of medieval men objected to the use made of imprisonment. It was a social and legal necessity. As well as being a tool of secular rulers it was popular with ecclesiastics. The clerk who was unable to purge his felony by oath might be condemned in a church court to life imprisonment. From 1352 the bishops were bound to enforce this penalty. When there was a likelihood of a clerk of known criminal connection and record being able to clear himself, bishops might delay purgation until the suspect had suffered a lengthy period of imprisonment. The king pressed the church hard on the issue of criminous clerks: in 1377 bishops were ordered not to permit the purging of notorious felons at all.[7] Much use was also made of imprisonment in the towns, both for the purpose of keeping men in custody and as a punishment. In trading centres there were bound to be debtors who could not pay, and urban authorities believed that prison was the best place for them. There were also those who drew profit from moral iniquity—the whores and the brothel keepers. They were regarded as particularly suited to imprisonment, as the borough custumals clearly testify. In an urban ordinance of June 1419, for the abolition of Ludgate gaol, we discover most clearly what medieval society expected of its prisons. The prisoners, who in this case were poor freemen of the city, were 'to dwell in quiet, to pray for their benefactors [those who had been responsible for the building of the gaol], . . . and in increase of their merits, by benign suffrance, in such imprisonment pass their lives if God should provide no other remedy for them'.[8] Prison was not intended for correction but as the place where the misdoer should suffer passively society's revenge. Furthermore, in that the prisoner was hidden from society at large, imprisonment was not a deterrent of the primitive sort but symptomatic of a more advanced society.

Buildings used for purposes of imprisonment must have existed in Saxon times and some may even have been constructed solely for that purpose. Most important for the general provision of prisons was the seventh chapter of the assize of Clarendon of 1166, which commanded that they should be erected in counties where there were

[6] *Cal. Pat. Rolls, 1348–1350*, p. 222.

[7] *Rot. Parl.*, iii, 23.

[8] *Memorials of London and London Life in the Thirteenth, Fourteenth and Fifteenth Centuries*, ed. H. T. Riley (London, 1868), p. 673.

none. They were to be sited in a borough, or one of the king's castles, and presumably near to the shire house, the headquarters of the sheriff. In addition to the king's county gaols, there existed by the end of the thirteenth century a good number of town gaols, constructed in the main under privileges granted by Henry III and Edward I. The custodians of these were appointed by the municipality although the prisoners were delivered by the king's justices. In the fourteenth and fifteenth centuries, keepers of county gaols were usually appointed by the king himself, thus often depriving the sheriff of a former power. A few gaols had been and continued to be in the custody of tenants in serjeanty.

There are some indications that medieval society took into consideration the personal qualities of a prison keeper. Town dwellers were concerned that he should be a man of a decent sort. In 1356 the London city council ordained that the keeper of Newgate should be of good character and should swear not to act extortionately. From 1431, probably because of fears of misbehaviour, the same keeper was supposed to be chosen annually, although it seems most unlikely that the office actually changed hands so often.[9] The post of keeper never lacked for men to undertake it, even if payment was by fees extracted from the prisoners rather than a salary from the authorities. It is, in fact, quite probable that the opportunities for extortion were what made keeperships attractive propositions. Thus men were willing to pay for the office and succeeded in purchasing it despite it being common knowledge that 'gaylors buying theire offices will deale hardly with pitifull prisoners'.[10] Regulations about forfeiture of office for such conduct and rules like the one at Newgate that keepers must swear they would not extort were no proper safeguard. Some keepers of prisons were enterprising and influential enough, so we are told, to get themselves appointed as justices of oyer and terminer and of the peace; their intention was apparently to promote the indictment of various innocent persons so as to have more prisoners in their gaols and thus the greater opportunity to extort.[11] The saddling of some keepers with responsibility for the repair of the gaol buildings may have contributed to their oppressive behaviour.

Few counties or towns can have possessed more than a single gaol

[9] *Calendar of Letter Books of the City of London*, *G*, ed. R. R. Sharpe (London, 1907–12), p. 74; *ibid.*, *K*, p. 127.
[10] J. Stow, *A Survey of London*, ed. C. L. Kingsford (Oxford, 1908), i, 351.
[11] *Rot. Parl.*, ii, 265; iii, 335.

which was in continuous use, though there was accommodation in castles in an emergency and in some areas there were special forest prisons. Because of the paucity of gaols they had to be of the omnibus variety, prisoners of all types being confined in the same premises, though not necessarily in the same rooms. The exception was London where, because there were several gaols, there developed a degree of specialization in various classes of prisoner. The largest London prison was probably Newgate. Although constructed in the twelfth century for confining men of London and Middlesex, it was soon also used for approvers in general and for those against whom they laid charges. In the fifteenth century in particular Newgate received more than its fair share of persons whose offences were thought by the king to be especially serious, either because of their station in society or because, like treason or heresy for example, they touched on the safety of the realm. Newgate was never famous for the number of debtors imprisoned within its walls but it usually had a fair sprinkling. More notorious in the latter respect was the Fleet prison, which contained quite a large percentage of that type of offender.[12] This was because from the early fourteenth century the Fleet was the gaol of the exchequer and the court of common pleas, where cases involving debt were often heard. The influx of debtors into the Fleet may have been consequent on statutes of Edward I and Edward III, for example the statute of Acton Burnell (1283), the statute of merchants (1285), and 25 Edward III st. 5 c. 17, which dealt with the recovery of debts by creditors and in some cases permitted the debtors' imprisonment. From the reign of Richard II the Fleet was much used by chancery and council. Like Newgate, it had been originally a gaol for the men of London, being the first proper prison in the capital and for half a century the only one. Chancery and particularly council were likely to send to the Fleet persons whose offences were not of the common sort. Sometimes these were not crimes at all under the common law: what they had in common was that they caused embarrassment to the king.

In contrast with Newgate and the Fleet, which eventually took their prisoners from all over the kingdom and for a wide variety of offences, Ludgate gaol, founded about 1380, was a place used very

[12] For a general survey of the medieval history of these two prisons see M. Bassett, 'Newgate Prison in the Middle Ages', *Speculum*, xviii (1943), 233–246, and 'The Fleet Prison in the Middle Ages', *University of Toronto Law Journal*, v (1943–4), 383–402, and the comprehensive study by R. B. Pugh, *Imprisonment in Medieval England* (Cambridge, 1968).

much for London freemen, particularly if their offence was a fairly modest one.[13] Trespassers were common but there were few felons, either suspect or proven. The two London Counters, which in the fifteenth century had come to reside in Cheapside and in the Poultry, were prisons used by the sheriffs of London and Middlesex to hold men accused of virtually any sort of crime. No particular category of offence predominated, nor can it be said that the prisoners were there temporarily while en route to another gaol. Maybe they were overflow prisons. The remaining London prisons were largely specialist in function. The marshalsea of the king's bench, until the early fifteenth century, was away from London for most of the time, perambulating with the justices of that court. Thereafter, with the king's bench remaining more often in the capital, it was to be found in Southwark. It held prisoners awaiting trial or already convicted. It was much used as a place where outlaws surrendered either with, or in expectation of, a pardon. The Tower of London, in contrast, was used in the later middle ages for the imprisonment of foreign dignitaries captured in the wars and for most prisoners of noble rank. Often there was suspicion of treason against those who were confined there. Those incarcerated in the marshalsea of the king's household seem to have been there for crimes committed against members of the household or because they were connected with some illegal commercial transaction involving it. Finally, the Tun, on Cornhill, was nothing more than a temporary prison for those caught defying the city curfew at night:[14] most of these were whores, their employers, and their clients.

Conditions in gaols varied enormously but only rarely can the prisoners have found them comfortable. The number of inmates in any one gaol was never great. Most keepers must have reckoned their total complement at between a dozen and a hundred: three hundred was quite exceptional. Prisons in early medieval castles must have been very grim but those in fortifications of the gatehouse type were much better. Newgate prison, which until the fifteenth century used part of the London city gate of that name and some adjacent buildings, displayed the medieval genius for making new use of old structures. The Fleet, on the other hand, was a prison designed for that purpose and was surrounded by a moat, with the keeper's house

---

[13] *Calendar of Letter Books of the City of London, H*, p. 97.
[14] *Munimenta Gildhallae Londoniensis*, ed. H. T. Riley (Rolls Series, 1859–60), i, 275–6.

next door. Such extravagance was exceptional, although buildings of a modest type constructed solely to hold prisoners must have been fairly common. There was some effort made to segregate prisoners, both according to the crimes committed and to the misdoer's social status. In 1293 the chancellor of Oxford university asked the king to allow Oxford gaol to be enlarged by adding another floor to it,[15] then serious offenders might be assigned the ground floor, petty criminals the top, and women, so 'they might avoid sin', the other one. In towns, it was not uncommon for citizens charged with less serious offences to have their own area within the gaol. 'No citizen,' says a fifteenth-century Worcester custumal, 'be putt in comyn prisone but in oon of the chambours of the halle, save it be for felony or man's death or heinous trespass....'[16] Quite the most sophisticated system of segregation about which we have information was in Newgate. In February 1431, the London common council decreed that freemen and other honest persons were to live in chambers north of the hall, freewomen in those on the south, strangers and persons of inferior rank in what were termed 'less convenient chambers', while felons and those suspected of the most serious sorts of crime were to be kept underground and not allowed to mix or communicate with the other prisoners.[17] This last stipulation, and the exception made at Worcester about homicide and heinous trespass, suggest that medieval man was quite aware that the persistent or brutal offender could corrupt persons of less evil disposition and entice them into a life of crime. There is unfortunately nowhere a categorical statement to this effect. The lodging of those suspected or convicted of felony or other serious crime in darker and less pleasant parts of the prison, while those charged with lesser offences were put in lighter parts, was admittedly to some degree a calculated punishment, but it was not the sole reason. Within each different group of prisoners there were no obstacles to mixing. Solitary confinement was not unknown but it was rare, even for political prisoners.[18] Usually it was in a dungeon below ground or a chamber entered by a trap door from above. Here the prisoner might be in almost perpetual darkness. Not all prisons

[15] *Select Cases in the Court of the King's Bench, Edward I*, ed. G. O. Sayles (Selden Society, 55, 1936), ii, 151.

[16] *Borough Customs*, ed. M. Bateson (Selden Society, 1904–6), i, 66.

[17] *Calendar of Letter Books of the City of London, H*, pp. 124–7.

[18] See, for example, the royal account of the plotting while in captivity in 1499 in the Tower of London of the earl of Warwick: *Third Report of the Deputy Keeper of the Public Records* (London, 1843), app. ii, pp. 216–18.

were equipped with dungeons. Newgate had an inner prison, much feared, called 'Julianesboure', but the most secure place in the Fleet was Bolton's ward, which although men called it a dungeon was, according to one early seventeenth-century writer, 'noe more dungeon then any roome on the floore or ground of the Fleete, or of the aforesaid Wards, being without descent, onely somewhat stronger, retyred or private, and used for to sett in Stocks, bolts and Irons such as are unruly'.[19] It had 'convenient, light, chimney and place of ease.' In most prisons day-to-day existence must have been made very unpleasant by lack of heat and drinking water, the absence of fuel and fireplaces, and difficulty of access to a lavatory and the like; yet these conditions were not universal. In Newgate there were rooms with chimneys and privies, and what were referred to as pleasant chambers in the turrets of the gate. The roof of the gate was flat and was used by prisoners for recreation. Such generous provision of amenities was unlikely to be found in many other gaols.

Gaol life could be made reasonably pleasant if the prisoner had money, since keepers would provide almost anything for a price. The medieval prison functioned through a system of payments in return for services rendered: the purchaser was the prisoner, the entrepreneur the keeper. The first fee extracted was often at entry, though how a gaoler was entitled to it is not really clear. Perhaps it was a form of surety that the prisoner had been properly accused and arrested and would not escape, being forfeitable if he tried. It probably reflected the fact that the gaoler could himself suffer penalties if he was found guilty of imprisoning falsely or found responsible for the escape of a prisoner. Once incarcerated, the prisoner discovered he must pay the keeper for virtually all features of his new life. He must pay if he wished to be placed in a pleasanter area than custom dictated. He must pay for fuel for fires, for light, for food and drink, and for bedding. When he was acquitted by a court or when his term of imprisonment had expired, he must pay a fee in order to be released, for this was not automatic. Many gaolers demanded from their prisoner on commitment a fee for not fitting him with irons, and in the Fleet, at least, the newcomer gave the warden a bond for his good behaviour and to prove that he or his friends had money; then the prisoner paid the clerk who drew up the bond for that service and

[19] *The Oeconomy of the Fleete*, ed. A. Jessopp (Camden Society, New Series xxv, 1879), pp. 88–9.

for entering his name, with the reason for commitment, in the gaol register. He was also introduced to lesser officials like the porter and the chamberlain, to whom he also paid a fee. In many cases the sum of money demanded for a service was related to the social status of the prisoner and his ability to pay. Thus in the Fleet in the sixteenth century, to avoid being put in irons a hypothetical archbishop would have had to pay £10 but a yeoman only 13s. 4d. It has been calculated that at this time, while it would cost the yeoman about 19s. to enter the Fleet, an archbishop, duke, or duchess would be charged £13 5s.[20]

The king and those who possessed franchises, because they refused to pay proper wages to the keepers of gaols and would not appoint a proper staff of warders, were forced to sanction many of these payments while at the same time seeking to make them reasonable in amount. This must have stemmed from public outcry rather than penological conviction. In 1319 a Newgate gaoler, Edmund le Lorimer, was accused of several varieties of oppressive behaviour, including blackmail and torture, and was condemned by a jury which added that he took fees from prisoners on entry contrary to the statutes.[21] In 1444 fees were limited throughout the realm to a total of 4d. a head, and thereby were made quite legal. The keepers of the London and the borough gaols had been restricted in the amount they could take in fees from sometime earlier. In 1393 the London common council ruled that the keeper of Ludgate should not charge prisoners at all for their beds and lamps and that, except for those suspected of treason or felony, the discharge fee should be 4d. For removing prisoners' irons the gaoler was to receive what was called 'a reasonable *suurette*' of 100s. The regulations compiled for Newgate in 1431 said that the keeper might take a reasonable fee from freemen and freewomen, imprisoned on what were described as graver charges, when he removed their irons. The charge for supplying a prisoner with bed, sheet, and blankets was to be a penny a night; for a couch the cost was a penny a week.[22] Each prisoner was to pay 4d. towards the upkeep of the gaol lamps, and on discharge make a payment of 8d., if he was suspected of lesser crimes, or 2s., if he was accused of felony. Whether the keeper of a gaol should sell food to his prisoners was obviously a vexatious issue. The keeper of Ludgate was so per-

[20] *Ibid.*, p. 152.
[21] *Chronicles, Edward I and Edward II*, ed. W. Stubbs (Rolls Series, 1882–3), i, 285.
[22] *Speculum*, xviii (1943), 240.

mitted by the regulations of 1431, and in the Fleet the warden ran a kitchen and a taproom. In that gaol prisoners were not permitted, as sometimes they were elsewhere, to have food sent in from outside, except by special permission. It was the Fleet which offered an inclusive price for board by the week, the cost being decided not only by the amount and quality of the food but also by the prisoner's rank and where he took his meals. A person of noble status would pay £1 13s. 4d. a week, a knight 18s. 6d., gentlefolk 10s., and lesser persons 5s. For food this seems to have been the most expensive of gaols.[23] In other London prisons the cost might be only 3s. per week for gentlemen and 2s. for the lower classes of society, and in the provinces it might be less still.

For the prisoners who could not afford to purchase these services and comestibles the outlook was black. Approvers, prisoners of war, and hostages were often allowed wages by the king, and the bishops paid a small sum to the prisoners in their gaols, but those held on suspicion of trespass and felony had to pay themselves for what they needed. If they had no money or possessions to turn into funds they had to rely on the generosity of friends. Convicted debtors were in some ways luckier, since they were supposed to be provided with bread and water by their creditors. In practice their needs were often forgotten and they were left to starve with the other unfortunates. Deaths in gaol from starvation were undoubtedly numerous, though disease probably helped the victims on their way. In June 1295 Edward I ordered York gaol to be delivered by his justices because many persons in exigend, who had surrendered themselves there, had died, and the remaining prisoners were in danger of dying in the near future.[24] A petition to the king by the commons of Berkshire in 1315, complaining about the remoteness of the county gaol at Windsor, pointed out that the inhabitants were so 'weak' that the prisoners there could not be supported by their alms and frequently died before trial.[25] In July 1443 the king admitted that so great was the concourse of prisoners in the county gaol at Nottingham that they were oppressed by hunger, want, and other miseries, and could not 'abide there

---

[23] *University of Toronto Law Journal*, v (1943–4), 396. In Ipswich gaol the cost of food in 1465 was 1s. 8d. per week: *Paston Letters*, ed. J. Gairdner (Edinburgh, 1910), no. 505. In some London gaols, though not in the Fleet, the sale of food was stopped from time to time during the fifteenth century: apparently the sale of liquor was never interfered with.
[24] *Cal. Pat. Rolls, 1292–1301*, p. 161.
[25] *Cal. Pat. Rolls, 1313–1317*, p. 328.

long having no support and refreshment'.[26] The Windsor and Nottingham examples show that the only way prisoners without money might be able to survive was by alms. The Nottingham prisoners were given permission by Henry VI to supplement the alms, collected in that town on their behalf three days a week, by sending two men to beg in any other part of the Nottinghamshire and Derbyshire shrieval bailiwick. Some of the prisoners of Ludgate and Newgate were allowed to solicit for themselves and their fellows in the London streets, and it was men and women in Newgate who earned their food by performing tasks for the keeper and even by selling small articles they had manufactured. Occasionally prisoners received a life-saving windfall in the form of gifts made by private persons in their wills, or while still living. In 1407, for the use of prisoners in Bury St Edmunds' gaol, John Caxton left a cauldron weighing 34 pounds and a cooking pot; and Margaret Odiham, for the use of the poor prisoners there, bequeathed a lamp and a yearly gift of wood.[27] Bequests in the form of money or actual food became increasingly frequent towards the end of the fifteenth century, some benefactors even establishing trusts to dispense their charity. From time to time we hear of municipal authorities providing for the poor prisoners food which had been confiscated from its owner for some contravention of economic regulations. Thus in 1464 herrings, which had been packed in a manner adjudged fraudulent, were handed over to the Ludgate and Newgate inmates. The king himself might part with money if he was aware that the plight of those in gaol was desperate. In 1357 Edward III was petitioned to assign to the support of the prisoners in the Fleet a due called 'Godspence', paid in the port of London by merchants on hides and wools.[28] This, as its title suggests, had been allotted to the poor before, and indeed may have been originally intended for charitable purposes. The king agreed to the request and ordered it to be given to the warden: the money was to be divided among prisoners of proven poverty and any surplus was to provide for a chaplain in an oratory near the prison. There seems to be little evidence of alms being given by the ecclesiastical authorities to prisoners in lay gaols.

For most prisoners the period in gaol must have been a time of

[26] *Cal. Pat. Rolls, 1441–1446*, p. 192.
[27] M. D. Lobel, 'The Gaol of Bury St. Edmunds', *Proceedings of the Suffolk Institute of Archaeology*, xxi (1931–3), 203.
[28] *Cal. Pat. Rolls, 1354–1358*, pp. 515–16.

infinite boredom, punctuated by moments of great concern. They must have wondered if they had not been forgotten by the outside world and the authorities who had put them there. The fear probably assailed them that their money, or that of their friends, would soon be expended. For some prisoners the suffering was much greater than this. There were the pangs of actual starvation and there were the pains imposed on them by gaolers, as for example to coerce the prisoner into signing a deed or paying money. The imposition of physical duress could be incidental, even accidental, as when a prisoner was restrained to prevent escape or from doing violence. For the latter purpose stocks were much used both inside and outside the prison buildings. A long spell in the stocks could do grievous harm. In 1384 the keeper of Sarum gaol was tried in the king's bench for keeping prisoners in the stocks for so long in winter that their feet rotted off.[29] Something similar must have occurred in the case of a suspected sheep stealer, William de Lodne, who was imprisoned in the Tolhouse, Norwich, in Edward I's reign. A fellow prisoner, while effecting his own escape, carried William, whose feet had putrefied by the duress of prison, to a place of sanctuary on his back.[30] If there was danger of the prisoners escaping there was no objection to the use of irons. The gaol keepers used this laxity for their own profit. For the purpose of restraint in general, or even perhaps to make prisoners think again about paying a fee in order to be excused them, various forms of chains and iron attachments were used. In 1350 the king's bench had at least 21 pairs of fetters available for use, and a fifteenth-century inventory of the gaol of Bury St Edmunds, which served both the abbot and the town, shows, in addition to 6 pairs of stocks, 46 pairs of fetters, 7 collars with chains and staples, and 4 pairs of manacles.[31] Examples of duress inflicted deliberately in order to coerce were less frequent but not rare. In 1327, in Bury St Edmunds gaol, Robert Cok was hung up by the arms by the gaoler and the coroner of the liberty until he had promised to pay them half a mark.[32] In 1319 Edmund le Lorimer, the Newgate

---

[29] B. H. Putnam, *Proceedings before the Justices of the Peace, Edward III to Richard III* (London, 1938), pp. 398–9.
[30] W. Rye, 'Notes on Crime and Accident in Norfolk temp. Edward I', *Archaeological Review*, II, ii (1888), 210.
[31] *Select Cases in the Court of the King's Bench, Edward III*, ed. G. O. Sayles (Selden Society, 82, 1965), p. xliv; *Proceedings of the Suffolk Institute of Archaeology, ubi supra*, 203.
[32] *Ibid.* It is sometimes difficult to tell how deliberately intended physical

gaoler, was accused before a commission of enquiry of, among other things, loading prisoners with iron and torturing them in order to obtain money. In 1370 a clerk named John Baumburgh claimed that while in Newgate a sergeant-at-mace had caused him to be put in fetters, made sport of, and tortured for five weeks. An inquest at York in February 1328 found that John Brumpton had been put in the castle gaol there, stripped to his shirt and breeches, and fastened to the bare ground by two pairs of irons for three days, 'until by the duress of prison and in order to save his life' he agreed to enfeoff Hugh Despenser the younger of a messuage, a mill, a carrucate of land, and other tenements in Shipton, Oxfordshire. These cases were typical.[33] The duress, because it was illegal, was of the *ad hoc* variety, there being in England, as we have seen, no proper provision for torture or of devices constructed specifically to inflict it.

The king and the community at large knew well enough of the evils of the prison system, and exhortatory statutes were passed to curb the coercive practices of the keepers. Unfortunately there was no proper surveillance system instituted at a national level to make sure the law was obeyed. There was, in London, something which resembled periodic inspection, but it was intended to reveal extortion in regard to the supplying of food and comforts and the distribution of alms, rather than the deliberate application of physical duress. The Newgate ordinances of 1431, which also applied to the two Counters, commanded that two London parish priests and two commoners, in addition to enquiring if alms were being distributed fairly and inspecting the water supply, should hear prisoners' complaints and find out why each was detained.[34] Since the inspectors were to be elected annually, prison visitations must have been intended to take place with the same frequency, although we only have definite reference to those of 1471, 1483, 1487, and 1488. Just occasionally there seems to have been another, more important, sort of inspection in London. In 1448 two aldermen were ordered by the London common council to visit Newgate, Ludgate, and the Counters, and report on the con-

---

[33] *Speculum*, xviii (1943), 236–7, 238n; *William Salt Archaeological Society*, xiv (1893), 41.

[34] *Calendar of Letter Books of the City of London, K*, pp. 124–7.

---

suffering was. For example, in 1315 Richard Lambert, a merchant of Lynn, was thrown by the sheriff into the depths of Wisbech gaol, among thieves, where by toads and other venomous vermin he was so inhumanly gnawn that his life was despaired of: so says an entry in *Cal. Pat. Rolls, 1313–1317*, p. 318.

duct of the gaolers. Perhaps it was a result of this visit that in 1449 William Arnold, the Newgate keeper, was imprisoned for violating a female prisoner. Few prisoners can have been without the hope of escape. In some gaols there were opportunities for the inmate to renew his acquaintance with the outside world from time to time, a privilege which must have been highly prized. Some prisoners were allowed to leave the gaol so as to beg on their fellows' behalf, and others were let out without bail in order to attend mass at churches nearby. Debtors imprisoned in the Fleet possessed, by the end of the thirteenth century, the privilege of going out and attending to their business accompanied by a baston or keeper. For this they paid a fee of 10*d.* per half day. In 1377 it was reported that debtors were away from the prison for days at a time. A statute of that year therefore decreed they should not be allowed out without the consent of those whose suits had got them committed to gaol, and that if they were, then action should lie against the warden of the prison. Allowing prisoners to be at large without giving bail was not a practice associated solely with the Fleet. Margaret, the widow of Henry Higham, appealed Alan Osmund of her husband's death and he was put in the custody of the deputy of the marshal of the king's bench. On 3 July 1293 she saw Alan in the Friars Preachers' church in London and at another time in St Pauls, 'as if he were someone accused of no crime [at all] and rambling and wandering about streets, squares, and inns of London, without irons'.[35] In the petition to the king by the commons of Berkshire in 1315 it was said that persons indicted of felony and sent to the gaol of Windsor were permitted to go forth from the prison where they wanted, and as a result the men of those parts feared to indict anyone. In 1342 an investigation showed that ninety-one indicted persons who were supposed to be confined in the marshalsea of the king's bench were at large.[36] We may conclude that many of these absences, although not based on bail proper, were allowed by gaolers or their subordinates under a system of sureties and agreements operated by themselves.

Actual escape from gaol was also fairly common. It was often achieved with no great difficulty. We hear of tunnels and of breaches made easily in stone walls. References made to the need for the repair of the gaol fabric suggest it was the maintenance of the structure

---

[35] *Select Cases in the Court of the King's Bench, Edward I*, i, 149.
[36] *Select Cases in the Court of the King's Bench, Edward III* (1965), p. xliv.

which was defective rather than the vigilance of the keeper. Perhaps there was no regular inspection by the keeper of the prisoners and their quarters, although this was not true at Newgate, where a form of check-up took place every night. The big break-outs occurred mostly at times of popular insurrection, such as 1325, 1381, and 1450, when London gaols were opened from the outside rather than from within. Such assistance was available at other times as well. In 1363 the king had cause to complain that his prisons at Stamford and Sleaford had been broken into by evil-doers and a number of felons released.[37] Prisoners of state were perhaps more likely to escape than most. They were often possessed of wealth and high rank and could count on friends on the outside as well as sympathizers within. The relative ease of their confinement usually allowed them ample time and opportunity to plot together.

Keepers of gaols feared all escapes. This was not simply on account of the loss of prisoners' fees but rather because they knew the king would punish them for what he considered was their negligence. If an escape seemed particularly culpable a special commission would be ordered to investigate and punish. If the negligence was less heinous then, after 1357, the justices of the peace would probably be expected to enquire, as would justices of gaol delivery: in the thirteenth century it had been one of the standard tasks set the eyre. When enquiry showed the gaoler had indeed been neglectful, then he would probably be fined and he might lose his office: if he served in a liberty then the franchise might be lost. If the escapee had been an approver, or other prisoner of great value, the gaoler might be imprisoned. The fines imposed varied from small to very large. In 1475 the sheriffs of London and Middlesex were threatened with having to pay 6,000 marks if a man escaped, and gaolers were faced on several occasions with having to pay sums of several hundreds of pounds if a particular prisoner or group of prisoners broke out. When clerks escaped from ecclesiastical prisons the bishop was treated by the king with a similar severity, fines of £100 being imposed and collected. Escape, if it was not successful, could bring disaster for the prisoner. Until the middle of the fourteenth century a prisoner who was originally suspect of felony might, on recapture, be executed without proper trial. This was because by his flight the man was held to have admitted his guilt. In 1423 the rule was extended to treason: suspect traitors who escaped were guilty of treason. The person accused of trespass who escaped

<hr>

[37] *Cal. Pat. Rolls, 1361–1364*, p. 450.

was thus guilty of trespass but no more: if retaken he might suffer a beating but there was no serious danger to life or limb.

The need to clarify the laws relating to escape from prison was met only at the beginning of the sixteenth century. The so-called statute of escapes (19 Henry VII c. 10) suggested that many escapes were connived at by gaolers in return for bribes, the gaoler reckoning the fine he must pay to the king would be less than the bribe. Therefore, in future, fines were to match the heinousness of the escaper's suspected offence, the degree of connivance or negligence on the part of the gaoler being ignored.[38] Ability to prevent escapes was to be all-important. Gaolers therefore must have been tempted to ensure that the prisoner who was suspected of a serious crime was allowed as little freedom in his movements within the gaol as could be contrived.

Whatever the feelings of the king, there was a popular notion that no prisoner ought to languish long in gaol before being put on trial. The government acquiesced: gaols were delivered by justices according to a proper plan and usually twice a year. The judges who most frequently performed the task were, from the end of the thirteenth century, justices of assize, although a substantial part of the work was also done by king's bench judges and by special commissions. The justices of assize tried the prisoners in local gaols after they had held their assize sessions and often delivered both the prisons of the king and those of the franchises.[39] From 1394 justices of the peace were allowed on commissions of gaol delivery provided they had had legal training, but coroners and sheriffs were permanently excluded. Very probably the justices of the peace had been delivering prisoners for half a century or more without specific authorization. There were occasions when the king wanted the immediate delivery of a single or a group of important prisoners. Those who were put on the special commission in such circumstances might include magnates, chief citizens, and royal servants, not merely judges of the two benches or lawyers. One hindrance to the smooth operation of gaol delivery was the reluctance of jurors to attend sessions which were held within the prison itself. What they feared was not mutiny, though this was not unknown, as the seizure of Newgate by its inmates in 1456 testifies, but gaol disease. The sessions had either to be held in a hall nearby or the jurors to be provided with free wine.

[38] For escape from gaol in general see R. B. Pugh, *Imprisonment in Medieval England*, pp. 218–54.
[39] Despite some opposition from the lords of the liberties in question.

Life in English prisons in the later middle ages could be hard but it could also, as we have seen, be quite comfortable providing the prisoner was not distressed by the deprivations or by the company of his fellows. John Paston, who was confined in the Fleet on three different occasions, was visited at one time by his wife Margaret and confided to her that 'the Flet is a fayir preson'. All he had to complain about was the lack of liberty, 'for ye must nedys aper when ye wer callyd', and the personal qualities of some of his fellow prisoners. 'I have non fansey with some of the felechipp', he was moved to comment. Much more common than John Paston's relative comfort must have been the plight of a correspondent of the Pastons, John Perse, who begged that Richard Kowven should 'sende . . . the money that is betwen hym and me in all the haste that he maye, for in goode feythe I hadde never more neede for to have help of my goode as I have at this tyme for, Godwot, it stonde right straunge with me; for the false chayler that kepeth me entreteth me worse thanne it weere a dogge, for I am feterid worse thanne ever I whas and manacled in the hands by the daye and nyght for he is a feerde of me for brekyng a weye'.[40] However unhappy his plight, there were two things in which any prisoner in an English gaol in the fourteenth or fifteenth century could find consolation. One was the knowledge that he would not be led straight to execution without appearing in court;[41] the other was that his death was not likely to go unnoticed. Even if he was the most hapless of wretches his demise must be reported to the coroner.

That all criminals should be punished was an axiom which few men denied. Most medieval Englishmen would have agreed that on conviction a misdoer should be punished as quickly as possible and that the punishment should be so arranged that all should notice it. This was probably why a term of imprisonment, although it was inflicted more and more as time went by, was not the predominant

---

[40] *Paston Letters*, ed. Gairdner, nos. 363, 693.

[41] No doubt there were a few cases but the only contemporary reference I have noticed is in *Polychronicon Ranulphi Higden*, ix, 49. The chronicler says that in September 1384 nineteen prisoners were let out of Newgate by a royal valet, whom they had robbed, to 'Fouleoke, in Kent and beheaded as notorious thieves. Some of the prisoners complained bitterly they were being put to death without proper legal process and judgment. No doubt King Richard, on whose order the executions were performed, would have argued that the sheer notoriety of the criminals' misdeeds did away with the need for proper trial. However, such notoriety, as Plucknett pointed out, only worked an instant conviction before the mid-fourteenth century and it did not do away with the need for a trial.

penalty for law-breaking but used only when circumstances would permit no other type. The immediacy and the overtness of most punishment suggest that the intention of the king, above all else, was to deter would-be malefactors. The idea of retribution was probably more in the minds of the offenders' victims and their friends than in those of the king and his justices, although they had by no means discarded it. No contemporary writer bothered to describe the philosophy of punishment which prevailed at the time. There is an almost total lack of comment on the subject, extending from the writers of legal treatises of the thirteenth century to the Tudor chroniclers. We may surmise that the church, especially the ecclesiastical doctrine of penance, must have had an influence on men's minds but actual proof and examples of this are most difficult to discover.

Judged against the Norman and Tudor periods, the English later middle ages was a time when penal brutality was uncommon. The commons of parliament might petition repeatedly about the low level of public order, but their complaints and suggestions concerned the powers of justices, the corruption of officials, the evils of maintenance and livery, and the abuse of pardons and benefit of clergy. Only rarely did they suggest that better public order could be attained through the use of more terrifying punishments. The king also, whatever his personal opinions, hardly ever in act, ordinance, or writ showed that it was the purpose of punishment to terrify. Indeed, the instructions of Edward II to his judges in July 1316, ordering such punishment on the men of Yarmouth and the Cinque Ports who persisted in their quarrel that should cause terror to them and to anyone else who ignored his proclamations, seem to have been unique. [42] By the mid-thirteenth century the old Norman punishments of mutilation had become neglected. In thirteenth-century legal treatises there occur, it is true, references to castration and blinding in connection with both rape and felonious wounding, but in practice, like lip removal, they had probably ceased by the turn of the century. A thief found guilty of petty larceny might still, in the middle of the thirteenth century, lose an ear or a thumb but even this practice was in decline. The writer who could easily have told us about physical punishment two centuries later, Sir John Fortescue, mentions only hanging. If there were, in fact, no other penalties of the body in the fifteenth century, they were nonetheless most common again under the Tudors. Holinshed talks with some relish about branding, the

---

[42] *Cal. Pat. Rolls, 1313–1317*, p. 520.

cutting off of ears and hands, and execution by means of boiling, and laments the penance and ducking of harlots as being woefully light. This is a far cry from an age when, according to one writer, 'conviction for trespass means financial penalties usually; occasionally punishment in the stocks; conviction for felony means hanging'.[43]

In the fourteenth and fifteenth centuries punishments of a physical nature which could be inflicted under the common law and outside liberties and particular jurisdictions were very limited in number. Apart from imprisonment, *peine forte et dure*, and execution, they seem to have been confined to branding, the cutting off of a hand for certain offences committed actually in the king's courts, the use of the stocks and, most rarely, of the pillory. Stocks, which as we have seen were part of the equipment of every gaol, were supposed to have been set up in every village not having them, under the statute of labourers of 1351. They were intended to serve as an open gaol for runaway servants and labourers, securing them until they were claimed by their masters. The display of the prisoners in the village or town would ensure that information of their whereabouts reached the ears of their employer. A period in the stocks was intended only as a prelude to trial later on, but some of those who sat in them did not survive to be tried, whereas others lost a foot as a result of the interference with the circulation of the blood. Branding, like the general provision of stocks, seems to have originated in, or at least been revived by, the labour legislation of the mid-fourteenth century. The justices were instructed to brand recalcitrant labourers with the letter 'F' but, according to B. H. Putnam, there is no evidence that they made use of this authority.[44] The cutting off of a limb was a very infrequent judicial penalty and reserved for those who displayed open contempt for the king's court by attempting to stop its proper functioning. On 27 June 1345 Richard Carlisle of London and Alan of Cambridge, both tailors, threatened the members of a jury which had just delivered its verdict and then pursued them across the Thames and wounded and ill-treated them.[45] Richard was arrested, confessed, and because it seemed to the chancellor and the judges of the benches that the trespass was a most grievous contempt of the king and his crown and in prejudice and disparagement of the law of the land, he was

---

[43] R. Holinshed, *Chronicles of England, Scotland and Ireland*, i, 311; Putnam, *Proceedings before the Justices of the Peace, Edward III to Richard III*, p. cv.
[44] *Yorkshire Sessions of the Peace, 1361–1364*, ed. B. H. Putnam, p. xxxvii.
[45] *Select Cases in the Court of the King's Bench, Edward III* (1965), p. 41.

sentenced to life imprisonment and the loss of his right hand. The second penalty, however, was to be postponed until the king's will had been ascertained, an indication that Richard was probably excused that part of the judgment. In 1461 this form of punishment was actually carried out in Cheapside on John Davy. He had struck a man before the judges at Westminster 'wherefore', said Stow, 'the king commanded him to have the law in example to others'.[46] Exactly how punishments involving dismemberment were carried out in medieval times is unknown, but arrangements made in June 1541 for the amputation of the hand of Sir Edmund Knevet, who was found guilty of striking a servant of the earl of Surrey in the king's tennis court, gives us some indication. Holinshed tells us that when the sentence had been given there was 'called to doo the execution, first the sergeant surgion with his instruments apperteining to his office: the sergeant of the woodyard with the mallet and a blocke whereupon the hand should lie: the maister cooke for the king with the knife: the sergeant of the larder to set the knife right on the ioint: the sergeant ferrer with the searing irons to sear the veines', and several other servants of the royal household.[47] There were no statutes to limit the type of physical punishment awarded by the king and his judges, nor did the jury have any say in the matter: the jurors merely returned a verdict of guilty or not guilty. In theory only custom limited the justices' choice of penalty in most cases, yet the late medieval kings do not seem to have been guilty of seeking to increase the severity of physical punishment or to extend its application, not under the common law at least. The single parliamentary act of the period which touched on maiming, the cutting out of tongues, referred not to its use by the king but by criminals. Even the greatest of crimes, treason, was unregulated in this respect, although defined by statute in most other ways.

To say that physical punishments, apart from execution, were rare in this period is untrue. They were few enough over the countryside as a whole, but in a number of towns they were still flourishing in the fifteenth century. In legal matters, sheltering behind the formulae of early custumals, the townsmen showed a most marked conservatism, and the penalties which their courts had the power to inflict were frequently intended to cause not only pain but the greatest amount of

[46] J. Stow, *Annales or A Generall Chronicle of England* (London, 1631), p. 416.
[47] Holinshed, *Chronicles of England, Scotland and Ireland*, iii, 820. See also *Statutes of the Realm*, iii, 847.

embarrassment and public ridicule. The aim was to warn the populace against the illicit practices of the accused, and often to make him so well known by some disfigurement inflicted by the authorities that he would be unable to perpetrate the same offence a second time. By modern standards most of the physical penalties were barbaric. Abscission, though not common, was by no means forgotten. At Portsmouth, for example, the customs of the borough allowed a thief to be 'scalde and his eyen put owte': if the culprit was a woman 'her tetys shall be kyt of at Chalcrosse'.[48] The use of stocks in towns was not common but the pillory was. In London, men were put in the pillory for scores of different offences, a great proportion of which concerned deceitful trading practices: for example selling sacks of coal deficient in weight, or oats which were good at the top but bad below, or fraudulently raising the price of corn. A baker who appeared in the king's bench in the reign of Edward I had been so frequently detected in this sort of malpractice that he had won for himself the nickname 'Pillory'.[49] Offences punishable by the pillory not connected with trade were also numerous and included such deceptions as pretending to be a king's officer, begging under false pretences, playing with false dice, the use of magic, and the forgery of letters, bonds, and deeds. Those who gave insults to civic dignitaries, or propagated lies and scandal, were often punished in the same way. A man found guilty of the latter offence in the reign of Edward III was imprisoned for a year and a day and compelled every three months to stand for three hours in the pillory with a whetstone hanging round his neck. It was recognized that prolonged exposure in the pillory could be fatal. In November 1380 John Bernard of Bishops Hatfield, Hertfordshire, a fraudulent charcoal seller, was sentenced to the pillory and to have the sacks used burned under his nose. Since he was an old man and there was doubt as to whether the judgment could be implemented without causing his death, the sheriff was told that John should only remain in the pillory until the sacks had been consumed.[50] The burning of false goods before a seller in this way was commonplace and reckoned most appropriate. Similar to the pillory was the thewe, which was used in London as a punishment mainly for whores and brothel keepers. From 1384 male and female

[48] *Borough Customs*, i, 77.
[49] *Select Cases in the Court of the King's Bench, Edward I*, iii, cvi.
[50] *Memorials of London and Life in the Thirteenth, Fourteenth and Fifteenth Centuries*, p. 446.

keepers of brothels on conviction had their hair cropped and were led to the thewe, accompanied by musicians. Prostitutes were treated similarly but carried a cloth hood over their head on the journey and a white wand in their hand. Procurers and procuresses were taken to the thewe carrying a distaff dressed with flax, and remained there at the discretion of the mayor and aldermen.

The pillory, if not the thewe, was known in other towns besides London, although references are far less frequent. A law of Dover stated that any cut-purse captured with the *mainour* was to be led before the mayor and bailiff, and if he could not offer a reasonable excuse be set in the pillory 'and all the peple that will come ther may do hym vylonye; and after that they may cut off hys one ere'. A law of Portsmouth was of a similar brutality. A person convicted of taking goods worth less than a shilling was to have an ear nailed to the pillory, 'he to chese whether he woll kytt [i.e. cut] or tere it of'. Similar to the punishment of the pillory and the thewe was that of the cucking stool. This was a form of chair, and it was set either at the culprit's own door or in a public place. It was used mainly for dealing with scolds, that is, nagging women. The laws of Hereford said that the scold must stand with bare feet and her hair let down 'during such time as [she] may be seen by all passers-by upon the road'.[51] Then she would be set free after paying a fine. A similar form of punishment, the ducking stool, seems to have been post-medieval in its origin. Although exhibitory punishments of the pillory type were largely inflicted according to urban custom, the king occasionally made use of them himself. This was done not after conviction under the common law but on the orders of his council. In June 1438 John Forde, a London mercer, who had admitted to illegally selling wool to an alien, was sent in a cart from Westminster to the Tower.[52] Where the citizens were congregated in the greatest numbers along the route his guards stopped and proclaimed his confession. From the Tower he was taken to Cornhill, set in the pillory for an hour, and then carted back to prison. It seems to have been on the orders of the council similarly that the sorcerer, Roger Bolingbroke, on 25 July 1441, was exhibited with all his magical accoutrements around him in the churchyard of St Pauls.[53]

Borough individuality in matters of physical punishment extended even as far as methods of execution. Often the geographical location

---

[51] *Borough Customs*, i, 79–80.   [52] *Cal. Close Rolls, 1435–1441*, p. 221.
[53] Stow, *Annales*, p. 381.

of the town and the nature of the crime appear to have played a part in determining the way the penalty was inflicted. The customs of Sandwich decreed that all who were condemned for homicide should be buried alive in a place allotted for this purpose at Sandown, called the 'thiefdowns'. At Pevensey any man 'of the franchise' found guilty on a plea of the crown was to be taken to the town bridge at high tide and thrown over into the harbour. At Portsmouth any man who slew another was burned.[54] At Halifax execution of thieves was by means of the original guillotine. An axe, which had been fastened with iron into a piece of wood, was drawn up by a rope to the top of a frame. 'The head blocke', says Holinshed, 'wherein the ax is fastened dooth fall downe with such a violence that if the necke of the transgressor were so big as that of a bull it should be cut in sunder at a stroke and roll from the leadie by an huge distance'.[55] If the offender had stolen a beast, the rope attached to the pin retaining the axe aloft was tied to the animal, which by moving executed its own abductor. The customs of Hastings, as redacted in the reign of Edward IV, suggest that towns were fully conscious of how much their methods of execution differed from the standard practice and that furthermore they had begun to see the need for conforming. In olden times, so the editor of the customs noted, those condemned of felony were thrown over the cliff at Stortisdale but now and hereafter the town would use 'suche execucyon as ys accordyng to the commune lawe of Inglonde as hangyng on galowes'.[56] The English kings were disinclined to allow peculiar methods of execution if the town customs did not warrant it. In June 1390 the mayor of Dartmouth had to purchase a pardon for burning to death a condemned poisoner, Denys Beaumont, without the express commission of the king.[57]

Unless the offence was committed in a town with its own peculiar death penalty, those who were convicted of felony could expect that very soon after the verdict they would be executed by hanging. An oak tree at a cross-roads was the customary gallows. In London, by the fifteenth century, the much used elms at Tyburn may have been replaced by the first scaffold, made from a beam placed across the branches of two trees. This beam against which, so it is said, was set a ladder draped with a black cloth, enabled as many as ten men to be hanged at once. Although references to executioners' methods are

[54] *Borough Customs*, i, 74.
[55] Holinshed, *Chronicles of England, Scotland and Ireland*, i, 312.
[56] *Borough Customs*, i, 76.   [57] *Cal. Pat. Rolls, 1388–1392*, p. 253.

few, it seems that the condemned men and women stood on a platform like a bench or cart, which was then pulled away to leave them swinging by the neck. Hanging by being hauled from the ground by a team of men was rare enough to excite comment. There is little evidence before the sixteenth century of men being hanged alive in chains, or of the practice, mentioned by Holinshed, of those who were convicted of manslaughter having their right hand cut off prior to execution. The sheriff or his officer was always in attendance at the gallows to see the condemned men die. While the tithing groups existed, the 'headboroughs' of the locality were supposed to wait at the gallows until those executed had breathed their last. The job of executioner was not one which men coveted. This is suggested by the rule in some borough custumals, as for example of Romney, that the successful appellant should be responsible for finding a hangman; if he could not, then he must put the convicted felon to death himself. If he refused to do this, he was to be placed in prison with the felon until he changed his mind. In the counties of Caernarvon, Merioneth, and Anglesey, the hanging and execution of felons was the business of the king's bondsmen, but by the mid-fifteenth century they found the duty so obnoxious that some of them decided to flee to other parts of England.[58]

For the condemned man, even as he trod his way to the gallows, some hope of survival still remained. Escapes were effected up to the very last moment, usually through the interference of friars. Late in 1317 John, son of William Tynhide, who had been convicted in Wiltshire before the justices of oyer and terminer and sentenced to be hanged, was set free from the bailiffs by a number of Friars Preachers when being led bound through Fisherton to his execution.[59] The condemned man might also escape death in another way. This was through the lack of expertise on the part of the hangman. A fair number of hanged men and women revived on being cut down or when being buried. This was because medieval hanging was intended to strangle the victim, rather than break his neck. One man, whom the chronicler Knighton calls Walter Wynkeburne, was hanged in 1363 on the Leicester gallows, but revived when being carried to the cemetery for burial.[60] Sometimes the revival occurred a good many hours

---

[58] *Borough Customs*, i, 74; *Cal. Pat. Rolls, 1441–1446*, p. 426.
[59] *Cal. Pat. Rolls, 1317–1321*, p. 69.
[60] *Chronicon Henrici Knighton*, ed. J. R. Lumby (Rolls Series, 1889–95), ii, 119.

after the condemned person had first mounted the gallows. In 1264 Juetta de Balsham was hanged for receiving thieves. According to the king's records she continued to hang from the ninth hour on Monday until sunrise next morn, yet she lived. Those who survived in this remarkable way usually received a pardon when testimony about the 'miracle' reached the king, but it was by no means automatic. Wynkeburne was kept in a church by the clergy so he should not be seized by the lay authority and hanged a second time. The same year (1363), Adam Trop was hanged in Dublin for felony and, after being cut down as dead by the sheriff's men, was carried on a bier to a church for burial. The next morning he rose from the bier on which he had been left, broke open the doors of the church, and departed. However, in this case the sheriff pursued him to county Kildare, brought him back, and hanged him again, this time successfully.[61]

The only capital offence under the common law which did not have solely hanging as its physical penalty was treason. Both for high treason, that is treason committed against the king, his family, and certain high officials when performing their office, and for petty treason, which was the murder of one's master or mistress, offenders were dragged to the place of execution on a hurdle. Men were then hanged but women were burned. The hurdle, Maitland suggested, was intended to give the executioner a living body. In the earlier middle ages the condemned person was probably tied by legs or arms to the horse's tail directly, with nothing to protect his body from the ground. In one instance, which seems unique, there is reference to the traitor being accompanied on his last journey by tormentors dressed like devils.[62] From at least as early as the mid-thirteenth century victims were sometimes disembowelled after hanging and later the body dismembered. The traitor was not necessarily dead when the executioner began the evisceration, since the hanging lasted for only a minute or so. There might be explicit instructions from the king saying the victim should be let down alive, and the descriptions of the chroniclers confirm that this was in fact done. Waurin tells the macabre story of how, in 1400, when the executioner was busy burning Sir Thomas Blount's entrails before his eyes, someone asked the knight if he would like a drink and received the reply that he would,

---

[61] *Cal. Pat. Rolls, 1258–1266*, p. 342; *ibid., 1361–1364*, p. 430.
[62] *Bartholomaei de Cotton Historia Anglicana*, ed. H. R. Luard (Rolls Series, 1859), p. 439.

but he had nowhere to put it.[63] Finally the corpses of dead traitors were cut into quarters, tarred, and dispatched for display on gates, gallows, and pillories in towns which had been connected with the victims and their schemes.

By the sixteenth century at least, English criminals had a reputation for going to their executions with great composure. Holinshed held that 'our condemned persons doo go so cheerefullie to their deths for our nation is free, stout, hautie, prodigall of life and bloud'. Sir Thomas Smith thought the same: 'In no place shall you see malefactors goe more constantly, more assuredly, and with less lamentation to death than in England.'[64] There are no references to felons and traitors being allowed to make a lengthy speech from under the gallows, although confessions were quite in order. Jack Straw, the peasant leader of 1381, is reported as having confessed his crimes in return for the saying of masses for his soul. In 1400 John Holland earl of Huntingdon, admitted a degree of treason to the crowds of people gathered to watch his execution, saying that he had sinned by allowing himself to become embroiled in the machinations of certain lords and not protecting his king. He asked for forgiveness of the wrong he had done them and for their prayers.[65] No convincing argument can be made out of the silence on the part of the chroniclers, but it does seem that most condemned felons and traitors made no public confession, if they were allowed to address the crowds at all. Those executed in England in the fourteenth and fifteenth centuries seem not to have realized, or been instructed about, the benefits to be gained by a declaration from the scaffold that they had sinned against God and the king, had been judged by the law of the land, and were content to accept the penalty. This realization seems to have owed its appearance to the adroit statesmanship of the Tudor kings, who used executions as a major method of advertising the merits and rewards of loyalty to the sovereign.[66] There was always the chance that the condemned man would be pardoned at the foot of the gallows, which was one reason, or so it has been argued, for

[63] *Recueil des Croniques par Jehan de Waurin* (Rolls Series, 1864–91), ed. W. and E. L. C. P. Hardy, ii, 41–3.
[64] Holinshed, *Chronicles of England, Scotland and Ireland*, i, 310; T. Smith, *De Republica Anglorum*, ed. L. Alston (Cambridge, 1906), p. 105.
[65] *Johannis de Trokelowe et Henrici de Blaneforde Chronica et Annales*, ed. H. T. Riley (Rolls Series, 1865), p. 328.
[66] See L. B. Smith, 'English Treason Trials and Confessions in the Sixteenth Century', *Journal of the History of Ideas*, xv (1954), 471–98.

the great crowds which thronged to see any execution. In 1447 five members of the household of Humphrey, duke of Gloucester, were on the scaffold, condemned for petty treason, when the writ was delivered giving them pardon. Sometimes the pardon was delivered, quite deliberately, when matters had gone a stage further. Some traitors were drawn, hanged, cut quickly down, and marked on the body with a knife as if disembowelling was to follow and then pardoned.[67] The punishment of the criminal found guilty of treason or felony did not finish with his death. If his crime had been felony or petty treason, his lands escheated, after the king's wasting of them for a year and a day, to his immediate lord. In this case the king received eventually only the offender's chattels. If, on the other hand, the crime was high treason, the king obtained by forfeiture everything the convicted man possessed. It was of course essential that the criminal be convicted according to proper judicial process. If a misdoer, on being taken in flight, was executed summarily by his captors, none of his possessions went to the king.[68] This virtually assured all criminals of a proper trial.

Medieval English kings delighted in being known for their maintenance of law and order, but equally they delighted in the profits which the administration of justice provided. Fines were common even in Anglo-Saxon times and from the thirteenth century the king's courts committed criminals to prison intending the imprisonment might be commuted to a fine. If a man could pay, so much the better for him; if not he would languish a year or two more in gaol. The fine was really the result of a bargain for release struck between the king and the offender. The sentence was not 'pay a fine or suffer imprisonment' but 'go to prison and then if you can offer the king sufficient financial inducement you may obtain release'. The deal was made quite easily, since the king was wont to be satisfied with a fairly small amount of money. The size of the amercement was usually decided not by the king or his justices but by the accused person's peers, perhaps the jurors of presentment or the more substantial men of the hundred. The only exception was in the later fourteenth century, when the justices were given power of punishing labourers with

[67] *Cal. Pat. Rolls, 1446–1452*, p. 68; *ibid., 1441–1446*, p. 278.
[68] Thus in February 1352, some time after Adam Peshale had been beheaded by men sent to bring him before the council, Edward III felt obliged to order that since Adam had not been convicted of any felony his lands and issues should go to his son and heir Richard: *Calendar of Close Rolls, 1349–1354* (Record Commission), p. 406.

fines, and in the fifteenth century, when justices of the peace were given summary powers, including the ability to fine, in order to deal with forcible entries and riots. The sum 'afeered', as the process of assessment was called, was usually very reasonable, being often no more than two marks. To all appearances it was graded to what the offender's position in society allowed him to pay. There are a number of cases recorded in which the justices expressly stated they had taken the poverty of the prisoner into consideration. There were also examples of justices who admitted they were influenced in the bargain they made with the prisoner by the amount of time he had already spent in prison.[69] Furthermore the king, through the exchequer, allowed for fines of any real size to be paid off in instalments at so much per year. Lord John Fitzwalter took ten years to pay off his. Fines, and they were heavy ones, were only 'imposed', that is to say fixed, by the king, in the case of delinquent officials. These were often men who had benefited financially from their abuse of office or had particularly annoyed the king. Thus, early in the reign of Henry V, Simon Kampe, the lieutenant of the constable of the Tower, was condemned by a judgment in the king's court to a fine of 1,000 marks.[70] There were a few occasions when the king resolutely refused to be satisfied with fining offenders. This might happen when a region had been particularly lawless or in open insurrection. On these occasions the commissions to the justices would state that fining was not permissible. Instances of this are few, and in any case the instructions were sometimes countermanded after sufficient example had been made of the misdoers by more draconian methods of punishment. There can be little doubt that when he tempered justice with mercy the king was frequently being influenced by mercenary motives. Fines provided him with a steady and sizeable annual income, one which has been calculated as amounting to a sixth of his revenue in the mid-thirteenth century.[71]

Between the payment of a fine and the purchase of a pardon there was little difference. Fines might be agreed on and paid even before arraignment, but pardons similarly were on occasion purchased in anticipation of future difficulties. Sometimes, as in the purchasing of

[69] *Crown Pleas of the Wiltshire Eyre, 1249*, pp. 106–7, 113–14; Pollock and Maitland, *History of English Law*, ii, 517; Putnam, *Proceedings before the Justices of the Peace, Edward III to Richard III*, pp. xxi, xxv; *Select Pleas of the Forest*, ed. G. J. Turner (Selden Society, xiii, 1901), pp. 29, 30.
[70] *Cal. Pat. Rolls, 1413–1416*, p. 191.
[71] *Crown Pleas of the Wiltshire Eyre, 1249*, p. 112.

land, it was cheaper to break rules and use a pardon than to follow proper legal procedure. Pardons were granted not by justices or parliament but by the king himself, it being a prerogative he retained largely unimpaired in this period. For example, in March 1383 John Awedyn of Essex was pardoned by Richard II of all his felonies and treasons despite the fact that, as one of the peasant leaders in the recent rebellion, he had been excepted from pardon by several parliaments.[72] When in the fifteenth century men were convicted of felonies, treasons, and other offences by act of attainder, the king still pardoned them and used nothing more than letters patent to do so. Not until the reign of Henry VII does the doctrine seem to have arisen that an attainder act could only be annulled by another parliamentary act.

To obtain a pardon there nearly always had to be a payment on the part of the recipient. The profit provided was of major importance to the king although he gave numerous other reasons for his generosity. The pardon, which was given, according to the king, because the accused was conclusively discovered either before trial or after conviction to be innocent, was not of a common type. Neither perhaps were those granted because of the criminal information the recipients were able to offer, but both occurred from time to time. Fewer still were pardons which resulted from the insanity of the accused, or from the inadequacies of the process of trial, as for example the inability of a man both deaf and dumb to plead, or the inability of *peine forte et dure* to either gain a plea or kill. In contrast, a fairly frequently granted pardon, especially in the fifteenth century, was that which stated it had been given because the recipient had been accused out of malice. We do not know how many times these statements were true, or how often they were offered by petitioners who had no other excuse to make. In the last ten years of the reign of Edward I, during the first half of that of his grandson, and after the Agincourt campaign, a great many pardons were granted, so their terms stated, in return for military service. At the beginning of March 1296 the chief justice, Roger Brabazon, was appointed to receive from persons in prison, or outlawed and at large, who were charged with homicides, robberies, and other offences, sureties that they would go to Scotland on the king's service. For their military duties they were to be paid at the normal rates. On return to England, the date of which was not specified, they were to stand trial if they

[72] *Cal. Pat. Rolls, 1381–1385*, p. 239.

had been appealed. When the pledges had been given the prisoners and the outlaws were given their pardons.[73] In 1343 Edward III, when about to set out to Brittany, ordained that all men accused of homicides, felonies, or robberies who embarked with him and served for a year at their own expense, and who found sureties for the same in chancery, should receive charters of pardon. Apparently pardons were on offer to any soldier who served in the king's army abroad. John Mast took advantage of the system, after he had fought at Crécy, to get a pardon in the name of his brother Walter, who was indicted of murder and a prisoner in Scarborough gaol at the time.[74] Unfortunately for both of them the device was detected, yet it must have succeeded on other occasions. Another reason for which the king said he granted pardons was his devoutness and Christian conscience. In January 1413 Henry IV pardoned William Longe, then imprisoned in the Tower of London, out of his 'reverence for one of whom he has firm hope of grace and mercy'. The later medieval monarch most prone to give this type of reason for his clemency was Henry VI. The grounds on which, in July 1447, he pardoned Sir Roger Chamberlain, Thomas Herberd, and three others of their conviction of petty treason was his 'reverence for the passion of Christ and the Virgin Mary whose assumption will shortly be celebrated by the whole catholic church and specially in the college of St Mary, Eton'. Thomas Michell, a Kentish supporter of Jack Cade, was pardoned in April 1451 of his treasons and felonies because King Henry wanted to show himself to his subjects as he desired God to be to him.[75]

The procedure for obtaining a pardon varied. Some were issued by chancery virtually as a matter of form and without royal warrant following a jury verdict of 'killed by misadventure' or 'in self defence'. Those which have been described above were granted for the most part on an individual basis. The supplicants had petititoned the king directly and he had considered each case on its merits. In contrast, there were the pardons granted after the king had announced they might be obtained during a limited period by anyone who wanted one and had the wherewithal to pay. This type of offer was made on at least three occasions in the reign of Henry IV, and six times in

---

[73] *Cal. Pat. Rolls, 1292–1301*, p. 186.
[74] Pike, *A History of Crime in England* (London, 1873–6), i, 295.
[75] *Cal. Close Rolls, 1409–1413*, p. 375; *Cal. Pat. Rolls, 1446–1452*, p. 68; *ibid.*, p. 461.

twenty-three years when his grandson was king. For a payment of 16s. 4d. anyone could obtain a pardon covering virtually every offence. Those who petitioned the king for an individual pardon would often rely on the intercession of some important man to win the king's favour for their request. Judges, although they could not give pardon themselves, could be the agents whereby pardons were obtained. More often noble laity were used, even if their connection with the misdoer was sometimes of the most tenuous sort. Any man indicted of a crime needed both money and time if he was to present a pardon when he came to be arraigned. A prisoner might even become an approver to gain the time. The adjournment of cases from the local peace sessions to the king's bench seems sometimes to have been intended to allow indicted persons time to purchase their pardon. The sum of money asked for a pardon was in most cases modest enough. One statute (1390), it is true, said that if the offender was of noble rank and his offence was treason, rape, or homicide by ambush, stealth or from malice, he should pay up to £1,000, yet there is doubt if such amounts were exacted in practice.[76] Purchasing a pardon was a routine pecuniary transaction for many offences and offenders but there was often involved a matter of pounds rather than shillings, as the sureties demanded of mainpernors show. It was not unknown for the bond of each pledge to be posted at £40, with another £20 as guarantee the offender would not injure the presenting jurors. When eventually the charter of pardon was offered in court and allowed it seems a writ was issued for a proclamation that the recipient was once more in the king's peace. From 1336 all pardoned felons had to find sureties within three months of getting their pardons. The number was normally six, though on occasion only four. This suggests that the king was not being foolhardy in his granting of pardons, and we must remember also that it was common for the justices of the peace to be ordered to take an inquisition to ascertain the reputation of the would-be recipient before a pardon was granted. With these safeguards it might be imagined that no notorious and persistent offender would ever benefit, but there are instances which make us wonder. For example, in March 1383 a pardon was given to Henry Hermyte of Southstoneham, 'a common disturber of the peace, a highwayman and harbourer of felons who sleeps by day and watches by night'.[77]

Most pardons contained limiting clauses. They might cover only

---

[76] 13 Richard II st. 2 c. 1; *Statutes of the Realm*, ii, 68–9.
[77] *Cal. Pat. Rolls, 1381–1385*, p. 238.

misdeeds done before a certain date, or particular categories of offence. For example, it was not uncommon for treasons, escapes from prison, or particularly offensive felonies to be expressly excepted. In the thirteenth and early fourteenth centuries it was also possible that the pardon would insist on its purchaser standing to right if anyone wished to speak against him. Such pardons were issued to appellees and may have been a concession to the notion that although the king could abate his own suit he had no proper right to stop that of the appellor, or at least another appellor on the same facts at a later date. By the end of the thirteenth century no second appellors were daring to come forward for fear of the king's wrath, but the formula remained in the pardon for some time.

If the king liked the system of pardons some of his subjects did not. Loudest in their denunciations were the commons of parliament. There were, for example, petitions asking for the issue of fewer pardons for various types of homicide in parliamentary sessions in 1310, 1347, and 1390, and the statute of Northampton of 1328 decreed that charters of pardon should only be granted for homicide if the deed was committed in self-defence or by misfortune. In answer to the petition of 1390 came an act which instructed there should be no pardons allowed henceforth for treason, rape, murder, or homicide committed by ambush, assault, or from malice, unless the charter specified the crime exactly. If the pardon did not refer definitely to murder or homicide by ambush, assault, or from malice, then the justices were to enquire through an inquest of the neighbourhood about the manner of the slaying. If it was indeed murder or homicide of that type, then the pardon was not to be allowed. The same statute also carefully controlled how such pardons were to be issued. The chamberlain or under-chamberlain, who endorsed the petition, was to write on it the name of the supplicant before dispatching it to the keeper of the privy seal for warranty. The cost of pardons for treason, rape, murder, and the rest was carefully listed for each class of society: the price ranged from £1,000 for a duke or archbishop to 200 marks plus a year's imprisonment for a clerk, bachelor, or person of lesser rank. As yet we do not know for sure how strictly the act was enforced, although it has been suggested that during the minority of Henry VI (1422–37) only a modest fifteen pardons for homicide were issued from chancery and all the crimes had been committed in self-defence or by misadventure;[78] however, the picture changed for the

[78] By R. L. Storey, *The End of the House of Lancaster* (London, 1966), p. 210.

worse after 1437. The idea of writing on the pardon the name of the man who made the recommendation to the king was not new. The commons of parliament had suggested it in 1353. The king had agreed and ordered in addition that the judges before whom the charter was presented should have the power to make enquiry and, if they discovered that the recommendation was not well founded, they were to hold the pardon invalid. In a statute of 1404 (5 Henry IV c. 12) came an important addendum to the act. If the misdoer who had been provided with a pardon became a felon once more, the recommender of that pardon must pay £100 to the king. As well as asking for restrictions on the issue of pardons generally, the parliamentary commons on occasion demanded the withdrawal or annulment of one in particular. This would be when the misdeed or the misdoer's reputation was known to be infamous. They got little satisfaction since the king was very loth to repudiate his acts of clemency. The only later medieval monarch who withdrew pardons or deliberately ignored them was Richard II, and most were pardons for what were really political offences.

There were few ways in which a private person could baulk a pardon which he considered had been given unfairly, even if general pardons given by Henry VI stipulated that any recipient who had already been indicted must answer in a royal court if any person he might have injured chose to object. L. O. Pike held there was nothing to help the individual oppose a pardon save the power 'to institute an appeal against the wrong doer, and the law by which the accused, when captured, was detained for a year and a day in prison to await the private action before he was brought to trial on the indictment'.[79] He supported the latter contention by exemplification from the gaol delivery rolls of the reign of Edward III. A baulking device which seems to have found considerable favour was the civil action of trespass: it could cause inconvenience to the person pardoned for quite a long period. But none of these procedures was likely to have great success, and, although Fortescue turned a blind eye to it, there was a danger to public order through pardoned men seeking to renew feuds with their enemies and gain revenge on those who had accused them.

---

[79] As has been noted above, Plucknett argued that jurors classified crimes into more categories than were recognized in strict law from a desire to make it more difficult for a really bad offender to purchase a pardon: *Proceedings before the Justices of the Peace, Edward III to Richard III*, p. cxl; Pike, *A History of Crime in England*, i, 296.

That the king gave pardons too easily cannot be denied, yet what statistical evidence we possess suggests that they were by no means the greatest threat to the maintenance of public order. Of the 169 persons indicted of felony in the Warwickshire and Coventry peace sessions of 1377–97 whose later career we know about, only 16 produced pardons in court; and of 244 indicted of trespass but 5 were pardoned. Out of 215 felons indicted in Gloucestershire before the justices of the peace between 1361 and 1398, only 6 presented pardons when they were summoned before the king's bench, and only 4 of 142 indicted of trespass. Of 254 Lincolnshire felons summoned before the king's bench when it visited the county in 1396, 11 offered pardons in court; and of 186 Lindsey felons summoned to the same court for crimes committed between 1381 and 1388, only 2 produced pardons. In the west midlands at roughly the same period there were more pardons, but not many more. Thus in Shropshire, out of 156 persons indicted of felony before the justices of the peace between 1400 and 1414, 14 produced pardons when they appeared in the king's bench. In Staffordshire, among 158 felons whose offences were presented to the local justices between 1409 and 1414 there were not less than 19 pardons.[80] The 'general' pardons issued by Henry VI in six periods between 1437 and 1460, so it has been calculated, numbered more than 12,000, but the majority were never offered in court and must therefore have been purchased for reasons other than to save a criminal from the gallows.[81] Far greater in percentage than pardons were acquittals by juries, and so were non-appearances when summoned.

How far the English kings of the later middle ages were justified in their resorting to pardons cannot at present be evaluated. Some justification for the special pardon issued in return for military service is readily apparent. It rid the countryside of dangerous misdoers for a while and provided the king with both cash and men who had a proficiency in the handling of weapons. Of most other pardons the best that can be said is that they persuaded men to come to terms with the

<hr>

[80] These figures are drawn from *Rolls of the Warwickshire and Coventry Sessions of the Peace, 1377–1397*, p. lxvii; *Rolls of the Gloucestershire Sessions of the Peace, 1361–1398*, ed. E. G. Kimball (Transactions of the Bristol and Gloucestershire Archaeological Society, lx [1940]), p. 49; *Records of Some Sessions of the Peace in Lincolnshire, 1381–1396*, p. liv; *The Shropshire Peace Roll, 1400–1414*, p. 41; Putnam, *Proceedings before the Justices of the Peace Edward III to Richard III*, pp. 295–341.

[81] Storey, *The End of the House of Lancaster*, p. 216.

king and thereby allowed him the success of having brought some criminal cases to a close. Perhaps it could be added that because of the rather easily come by pardon, few offenders were irrevocably alienated from society and few men's careers were irretrievably blighted by a single crime.

VII

<hr>

Problems and Promise

<hr>

By the middle of the fifteenth century the machinery which was supposed to provide for the upkeep of public order in England was showing signs of stress. It is obvious from what has gone before that the causes of this malfunctioning were many and stretched from the inefficient rule of the king himself down to the failure to perform civic duties on the part of a great number of ordinary men. The degree of blame was not all the same, and some attempt must be made to apportion it.

However well designed the system for maintaining law and order, little could be achieved if the king was not a dominating force within the state, and if he did not interest himself personally and fairly often in the suppression of crime. A powerful king who was often away at war was almost as harmful as one whose personality lacked all qualities of leadership and authority. The king must forever be on the watch for corrupt administration by officials, an evil which was not to be suppressed by making offices rotate more quickly. The difficulties in bringing such malpractice to the notice of the king and obtaining proper satisfaction was a problem not to be solved in the middle ages.

One of the greatest areas for concern was the influence and power of the nobility, then perhaps at its zenith, and the way it was used to defeat the proper course of justice. Lesser men, when they took the livery of a magnate, were promised support in all their causes and frequently received it. It took the form of corrupting and intimidating jurors, the installation of protégés in local offices, the bullying of other lesser officials, and the provision of armed assistance in feuds. Why could not the king put the erring magnate on trial? Why were so few examples made? The personality of Henry VI and the divisions within his council are explanations of why, for a crucial period of thirty years in the fifteenth century, so little was done in this direction. It is true that a number of lawbreaking nobles were summoned before the king's council, but little more than moderate fines and promises seem to have been exacted. What was most rare in the fifteenth century was the magnate on trial under the common law for an offence which could cost him his life. For this there were probably several reasons. Noblemen did not themselves have to kill or rob for they had followers who would do it for them. Most important was the fact that in the two preceding centuries the rule had become accepted that they should only be tried and judged by their peers, and this usually meant the lords of parliament. Furthermore, the accusations against them had nearly always touched on treason. Very few noblemen of the fifteenth century appeared to answer to indictments of felony or trespass before the king's bench or commissions of oyer and terminer. The petty juries had always to be composed of men equal in rank to the accused, which was impractical. Even if this difficulty was overcome there was little chance of getting a conviction. There was strong *esprit de corps* among the English baronage; or, put another way, dog did not eat dog.

The giving of livery illegally, that is to say to a knight or an esquire not retained in the proper manner or to a yeoman, archer, or man of lesser estate not living in the lord's household, was a crime with serious consequences for public order, but the king failed to deal with it either fairly or firmly. Usually it was not the nobleman who gave it who was accused, but the lesser men who received it from him and those who gave it when their inferior social rank did not permit them to do so. We do not yet have a proper idea of how many livery cases were heard in the common law courts in the Lancastrian and Yorkist periods, but the fact that there are no more than about twenty references in the calendared rolls of chancery for that time does not suggest any great drive against it. One can hardly escape the conclusion that by the fifteenth century most kings were scared of making an example of an erring nobleman; yet it was a thing which badly needed doing. Only when the king felt that his person was directly threatened and that the nobility as a class was behind him because the crime was treason did he dare to move decisively.

'He cannot be found' was a stock response by the sheriff when asked to produce an accused man in court. The way in which those suspected of crime were able to avoid appearing before the justices and their relative unconcern, in the mid-fifteenth century at least, at being outlawed suggests that a proper police system was badly needed. If the law was to be respected it was all important to capture a good percentage of misdoers and put them on trial as soon as possible after the committing of their offences, when the deed was still remembered in the locality. As it was, in the more lawless decades of the later middle ages, a felon could consider himself distinctly unlucky if he was captured by the authorities. Policing was left largely in the hands of the local community. The maxim was not efficiency but financial economy, making the system of public order pay for itself. A king with no proper permanent army, and who could not pay with regularity the members of his own household, was not likely to be able either to visualize or to finance a proper police system. In any case the idea was quite alien to the popular ethos of the common law.

There was another weakness in the English system for maintaining law and order. Because the majority of criminal cases were heard in the first instance before the peace commissions, justices for the most part were country gentlemen and many had only a modest knowledge of the law. This deficiency could be remedied by insisting on the presence at all sessions of a number with legal training but little could be done about reducing the conflicting interests of these men. They were landlords, and as leading members of local society they had both enemies and allies. By the fifteenth century they had often developed a close affiliation with a magnate. Their prejudices were quite likely to affect their decisions, where they had summary powers, and their receiving of indictments, examinations, and sentencing where they did not. Even if they were not prejudiced, men must have thought they were. In the fourteenth century, to all appearances, the king had doubts about how much work he should entrust to the peace commissions, but eventually his reluctance was overcome. How far this was caused by the demands of the gentry for judicial authority and how far it was *faute de mieux* is not yet completely clear. There was another more pronounced popular element in English judicial administration. The thirty-ninth clause of Magna Carta had demanded that no man should be condemned without due process of law, and this had come to mean without proper accusation and trial. By the fourteenth century the jury dominated both of these legal processes and thus verdicts were, to a marked degree, in popular hands. This was a great bulwark against royal tyranny. If the king was particularly desirous of gaining a conviction he had either to avoid the common law altogether, or to exert himself greatly in order to convince the jurors. On the other hand, trial by jury was equally efficacious in acquitting a proportion of accused which was too high if public order was to be respected.

By the fifteenth century the English kings had begun to realize, if they had not before, that the popular control of trial procedure ought to be limited. There could be alteration of the functioning of the petty jury but in the matter of accusation, an area almost as crucial since the king could not prosecute a criminal himself, there was probably some successful interference in the form of prompting. The attention of indicting jurors was turned in particular directions and some suggestion probably made as to what it should discover. The rise of informing in the later fifteenth century was another move in this direction. There were several other loop-holes in the machinery for maintaining public order which the king periodically attempted to close. Benefit of clergy, which may have been claimed more frequently as education became more widespread, enabled many felons to escape virtually without penalty. It caused dissatisfaction at large because it was obviously so unfair, and it must have lowered the morale of many peace officers. Sanctuary was similar, if rather more local in its effect, while pardons were common and cheaply to be had at times. Efforts to limit each of these met with only slight success. Basically English law was not the king's law but the 'common' law, evolved by the whole community. It was difficult for the king to alter established common law ideas and processes because he must always carry the community with him. Novel ideas for the better maintenance of public order in the fifteenth century, like the taking of oaths from the upper classes, the issuing of writs of proclamation, a formalized use of arbitration and suspended attainder, were therefore introduced outside the common law, though they had the sanction and the assistance of parliament. Nor did the king dare to interfere with the common law of personal actions in order to speed up the dreadfully slow procedure and thereby diminish the number of feuds which turned into open warfare.

If the weaknesses of the English criminal law of the later middle ages were several, there was nonetheless a good side and some promise for the future. As we have already noted, if it allowed a high incidence of crime it helped prevent royal tyranny. The popular nature of the system meant that justices, local law officers, and jurors were amateurs, taking a turn of duty as required. They were therefore always in touch with society at large and likely to adjust the system where they could, when it did not hurt their own interests, in the cause of equity. Acquittals were too numerous but, as Fortescue noted, few men were condemned who were not guilty. Another creditable feature of English medieval justice was its relative lack of class bias. The justices, who were often drawn from the squirarchy, and the jurors, who were men of a moderate degree of wealth, might have been expected to administer the law in a way unfavourable to the lowest classes. This may have happened for a decade or so in the fourteenth century subsequent to the promulgation of the statutes concerning labourers and their wages, but it does not seem to have prevailed generally. Infringements of the forest laws may have been fairly numerous in court rolls in the early fourteenth century but they were relatively few a century later. This was not due entirely, or even mainly, to the enlightenment of the justices but rather to changing economic conditions and the new value set on a peasant's labour. One of the most beneficial elements of late medieval English government was that it did not usually seek to enforce antiquated laws or those which ran contrary to the wishes of the community as a whole.

In the England of the fourteenth and fifteenth centuries there was no effort made to increase the severity of the physical punishment inflicted on the condemned; rather there was a moderation of cruelty. In the towns, local barbaric customs such as abscission of bodily parts, burying of criminals alive, and the like were being supplanted by practices used more generally under the common law. The evisceration of traitors was practised periodically, it is true, but this refinement of execution, though more frequent perhaps and more noticed by chroniclers in the fourteenth and fifteenth centuries, dated from at least as early as the reign of Henry III. Only the use, on two occasions, of torture before trial in order to elicit information anticipated the severer use of physical duress to be made by the Tudors. The use made of imprisonment was increasing, but the general intention was to keep a man in custody until he could be tried or to punish him: the aim was rarely coercion. For the prisoner conditions varied a great deal but there was some concern, particularly in the towns, about the rigours of gaol life and in London at least there was some progress in the fifteenth century towards regular inspection. The same century also seems to have seen the end of trial by battle, both of the variety which stemmed from appeals by

203

ordinary appellants and those which originated in the accusations of approvers. Finally, it is possible to argue that the increased use made of pardons and fines in this period showed a novel approach to punishment, even if the king welcomed them as a means of royal profit and a way to reconcile to society offenders he was unable to bring to trial.

Select Bibliography

The ultimate source of the history of crime and public order in later medieval England is the legal records in the Public Record Office, London. The most profitable of these are probably the *coram rege* rolls (K.B. 27), the ancient indictments of king's bench (K.B. 9), the controlment rolls ('the memoranda rolls of the king's attorneys in the king's bench'; K.B. 29), the gaol delivery rolls (J.I. 3), and the assize rolls (J.I. 1). Also worthy of attention, if less rewarding, are the Early Chancery Proceedings, Series 1 (C. 1), Chancery Miscellanea (C. 47), Chancery Warrants for the Great Seal, Series 1 (C. 81), and (for pardons) the Supplementary Patent Rolls (C. 67).

Very little of this mass of material has found its way into print. The small part which has is largely the surviving rolls of the justices of the peace. A list of these publications to 1946 is to be found in the *University of Toronto Law Journal*, vi (1945–6), pp. 401–13. The records of the higher courts to be found in print are usually for a particular county or a very limited period. The William Salt Archaeological Society produced a translation by G. Wrottesley of the entries referring to Staffordshire in the medieval *coram rege* rolls: there is a transcript of the *coram rege* roll for Trinity term 1297 in its entirety (W. P. W. Phillimore, Index Library, 1898). A selection of pleas in the king's bench, dating for the most part from the thirteenth century, is to be found in *Abbreviatio Placitorum. Richard I to Edward II*, ed. G. Rose and W. Illingworth (Rec. Comm., 1811). There is included a list of other cases to Henry V. Some of the more interesting cases in the *coram rege* rolls are to be found in *Select Cases in the Court of the King's Bench*, I–VI, ed. G. O. Sayles (Selden Society, 55, 57, 58, 74, 76, 82, 1936–65).

There are many references to criminal cases in the calendared rolls of chancery, particularly in the patent rolls, the close rolls (until the beginning of the fifteenth century), and the 'miscellaneous inquisitions'. These need to be read in their entirety since the indexes, save in the volumes published in the last few years, offer little assistance. The *Rotuli Parliamentorum* (Rec. Comm., 1767–7) contain a great number of petitions pertaining to lawlessness and defective legal process; the *Statutes of the Realm* (Rec. Comm., 1810–28) show what laws were made but not if they were implemented. Another important source is the *Year Books*, which are best

205

examined in *Les Reports del Cases en Ley* (London, 1678–9). Although the knotty points of law discussed were usually the products of personal actions, there is much of interest about legal process in general. The *Proceedings and Ordinances of the Privy Council*, ed. N. H. Nicolas (Rec. Comm., 1834–7) give information about a number of criminal offences which came at some stage before the council; often they had political implications.

Chapter I: Crime and Medieval Society

The only work to attempt a general history of crime for this period is L. O. Pike, *A History of Crime in England* (London, 1873–6), which is still of value. It suffers from an over-concern with political 'crimes' and from being written before the rolls of the justices of the peace became readily accessible. This is compensated to some extent by a detailed examination of the *coram rege* rolls for 1348. Although concerned with an earlier period, F. Pollock and F. W. Maitland's *The History of English Law before the Time of Edward I* (Cambridge, 1895) has much to offer through its insight into police administration, judicial procedure, and the prevalence of crime. J. F. Stephen, *A History of the Criminal Law of England* (London, 1883), is now outdated; W. S. Holdsworth's *History of English Law* (London, 1903–72) should also be used with some caution for this period. Avowedly covering the whole of English legal history and from the social viewpoint, A. Harding, *A Social History of English Law* (Penguin, 1966), has some valuable things to say on the later middle ages and is easy to read. Of great value, both for the printed rolls it contains and for the introduction, is B. H. Putnam, *Proceedings before the Justices of the Peace in the Fourteenth and Fifteenth Centuries, Edward III to Richard III* (Ames Foundation, 1938). This work, in which wherever possible each case is followed through to its conclusion, includes an excellent commentary on the indictments by T. F. T. Plucknett. There are other valuable editions of peace rolls by B. H. Putnam, E. C. Furber, M. Gollancz, E. G. Kimball, R. Sillem, and M. M. Taylor: it is these studies which provide the material for purposes of regional and period comparison. The various volumes of the Selden Society which touch on public order in this period are also recommended, although their explanatory introductions are not all of the same quality.

Of the medieval legal treatises the most useful are: Sir John Fortescue, *De Laudibus Legum Angliae*, ed. S. B. Chrimes (Cambridge, 1942); *Henrici de Bracton de Legibus et Consuetudinibus Angliae*, ed. (a) G. E. Woodbine (New Haven, 1915–42), (b) T. Twiss (Rolls Series, 1878–83); *Britton*, ed. F. M. Nichols (Oxford, 1865 and Washington, 1901); *Fleta II, Prologue, Bk. I, Bk. II*, ed. H. G. Richardson and G. O. Sayles (Selden Society, 72, 1953); *The Mirror of Justices*, ed. W. J. Whittaker (Selden Society, 7, 1895). There survives an interesting tract demonstrating aspects of trial procedure in the thirteenth century: *Placita Corone*, ed. J. M. Kaye (Selden Society, Supplementary Series, 1966).

The medieval chronicles are not without value, although they often have more to offer on the niceties of monastic litigation than on the criminal side of the common law. Those which say more than usual about lawlessness are probably: Matthew Paris, *Chronica Majora*, ed. H. R. Luard (Rolls Series, 1872–83); *Chronicles of the Reigns of Edward I and Edward II*, ed. W. Stubbs (Rolls Series, 1882–3); *Chronicon Henrici Knighton*, ed. J. R. Lumby (Rolls Series, 1889–95); *Polychronicon Ranulphi Higden*, ed. J. R. Lumby (Rolls Series, 1865–86); 'Hardyng's Chronicle', ed. C. L. Kingsford, *English Historical Review*, xxvii (1912), 740–53. The Tudor historians Stow (*Annales or a Generall Chronicle of England*, ed. E. Howes [London, 1631]) and Holinshed (*Chronicles of England, Scotland and Ireland* [London, 1808]) are of considerable usefulness for the fifteenth century. Holinshed in particular had a personal interest in law, order, and the punishment of criminals. The authors of several fifteenth-century London chronicles provide information about notable crimes and trials with a London interest: for example *The Historical Collections of a Citizen of London in the Fifteenth Century*, ed. J. Gairdner (Camden Society, New Series, xvii, 1876), and R. Fabyan, *Newe Chronycles of England and of France*, ed. H. Ellis (London, 1811).

Corrupt practices by officials and the occasional enquiries into them by the king are perhaps best studied in: *State Trials of the Reign of Edward I, 1289–1293*, ed. T. F. Tout and H. Johnstone (Camden Society, 3rd Series, ix, 1906); D. Hughes, *The Early Years of Edward III* (London, 1915); L. Ehrlich, *Proceedings against the Crown* (Oxford, 1921); T. F. T. Plucknett, 'The Origins of Impeachment', *Transactions of the Royal Historical Society*, 4th Series, xxii (1942), 47–71. None of these is entirely satisfactory: there is a great need for a proper investigation, as there is into late medieval office-holding in general. The careers and the work of the professional judges are well exemplified in B. H. Putnam, *The Place in Legal History of Sir William Shareshull, Chief Justice of the King's Bench, 1350–61* (London, 1950), and in E. L. G. Stones, 'Sir Geoffrey le Scrope (c. 1285–1340), Chief Justice of the King's Bench', *English Historical Review*, lxix (1954), 1–17.

The value of the presence of the king as an antidote to local lawlessness is demonstrated in J. G. Bellamy, 'Justice under the Yorkist Kings', *American Journal of Legal History*, ix (1965), 135–55. Litigation and its attendant evils is best approached through M. Hastings, *The Court of Common Pleas in the Fifteenth Century* (Ithaca, 1947), and through a case study in P. S. Lewis, 'Sir John Fastolf's Lawsuit over Titchwell, 1448–1455', *The Historical Journal*, i (1958), 1–20. On later medieval developments in the law concerning homicide see J. M. Kaye, 'The Early History of Murder and Manslaughter, Part I', *Law Quarterly Review*, lxxxiii (1967), 365–95, and on treason, J. G. Bellamy, *The Law of Treason in England in the Later Middle Ages* (Cambridge, 1970).

On the vital issue of the relationship of lawlessness to 'bastard feudalism' there is very little writing which gives satisfaction. The *Paston Letters*, ed. J. Gairdner (Edinburgh, 1910), provide much excitement and some useful insights, but whether East Anglia at that time was typical of conditions countrywide has yet to be decided. One book that can be highly recommended is R. L. Storey, *The End of the House of Lancaster* (London,

207

1966); based on the ancient indictments of the king's bench it provides some excellent examples of feud, maintenance, illegal retaining, and corruption of the law in the mid-fifteenth century. On a lesser scale see R. A. Griffiths, 'Local Rivalries and National Politics: The Percies, the Nevilles and the Duke of Exeter, 1452–55', *Speculum*, xliii (1968), 589–632. For feuding in the fourteenth century see G. H. Tupling, *South Lancashire in the Reign of Edward II* (Chetham Society, 3rd Series, i, 1949).

Chapter II: Misdeeds and Misdoers

Despite the large number of serious offences committed, those which are well documented are few. Examples of cases about which more than the usual is known are perhaps best sought in *Select Cases in the Court of the King's Bench*, i–vi, in L. O. Pike, *A History of Crime in England*, and in the *Calendar of Letter Books of the City of London, 1275–1498*, Books A–L, ed. R. R. Sharpe (London, 1899–1912). The calendared rolls of chancery and the chronicles have one or two offenders and misdeeds of note but no more.

The robbery of the cardinals has been thoroughly investigated in A. E. Middleton, *Sir Gilbert de Middleton and the Part He Took in the Rebellion in the North of England in 1317* (Newcastle-on-Tyne, 1918). T. F. Tout wrote an interesting paper, based on the confession of the chief culprit, about the robbery of the king's treasure house at Westminster (*Collected Papers*, iii [Manchester, 1934]). The background to the killing of Nicholas Radford in 1455 has been clearly revealed in R. L. Storey, *The End of the House of Lancaster*. Apart from these, few medieval felonies have been the subject of special studies by historians.

Chapter III: The Criminal Bands

On misdoers confederating together there is very little in print, and that little is concerned mainly with the fourteenth century. E. L. G. Stones, 'The Folvilles of Ashby-Folville, Leicestershire, and Their Associates in Crime, 1326–1341', *Transactions of the Royal Historical Society*, 5th Series, vii (1957), 117–36, and J. G. Bellamy, 'The Coterel Gang: An Anatomy of a Band of Fourteenth Century Criminals', *English Historical Review*, lxxix (1964), 698–717, deal with the operations, structure, and allies of two north midland gangs. R. H. Hilton, *A Medieval Society* (London, 1966), has some useful information on one or two notable malefactors in the west midlands c. 1300. J. G. Bellamy, 'The Northern Rebellions in the Later Years of Richard II', *Bulletin of the John Rylands Library*, xlvii (1965), 254–74, covers the activities of William Beckwith and his followers in their feud with authority in Yorkshire c. 1388–92. For the fifteenth century the *Paston Letters* reveal something of the criminal activities of Charles Nowell, Robert Ledham, and their confederates, and more could probably be extracted from the Public Records. Of interest concerning the image cast by the persistent lawbreaker are: M. H. Keen,

The Outlaws of Medieval Legend (London, 1961); *Anglo-Norman Political Songs*, ed. I. S. T. Aspin (Oxford, 1953); *The Political Songs of England*, ed. T. Wright (Camden Society, vi, 1839); *The English and Scottish Popular Ballads*, ed. F. J. Child (New York, 1962).

Chapter IV: Enforcing the Law

The administrative side of English law in the fourteenth and fifteenth centuries is relatively well covered, albeit not as adequately as in the thirteenth century. On the office of sheriff at the beginning of the period under review there is a monograph by W. A. Morris (*The Medieval English to 1300* [Manchester, 1927]) and a short study by G. Templeman (*The Sheriffs of Warwickshire in the Thirteenth Century* [Dugdale Society Occasional Papers, 7, 1948]). *The English Government at Work, 1327–1336*, ed. J. F. Willard, W. A. Morris, J. R. Strayer, and W. H. Dunham (Cambridge, Mass., 1940–50), provides sketches of the roles of sheriffs, constables, and royal bailiffs at a time when lawlessness was rampant.

On the central theme of the peace commission A. Harding's 'The Origins and Early History of the Keepers of the Peace', *Transactions of the Royal Historical Society*, 5th Series, x (1960), 85–109, is a useful prelude to B. H. Putnam, *Proceedings before the Justices of the Peace in the Fourteenth and Fifteenth Centuries, Edward III to Richard III*, and her *Early Treatises on the Practice of the Justices of the Peace in the Fifteenth and Sixteenth Centuries* (Oxford, 1924). The workings of the king's bench are revealed in *Select Cases in the Court of the King's Bench*, i–vi, but there is room for a close examination of business over one or two terms in the fifteenth century. There is nothing extensive in print specifically on oyer and terminer commissions. Historians have been well served by J. F. Baldwin, *The King's Council in England during the Middle Ages* (Oxford, 1913), and *Select Cases before the King's Council, 1243–1482*, ed. I. S. Leadam and J. F. Baldwin (Selden Society, 35, 1918), but a new study of council as a court is now necessary. Some idea of the *modus operandi* of the Lancastrian and Yorkist council in judicial matters can be gathered from *Select Cases in the Council of Henry VII*, ed. C. G. Bayne and W. H. Dunham (Selden Society, 75, 1956).

Many books touch on medieval outlawry but none examine the process thoroughly. The best summaries are probably in T. F. T. Plucknett, *A Concise History of the Common Law* (London, 1956), and W. S. Holdsworth, *History of English Law*. The use of parliamentary sanctions to stiffen the processes of the common law has yet to be properly investigated. One or two examples relating to treason are to be found in J. G. Bellamy, *The Law of Treason in England in the Later Middle Ages*. Arbitration, an important factor in an age of interminable lawsuits, has as yet hardly been noticed by historians.

Sanctuary and abjuration from the realm have attracted more attention than almost any other aspect of medieval crime. On sanctuary, see particularly: N. M. Trenholme, *Right of Sanctuary in England*, University of Missouri Studies, i, part 5 (1903); J. C. Cox, *The Sanctuaries and Sanctuary*

Seekers of Medieval England (London, 1911); I. D. Thornley, 'The Destruction of Sanctuary' in *Tudor Studies presented to . . . A. F. Pollard*, ed. R. W. Seton Watson (London, 1924); *Sanctuarium Dunelmense et Sanctuarium Beverlacense*, ed. J. Raine (Surtees Society, v, 1837). On abjuration see J. C. Cox again, also A. Réville, ' "L'Abjuratio Regni", histoire d'une institution anglaise', *Révue Historique*, 1 (1892), 1–42, and especially R. F. Hunnisett, *The Medieval Coroner* (Cambridge, 1961).

Chapter V: Accusation and Trial

The basic types of accusation are well handled in *Crown Pleas of the Wiltshire Eyre, 1249*, ed. C. A. F. Meekings (Wiltshire Archaeological and Natural History Society, Records Branch, xvi, 1960), and B. H. Putnam, *Proceedings before the Justices of the Peace in the Fourteenth and Fifteenth Centuries, Edward III to Richard III*. Examination is a topic which has suffered almost total neglect by historians, although it was becoming a vital part of judicial process in this period. Similarly there is very little on the laying of information as a means of prosecution. For trial itself the material is scattered and fragmentary, there being nothing comparable to the account of sixteenth-century practice in Sir Thomas Smith, *De Republica Anglorum*, ed. L. Alston (Cambridge, 1906), and the thirteenth-century glimpses in *Placita Corone*, ed. J. M. Kaye. The best books available are probably J. Fortescue, *De Laudibus Legum Anglie*, ed. S. B. Chrimes, and J. B. Thayer, *A Preliminary Treatise on Evidence at Common Law* (Boston, 1898). Trial in the boroughs sometimes differed from the general practice, as is demonstrated by the custumals in *Borough Customs*, ed. M. Bateson (Selden Society, xviii, xxi, 1904–6), and C. Gross, 'Modes of Trial in the Medieval Boroughs of England', *Harvard Law Review*, xv (1901–2), 691–706.

On approvers and how they were used by the king for the accusation of others there is an interesting essay: F. C. Hamil, 'The King's Approvers: A Chapter in the History of the English Criminal Law', *Speculum*, xi (1936), 238–58. Late medieval judicial combat has drawn considerable attention from historians. For a battle well described by a contemporary, see J. G. Bellamy, 'Sir John de Annesley and the Chandos Inheritance', *Nottingham Medieval Studies*, x (1966), 94–105. There is a general account of this mode of trial in G. Neilson, *Trial by Combat* (Glasgow, 1890). T. F. T. Plucknett first drew our attention to the occasional use of the epithets 'common' and 'notorious' to describe those accused in indictments: 'The Origins of Impeachment', *Transactions of the Royal Historical Society*, 4th Series, xxii (1942), 47–71. The topic still awaits thorough examination and the same is true of summary trial by 'record'.

Coke was interested in the origins of English torture: E. Coke, *The Third Part of the Institutes of the Laws of England* (London, 1797). Apart from the general comments of H. C. Lea, *Superstition and Force* (Philadelphia, 1870), the subject has not attracted an investigator since D. Jardine, *Reading on the Use of Torture in the Criminal Law of England previously to the Commonwealth* (London, 1837). On benefit of clergy there is a competent survey by L. C. Gabel, *Benefit of Clergy in England in the Later Middle Ages* (Smith College Studies in History, 1928–9). Moral offences were the concern of the church, but unfortunately very few of the relevant records survive. Thus 'Records of a Ruridecanal Court of 1300', ed. F. S. Pearson, *Collectanea* (Worcester Historical Society, 1912), is of particular value. How the authorities of London dealt with misbehaviour of a moral nature is well illustrated in the *Calendar of Letter Books of the City of London, 1275–1498*.

Chapter VI: Prison, Punishment, and Pardon

On imprisonment the standard work is now R. B. Pugh, *Imprisonment in Medieval England* (Cambridge, 1968), but the pioneer studies by M. Bassett, 'Newgate Prison in the Middle Ages', *Speculum*, xviii (1943), 233–46, and 'The Fleet Prison in the Middle Ages', *University of Toronto Law Journal*, v (1943–4), 383–402, are still worthy of attention. Although concerned with prison abuses in the early seventeenth century the contemporary *The Oeconomy of the Fleete*, ed. A. Jessopp (Camden Society, New Series, xxv, 1879), provides some useful detail with a medieval relevance. Also of interest is M. D. Lobel, 'The Gaol of Bury St Edmunds', *Proceedings of the Suffolk Institute of Archaeology*, xxi (1931–3), 203–15. There are several references to the unpleasantness of gaol in the *Paston Letters*, ed. J. Gairdner, and a great many in the calendared chancery rolls.

Corporal punishment and execution in the later middle ages did not move men to compile descriptive accounts as was the case in later centuries; information is therefore scattered. *Borough Customs*, ed. M. Bateson, has much of interest on exotic urban practices. *The Chronicle of the Grey Friars of London*, ed. J. G. Nichols (Camden Society, liii, 1852), has a list of executions in London in this period and the *Calendar of Letter Books of the City of London, 1275–1498* has details of punishment inflicted there for commercial and moral offences. There are other references of value in the chronicles, in L. O. Pike, *A History of Crime in England*, and J. Fortescue, *De Laudibus Legum Anglie*, ed. S. B. Chrimes. On fines see *Crown Pleas of the Wiltshire Eyre, 1249*, ed. C. A. F. Meekings, and F. Pollock and F. W. Maitland, *The History of English Law before the Time of Edward I*. Pardons have been very much neglected as a subject for study. There is a short but informative discussion in R. L. Storey, *The End of the House of Lancaster*; B. H. Putnam, *Proceedings before the Justices of the Peace in the Fourteenth and Fifteenth Centuries, Edward III to Richard III*, has details of numbers of pardons proffered in courts, and there are comments of value in *The Shropshire Peace Roll, 1400–1414*, ed. E. G. Kimball. The reader's attention is also drawn to N. D. Hurnard, *The King's Pardon for Homicide before A. D. 1307* (Oxford, 1969).

Index

213